The Interwar Depression in an International Context

Schriften des Historischen Kollegs

Kolloquien
51

The Interwar Depression in an International Context

R. Oldenbourg Verlag München 2002

The Interwar Depression in an International Context

Herausgegeben von
Harold James
unter Mitarbeit von
Elisabeth Müller-Luckner

R. Oldenbourg Verlag München 2002

Das Historische Kolleg fördert im Bereich der historisch orientierten Wissenschaften Gelehrte, die sich durch herausragende Leistungen in Forschung und Lehre ausgewiesen haben. Es vergibt zu diesem Zweck jährlich bis zu drei Forschungsstipendien und ein Förderstipendium sowie alle drei Jahre den „Preis des Historischen Kollegs".

Die Forschungsstipendien, deren Verleihung zugleich eine Auszeichnung für die bisherigen Leistungen darstellt, sollen den berufenen Wissenschaftlern während eines Kollegjahres die Möglichkeit bieten, frei von anderen Verpflichtungen eine größere Arbeit abzuschließen. Professor Dr. Harold James (Princeton, N.J.) war – zusammen mit Professor Dr. Thomas A. Brady (Berkeley, Cal.), Prof. Dr. Christof Dipper (Darmstadt) und Dr. Felicitas Schmieder (Frankfurt a. M.) – Stipendiat des Historischen Kollegs im Kollegjahr 1998/99. Den Obliegenheiten der Stipendiaten gemäß hat Harold James aus seinem Arbeitsbereich ein Kolloquium zum Thema „The Interwar Depression in an International Context" vom 31. Mai bis 1. Juni 1999 im Historischen Kolleg gehalten. Die Ergebnisse des Kolloquiums werden in diesem Band veröffentlicht.
Das Historische Kolleg, bisher vom Stiftungsfonds Deutsche Bank zur Förderung der Wissenschaft in Forschung und Lehre und vom Stifterverband für die Deutsche Wissenschaft getragen, wird ab dem Kollegjahr 2000/2001 in seiner Grundausstattung vom Freistaat Bayern finanziert; seine Stipendien werden aus Mitteln des DaimlerChrysler Fonds, der Fritz Thyssen Stiftung, des Stifterverbandes und eines ihm verbundenen Förderunternehmens dotiert. Träger des Kollegs ist nunmehr die „Stiftung zur Förderung der Historischen Kommission bei der Bayerischen Akademie der Wissenschaften und des Historischen Kollegs".

Die Deutsche Bibliothek – CIP Einheitsaufnahme

The Interwar Depression in an International Context
hrsg. von Harold James unter Mitarbeit von Elisabeth Müller-Luckner. –
München : Oldenbourg 2002
(Schriften des Historischen Kollegs : Kolloquien ; 51)
ISBN 3-486-56610-5

Rosenheimer Straße 145, D-81671 München
Internet: http://www.oldenbourg-verlag.de

Gedruckt auf säurefreiem, alterungsbeständigem Papier (chlorfrei gebleicht)
Gesamtherstellung: R. Oldenbourg Graphische Betriebe Druckerei GmbH, München

ISBN 3-486-56610-5

Inhalt

Harold James

Introduction: Interpreting the Great Depression

The devastation of that Depression still exercises a colossal fascination. In the second half of the century, whenever there is an interruption to growth or a threat to prosperity, many people ask themselves whether we are not once more back in the grips of the Great Depression. In the mid-1970s, the recession that followed from the sudden quadrupling of oil prices was taken as a new world crisis, combining a threat to the economy with a threat to political democracy. The lessons learnt from the Great Depression at that time involved the desirability of a Keynesian demand stimulus. At the beginning of the 1980s, a recession in the industrial world and the Latin American debt crisis led to a new wave of pessimistic forecasts, and a new interest in the history of depression. Then the lesson was lower interest rates. In October 1987 in analyzing the stock exchange collapse, almost every major newspaper printed charts juxtaposing the developments of 1929 and 1987. Again, after the outbreak of an Asian crisis in 1997, and the contagion effects in Russia and then in Brazil, the parallels to 1929 recurred. Helmut Schmidt, who as Chancellor in the 1970s had been terrified of the possibility of a replication of the Great Depression, for instance now wrote: "The main parallel lies in the helplessness of many governments, which had not noticed in time that they had been locked in a financial trap, and now have no idea of how they might escape."[1]

No one has done more to explain the importance of providing an accurate account of the interwar depression and to warn against the dangers of contemporary solutions to economic policy questions of that time than the Munich economist Knut Borchardt. He has also been a source of great inspiration and encouragement to a large number of younger scholars, some of whom were present at this colloquium, held in the Historisches Kolleg on May 31 and June 1, 1999. Professor Borchardt was present for all of the discussion, and much of the debate revolved around the question he had posed twenty-one years earlier, in a lecture at the Bayerische Akademie der Wissenschaften[2], on the room for policy choice during the German depression. In addition, it was a special pleasure and honor for

[1] *Helmut Schmidt*, Vorsicht, Finanzhaie, in: Die Zeit, 42, 8. Oktober 1997, 3.

[2] A version with extended bibliographical apparatus was published as *Knut Borchardt*, Zwangslagen und Handlungsspielräume in der großen Weltwirtschaftskrise der frühen dreißiger Jahre: Zur Revision des überlieferten Geschichtsbildes, in: Wachstum, Krisen, Handlungsspielräume der Wirtschaftspolitik (Göttingen 1982) 165–82.

those attending the colloquium that this event also marked a celebration of Knut Borchardt's seventieth birthday.

The colloquium, and the ensuing publication, was expertly managed by Dr. Elisabeth Müller-Luckner of the Historisches Kolleg.

One peculiarity is worth pointing out. Many volumes of colloquia of the Historisches Kolleg have appeared in multiple languages. This is the first that appears only in one language, and all the German native speakers chose (without any prompting from the organizers) to give their presentations in English. Their choice is a reflection both of the development of the discipline of economic history, and of the globalized character of the issues they were discussing. Readers will also note the absence of an index, which was felt to be unnecessary as the individual contributions are heavily thematic and analytical.

These issues still have clear and obvious policy implications for the present. The final paper of the colloquium, by Barry Eichengreen, examines lessons from the 1930s in the context of current debates. The academic discussion was also followed immediately by a public debate about some of the current problems raised by depression-era issues (such as the choice of exchange rate regime and monetary policy), in which the participants were Professor Forrest Capie, Professor Barry Eichengreen, State Secretary Heiner Flassbeck, Bundesbankpräsident a.D. Professor Helmut Schlesinger, and Professor Lord Skidelsky. This part of the proceedings was generously supported by the Herbert Quandt Foundation.

The fundamental problem of why the great depression occurred (and whether it could be avoided) still remains a great intellectual challenge. Today, the depression raises a major issue: are events such as this likely to recur? Does this mean that the wave of global integration experienced in the last half of the twentieth century is reversible?

On the eve of the millenium, "globalization" became a global catchphrase. An increasingly close economic interconnection has led to a political and social revolution. Old certainties are cast into doubt. The nation-state, which was the decisive driving force of the past two centuries, is dissolving under the pressure of a cross-national integration, which develops with a dynamic and a momentum of its own.

Often we believe that this process is irreversible, that it provides a one-way road to the future. But historical reflections lead to a more sober and pessimistic assessment. There have already been highly developed and highly integrated international communities that dissolved under the pressure of unexpected events. The momentum was lost, the pendulum changed direction, and went backwards. In Europe, for instance, the universal erasmian world of the Renaissance was destroyed by the Reformation and its Catholic counterpart and separatism, provincialism and parochialism. My friend and colleague at the Historisches Kolleg in 1998–99, Thomas Brady, has given a beautiful account of how local thinking in the age of the Reformation shaped the subsequent history of central Europe.

In economic history, the late nineteenth century is a similar universal age, in which integration and progress went hand in hand. At the end of the nineteenth century, the world was highly integrated economically through a mobility of capital, goods and people. Capital moved freely between states and continents. Trade was largely unhindered, even in apparently protectionist states such as the German Empire. Above all, people moved. They did not need passports. There were hardly any debates about citizenship. These inter-related flows helped to ensure a measure of global economic stability. Some forty years ago, the economist Brinley Thomas brilliantly demonstrated an inverse correlation between cycles in Britain and the United States: slacker demand in Britain helped to make the Atlantic passage more attractive. The new immigrants stimulated the American economy, and hence also British exports, and the British economy could revive[3]. This integrated world bears a close resemblance to our world in which "globalization" is so hotly debated.

Did the guns of August 1914 explode these beliefs? It was certainly harder to be optimistic. But after the horrors of the war it was also hard not to have a nostalgic yearning for the internationalism and the security of the prewar world. The hope of the peacemakers was a "return to normalcy": the old certainties should be restored. But at the same time they should be secured and institutionalized through international institutions, the Covenant and the League of Nations, and treaties, such as the permanent pact of peace concluded at the initiative of the U.S. Secretary of State Frank Kellog and the French Foreign Minister Aristide Briand. Such a framework would allow the markets to operate: and indeed international capital resumed its flow. George Grosz in a memorable caricature saw the dollar as the sun that warmed the European continent. Migrations resumed. And markets, it was assumed, would make peace: every observer of the 1920s was struck, for instance, by how dependence on foreign capital imports made eccentric, destructive and belligerent figures such as the Italian leader Benito Mussolini into responsible and even pacific statesmen.

All of these beliefs – part hopes, part illusions – in the restoration of one market-driven world were destroyed by the experience of the Great Depression. In the 1930s the world descended into economic nationalism and protectionism. There were competitive devaluations. Autarky and war economy became national goals.

How and why did the interwar depression turn back the push of globalization? The search for new means of securing integration ended in the late 1920s with a series of shocks.

First, since the middle of the 1920s, raw material prices were falling, in large part as a consequence of the extension of the area of production during the World War, in part as a result of inept schemes for price manipulation, such as the Stevenson scheme which aimed to keep an artificially high rubber price (by making exports from the producer countries dependent on the price level), but which actually encouraged overplanting and eventually led to a price collapse at the end

[3] *Brinley Thomas*, Migration and Economic Growth (Cambridge 1954); *Brinley Thomas*, Migration and Urban Development (London 1972).

of the decade. This price decline made the situation for many capital-importing countries more difficult. But, from the perspective of the industrial countries, the results appeared beneficial, since raw materials and foods – at that time a much larger component of household budgets than currently – were cheaper. With additional available income, consumers might buy new products. Such calculations sustained the giddy glitter of the jazz age.

Secondly, the international political situation in Europe was burdened by an impossible conflict over war debts and reparations. Impossible, because the more credits flowed, the more inextricable the situation became. Germany was supposed to pay a substantial part of the burden of the war through the reparations imposed under the Versailles Treaty. France needed reparations not only to reconstruct, but also to pay the wartime debt to Britain and the United States. Germany – that is German corporations and the German public sector – borrowed substantial sums largely on the American market; this borrowing financed at least indirectly the reparations payments. But as the payments were made through the second half of the 1920s, it became increasingly apparent that this was not a game that could be played for ever: that at one moment, there would come a choice when either the United States could continue to receive reparation payments, or U.S. creditors could have their private loans serviced. At least some German policy makers, notably Hjalmar Schacht, President of the German Reichsbank, made this calculation in all cynicism, in the belief that the resulting debacle would demonstrate the folly of reparations. The reassessment of the reparations burden in 1929, in which at last a final term was set for the payment of reparation (payments were to continue until 1988), made clear to more investors the impossible nature of their bet and Germany's chances of external credit deteriorated dramatically. At the colloquium, and in this volume, Albrecht Ritschl presents an interpretation of the German stock market downturn of 1927, in which at this time investors already take into account the problems of the capital market and their implications for Germany.

Third, there was a tendency to react to economic problems in the 1920s by trade measures. The model for this was the U.S. Fordney-McCumber tariff act of 1922. It was not that the level of protection was especially high (most analysts now see that the overall level of protection was actually lower than before the First World War). But the possibility of such measures being applied in response to other, financial problems, and the increased popularity of non-tariff protection (quotas) made for a greater restriction of trade. The discussion of trade policy in the early 1930s is central to the paper by Carl-Ludwig Holtfrerich and Monika Rosengarten. Christoph Buchheim provides a survey of how the world economy collapsed in the 1930s, and contrasts that era with the post-1945 world, in which a hegemonic power, the United States, pushed for trade liberalization and in doing this created a new basis for global growth. Solomos Solomou and Forrest Capie both consider the costs of protection, and give different answers: Solomou is concerned to show how, given what else was wrong in the 1930s, the protectionist response was defensible; while Capie points out the very high costs.

There were plenty of economic problems in the world before the dramatic collapse of Wall Street in October 1929. Australia, with its dependence on exported wool, or Brazil, almost exclusively reliant on coffee exports, were deeply depressed. In Germany cyclical production indicators already turned round in the autumn of 1927 (the stock market weakness appeared even earlier, as Albrecht Ritschl analyzes in his paper). Gerald Feldman's contribution to this volume gives a diagnosis of problems in Austrian and German insurers. The UK suffered a recession as a consequence of decline in the export of traded services in 1928[4]. The story of what produced 1929 in the United States is still slightly mysterious, at least for believers in the rationality of markets. What did stock market investors know on "Black Thursday", October 24, 1929, that they had not known on Tuesday or Wednesday? There was "bad news" since early September: and the weight of evidence had accumulated to such an extent that there was a panic in the face of the likelihood of the future decline of stock prices. The only plausible answer for those who wish a rational account of the stock market collapse is that American investors were contemplating the likelihood of the implementation of a new piece of legislation, which went under the names of Hawley and Smoot. This tariff bill had begun as a promise in the presidential campaign of 1929 by Herbert Hoover to improve the situation of the American farmer (with the agricultural price collapse, the farmer was the major loser of jazz age prosperity). In the course of congressional debate, however, each representative tried to add on new items (there were 1253 Senate amendments alone). The result – a tariff with 21,000 tariff positions – was extreme protectionism: but worse, until the final narrow voting in June 1930, it was constant uncertainty about the future of trade policy.

If the story of the depression does not begin with the stock market crash and Smoot-Hawley, neither does it end there. There were some signs of recovery in 1930: stock prices in the U.S. rebounded, and the lower level of the market made foreign issues appear attractive again.

What made the depression the *Great* Depression rather than a brief-lived stock market problem or a depression for commodity producers was a chain of linkages that operated through the financial markets. The desperate state of the commodity producers along with the reparations induced problems of Germany set off a chain of domino reactions across national boundaries. In this sense the depression was a product of disorderly financial markets. Dietmar Rothermund's contribution shows how financial conditions on European and American capital markets affected territories literally on the other side of the globe: even Asian peasant producers were devastated by the turmoil on the international financial markets.

How does financial contagion operate? There are at least three separate channels. First, there can be a direct contagion, when bad loans to one country produce failures in banks in the lending country. Secondly, there is a "portfolio effect": when a bank is vulnerable because it has lost badly on its loans to one market, and

[4] *Solomos Solomou*, Themes in Macroeconomic History: The UK Economy 1919–1939 (Cambridge 1996) 95.

faces demands for withdrawals by its depositors, it will call in credits where it still can, in other words from sound areas. Such calls may then cause liquidity problems in that third country. Thirdly, financial markets may anticipate that their customers – or market sentiment – will caricature a whole area such as "Latin America" or "Central Europe" (or recently "East Asia") as a problem area, and withdraw credits from the region as a whole.

The sequence of the different aspects of crisis was different in each of the central European crisis economies, but the outcomes were surprisingly similar. In each case, capital movements across frontiers destroyed a banking system that had already been weakened by the effects of war and postwar inflations. And in each case, the concatenation of problems produced a policy paralysis. In his 1978 lecture, Knut Borchardt analyzed the limited room for maneuver, and warned against a retrospective optimism about the solubility of problems[5]. The astonishing feature of the world depression was how rapidly this paralysis was transferred across national frontiers. A similar contagion mechanism operated in Latin America. In mid-1930, rates on South American bonds had been only 1 or 2% above those on U.S. domestic securities. In the second half of the year, prices slid, as investors anticipated defaults. Bolivia defaulted in January 1930, Peru in March, Chile in July, Cuba in August.

A crisis in the creditor countries followed the problems of the debtors. In Britain, there were no fundamental problems with banks. But many investment houses suffered from the freezing of their credits in central Europe, and their depositors feared possible insolvencies. The German bank closures of July 1931 set off a run on sterling: the final event that tipped Britain off the gold standard were rumors of an impending Latin American default. On 21 September 1931 Britain announced that the pound would float: there was no longer a commitment to sell gold for sterling at a fixed price. The Bank of England refused to use all the instruments at its disposal – interest rate increases, or the use of its reserves – in defense of the parity, as it feared that allowing further transfers over the exchange would bring down at least some of the weaker London banks. The devaluation stabilized the British financial system because of its rather skillful management. The pound fell sharply on the exchange, creating expectations that the next movement would be up rather than down, and thus discouraging depositors from realizing their losses. It is important to note – particularly for those who suggest that this British style solution might have been appropriate for the central European or South American cases – that there it would have been harder, indeed impossible to find an exchange rate which would have given rise to the expectation of recovery.

The British panic had in common with the preceding debtor crises an abrupt reversal of expectations. Depositors and investors saw a danger of being trapped in a particular engagement, and – as they saw the door closing – rushed to get out. Once this mechanism had operated in one creditor country, it might apply to others. The United States was vulnerable, not because it had an external current

[5] *Borchardt,* Zwangslagen und Handlungsspielräume.

account problem, but because it was apparent that U.S. banks were vulnerable to losses elsewhere. The resulting capital movements, which set on quite suddenly after the sterling devaluation of September 1931, changed the possibilities for anticyclical measures. Before September 1931, President Hoover had been contemplating quite extensive measures to stimulate the economy through government expenditure. After the panic, in which as a result of experience elsewhere government deficits were synonymous with failures of confidence, the President started to assert the necessity of balanced budgets. But so, remarkably, did his Democratic opponent in the 1932 presidential race Franklin Delano Roosevelt, who made criticism of Hoover's deficits a focal point of his campaign. The withdrawals and the shocks to confidence only ended when Roosevelt, seeing every other alternative fail, took the dollar off the gold standard in April 1933. Again the dollar fell sharply, encouraging belief that it might be stabilized or even recover. Then the crises continued in the remaining gold standard countries, Belgium, France, the Netherlands and Switzerland, until in the end they too saw an abandonment of the parity regime as the only way of ending continual budget strain and bank panics.

What are the economic lessons of this dramatic experience of panic and failure? First, countries with high foreign debts and weak banking structures are vulnerable to deflationary shocks. Secondly, the mechanisms of financial contagion transfer the weakness even to creditor countries with sound banking systems. Thirdly, the most obvious transmission mechanism was the fixed exchange rate commitment[6]. As soon as Britain or the United States – or Belgium or Switzerland – abandoned the gold standard link, while preserving fiscal orthodoxy, the banking threat that had been a prime mechanism for the transmission of depression disappeared.

It might be though that only concerted international action could deal with these structural problems. There was a great deal of discussion, and even international institutions: but the papers given by Patricia Clavin and Harold James tell a story of rather dismal failure.

Many aspects of our analysis are not intelligible in terms of purely economic analysis. Why was the world of that time so vulnerable to crises? Do financial crises always have to have such a domino effect? In order to understand the institutions that played such a central role in the world depression – the state and its budgets, the central banks, the gold standard linkage – it is necessary to go back to the nineteenth century and the beginnings of globalization, and the concept of the nation-state as a protective barrier against the threats posed by global integration.

Globalization almost immediately in every country produced reactions against internationalism, and demands for protection from the effects of changes and crises coming from the outside. It was clear that in the 1920s and 1930s, previously

[6] *Barry Eichengreen*, Golden Fetters: The Gold Standard and the Great Depression 1919–1939 (New York 1992) 257.

successful remedies from the past were applied once more. Now everything was to be national – labor and goods, but also capital. John Maynard Keynes brilliantly described this development in his 1933 essay, "National Self-Sufficiency", which was quickly translated into German[7]. Keynes's leading biographer, Robert Skidelsky, provides a survey of Keynes's 1930s diagnosis of the problems of Britain and the United States in the 1930s, and concludes that we have actually learnt a great deal from the "lessons of the depression".

The collapse of the economy now brought a turning away from the market. Even moderate and pragmatic analysts, such as the director of the League of Nations' Economic and Financial Section, Sir Arthur Salter, believed that the future lay in regulation and control[8]. With the encyclical *Quadragesimo Anno* in the crisis year 1931, the Catholic church looked for a "third way" between capitalism and socialism.

Increasing regulation and planning encouraged those who saw the function of the state as being to externalize the costs of economic adjustment: to impose those costs on those outside the national community. The state's duty lay in protecting its citizens, and ensuring that the inhabitants of other national communities suffered as much as possible. This was of course quite the opposite of the traditions of classical economic liberalism, in which there is a mutuality of gains.

The path away from the market and toward control was also a path to political dictatorship. The most obvious examples were in Russia and Germany. But the sentiment that democracy had failed in fulfilling a basic social need was widely shared by many democrats. At this time, the nation-state and its control mechanisms was supposed to give guarantees against the threats from the world economy. But was not the protection more dangerous and destructive than the threat?

In the world of today, we do indeed immediately experience and react to distant crises.

The Great Depression was a consequence of a financial vulnerability that reflected a set of institutions which had originally been created as a protection against the impact of globalization:

1. Restrictions on immigration diminished the prospects for growth in the classic countries of immigration, and at the same time contributed to over-population and under-employment in the capital scarce countries of Mediterranean and Eastern Europe.

2. Tariff protection (especially the Hawley-Smoot Act) sent the wrong signals to the markets.

3. The gold standard linkage reduced rather than enhanced confidence in financial markets.

4. Central banking could no longer hope to control the capital markets.

[7] *J.M. Keynes*, Nationale Selbstgenügsamkeit, in: Schmollers Jahrbuch (1934) 565–6. On the German translation, see: *Knut Borchardt*, Keynes' Nationale Selbstgenügsamkeit von 1933, in: Zeitschrift für Wirtschafts- und Sozialwissenschaften (1988) 271–84.
[8] *Arthur Salter*, Recovery: The Second Effort (London 1932).

5. The interventionist state reached the limits of its capacity for action.

By a perverse logic, the most common response was increased control, nationalization, autarky, control of capital movements, exchange control, bans on immigration, ending with the expulsion and even genocide of whole peoples.

To sum up: in the nineteenth century, there had been a rapid process of globalization, which met almost immediate resistance. The interventionist state derived a great deal of its legitimation from the process of globalization, and became increasingly an impediment to integration. It was in the Great Depression that those who opposed the freedom of migration, and of goods and capital transactions, saw the opportunity to move the pendulum back. Are we now living in an age in which the attempt is being made to use – not a Great Depression, but the fear of one – as a justification for moving back away from the world of the internationalized economy?

Verzeichnis der Tagungsteilnehmer

Prof. Dr. Knut Borchardt, Icking
Prof. Dr. Christoph Buchheim, Mannheim
Prof. Dr. Forrest H. Capie, London
Dr. Patricia Clavin, Keele, Staffs (England)
Prof. Dr. Barry Eichengreen, Berkeley, Cal.
Prof. Dr. Gerald D. Feldman, Berkeley, Cal.
Dr. Marc Flandreau, Paris
Prof. Dr. Heiner Flassbeck, Bonn
Prof. Dr. Carl-Ludwig Holtfrerich, Berlin
Prof. Dr. Harold James, Princeton, N.J.
Prof. Dr. John Komlos, München
Prof. Dr. Albrecht Ritschl, Barcelona
Monika Rosengarten, Berlin
Prof. Dr. Dietmar Rothermund, Heidelberg
Dr. Jens van Scherpenberg, Ebenhausen
Prof. Lord Robert Skidelsky, London
Prof. Dr. Solomos Solomou, Cambridge
Prof. Dr. Reinhard Spree, München

Albrecht Ritschl

International Capital Movements and the Onset of the Great Depression: Some International Evidence

I. Introduction

Having rational expectations is not always comfortable. Archival historians tell us the story of the international central bankers' meeting at Long Island in 1927, where Benjamin Strong, then governor of the Federal Reserve Bank of New York, predicted that within two years' time, the worst depression in history would set in, the only question being whether it would break out in Germany or in the U.S. (see Link, 1970).

What concerned central bankers at the time was the stabilization of the gold standard in a heavily changed international environment. The pre-war monetary system had largely rested on Britain's unquestioned role as the world leader in capital exports. The flow of revenues generated by these overseas investments helped to stabilize the British balance of payments in times of recession. This, in turn, made it easy for the Bank of England to conduct the "international orchestra" of monetary policies (using a phrase coined by Eichengreen, 1987), even in the absence of large gold reserves of her own.

After World War I, these conditions no longer existed. Britain had used up many of its foreign investments, notably in the U.S., to finance World War I. In addition, large war loans had flowed from the U.S. to Europe. As a consequence, the U.S. converted into the world's largest creditor and would now have to assume the role of the orchestra's conductor. The fundamental difference to pre-war times was that Europe's recovery from the war was not satisfactory. Britain had suffered severely from the deep recession of 1920 and later followed deflationary policies to stabilize its currency at the pre-war parity. France had experienced inflation and turmoil, and by mid-1927 it was not yet clear that Poincare's stabilization of 1926 would be a success. Recovery in Germany had been severely hampered by the hyperinflation in 1922 and 1923 (Eichengreen, 1992). As a result, in 1927 neither Britain nor France had attained their pre-war levels of output per capita, and the same may have been true of Germany (Maddison, 1995). Thus, administering the gold standard was clearly not an easy task.

To make things worse, much of the stabilization achieved so far seemed artificial and unhealthy. The Dawes Plan of 1924 had brought recovery and stable money back to Germany, at a cost. In order to help Germany to re-stock and modernize its productive apparatus, fresh money had been injected into the German economy. However, instead of putting their house in order and starting to pay out reparations from trade surpluses, the Germans had begun to borrow abroad in almost unlimited quantities. During the Dawes Plan period from 1924 to 1929, Germany paid her reparations entirely on credit, and in addition to that ran massive import surpluses. Germany operated a credit pyramid, a veritable Ponzi scheme; even the interest on existing foreign debt was paid from new credits.

Worries about Germany's reckless foreign borrowing had already appeared in 1925 (Schuker, 1988). In 1926, the president of the Reichsbank, Schacht, started desperate attempts to gain control at least of a portion of public borrowing abroad, but only with limited success (James, 1985). By 1927, the debt was already so high that Germany was faced with a stark choice: authorities could either deflate the economy abruptly in order to ensure her future capacity to pay, or they would have to keep waiting passively until the bubble burst and the pyramid came crushing down to damage, not only the German economy but the international financial system along with it. No doubt, Mr. Strong had reasons to be worried.

This paper is about the international causation of the Great Depression, centering on the crucial year of 1927. Employing leading indicators for business-cycle activity, I provide evidence that the international depression did not start in the U.S. and that it was probably not caused by an "autonomous" decline in U.S. foreign lending to Europe, as conventional wisdom would have it. As soon as 1927, there are clear indications of a beginning downturn in the German economy, which came too early to be explained by a contraction of American lending. Both real and financial indicators point downward in Germany one or two years before they do so in the U.S. Cross-examining the results with data for Britain, it appears that the decline in the British economy comes even later.

I am clearly not the first to make this point. In a well-known paper, Temin (1971) argued from an examination of German investment data that there must have been a decline of investment demand before American lending dried up, which would refute the standard hypothesis. Temin's view was challenged by Falkus (1975) and Balderston (1977, 1982) on the grounds of measurement problems. Using different data, however, it appears that Temin's point must be re-established.

The rest of this paper is organized as follows. The next section looks at leading business indicators for the German economy, which all show a turning point already in mid-1927. Section III turns to the time profiles of German borrowing and American lending in order to find evidence on the transmission of the business cycle across the two countries. Section IV explores the issue of timing further by looking into turning points in U.S. capital formation. Section V traces the implications for interest rate differentials between Germany, Britain, and the United States. Section VI presents conclusions and implications for further research.

II. Turning points in the German business cycle of the 1920s

Looking at the moving forces of the German inter-war business cycle, we need to distinguish between domestic and foreign components. Considerable parts of Germany's economy, especially the large agricultural sector, were entirely home-oriented. But others, such as manufacturing, were not. Activity in this sector was influenced both by domestic and international demand, which during the inter-war period often moved in opposite directions. As a result, industrial production only partly reflected domestic demand trends. This is particularly true of the capital-goods industries. These are interesting to us as their activity also helps to predict investment in the German economy in later periods.

For this industry, we have monthly statistics on domestic and foreign orders, which come from surveys conducted by the German machine builders' association (VDMA) among its members[1]. As can be seen from Figure 1, domestic and foreign orders to German machinery industry followed a very different pattern in the late 1920s.

Note the marked phase shift between the two series: while foreign orders reached their maximum only in September of 1929, domestic orders peaked al-

Figure 1: Orders to German Machinery Indusry and Tobin's Q in the Berlin Stock Market

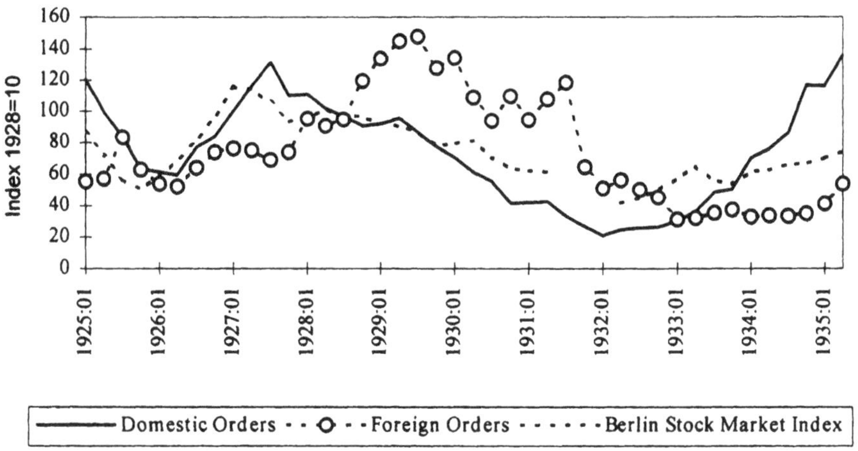

Domestic Orders: *Wagemann* (1935, p. 228, series 66).
Foreign Orders: *Wagemann* (1935, p. 228, series 67).
Berlin Stock Market Index: *Wagemann* (1935, p. 115, series 2, deflated by prices of equipment, p. 105, series 27).

[1] According to VDMA (1930), its membership represented 90% of the value added in machine building in 1928. The order series are also in *Wagemann* (1935).

ready in August, 1927, and declined thereafter almost without interruption[2]. This means that as far as business expectations were concerned, domestic capital formation was on the decline since mid-1927. Capital installment takes time to build, and therefore, the actual data on investment lagged behind. Here, we see that between 1927 and 1929 there is no clear tendency. This explains much of the debate about Temin's (1971) data. If one looks at realized investment rates only, the existence of a turning point of 1927 is not so clear, as it only can be affirmed that an investment boom came to an end, albeit still at a high level of activity. Only if we look at an early indicator of domestic investment demand, we can spot the turning point correctly.

There is further corroborating evidence. In Figure 1 the series of domestic orders is also plotted against the price-adjusted Berlin stock market index (or Tobin's q). Both series peak sometime in 1927 and decline thereafter. It is noteworthy how well the stock market data and domestic machinery orders correlate with one another[3]. In fact, the stock market appears to be a leading indicator for machinery orders, as predicted by economic theory[4].

The tight correlation between the stock market index and the domestic machinery order series is evidence against a bubble in the 1927 stock market. There existed fundamentals in the German economy which supported the previous stock market increases, and when the stock market declined, these fundamentals went down as well. Apparently, some fundamental change occurred in the German economy in 1927 which induced investors to become bearish about stocks and real capital investments as well.

If trouble was ahead for the German economy and if investors expected that, this should also be visible in the bond markets. A concept that has attracted increasing attention in recent years is the term structure of interest rates. Under normal business conditions, interest rates are higher in the long run. However, when investors expect a deflationary shock to occur, the term structure, or difference between long- and short-term interest rates, may become smaller or even negative. The term structure shown in Figure 2 provides an example of just this effect, and once again, the recessive impulse we are looking for is visible in 1927.

Unfortunately, our data do not permit us to focus more closely on the time horizon at which investors expected the deflationary shock to occur. Ideally, we should have interest rates on bonds of different maturity to be able to construct a yield curve over a time span of several years. This we do not have. The short-term

[2] From April 1928 to August 1932, domestic orders in each month are lower than in the respective month of the preceding year. The only exception is April 1929; otherwise the decline is uninterrupted.

[3] The tight correlation between these two series was first noted by *Donner* (1934). We note in passing that domestic demand follows a very similar pattern at the time. All series come from *Wagemann* (1935).

[4] The stock market data shown here are stock prices divided by machinery prices, which is an indicator for Tobin's q, the relative price of existing and new equipment. If this goes up, investment should rise, and vice versa. The seminal paper on this is *Hayashi* (1982).

Figure 2: The Term Structure of Interest Rates, Germany 1926–1935

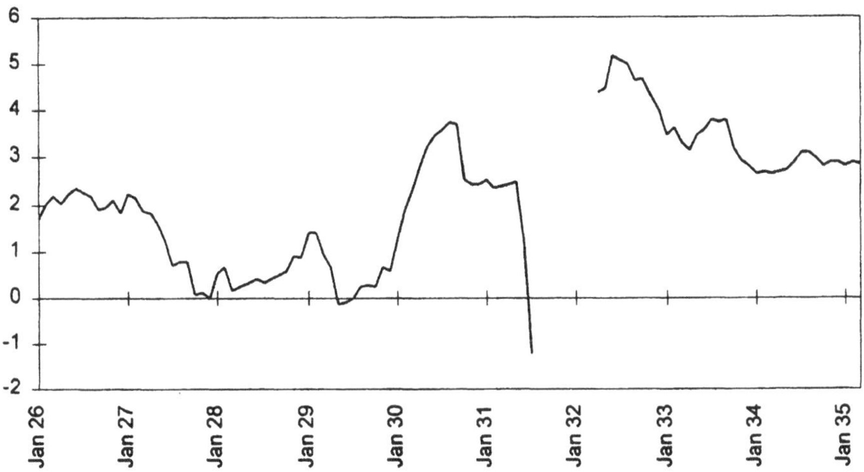

Term Structure: NBER Macrohistory database, series 13028 (yields on gold bonds), series m13018 (Berlin private discount rate).

interest rates are for three-monthly paper, while the long-term rates are on long-term gold bonds with unspecified maturity. However, even in these imperfect data we do see a dramatic deterioration in the term structure in 1927, two years before deflation actually set in. We note that, if investors predicted the depression correctly, they believed it to be short-lived: the span between the collapse of the term structure in mid-1927 and its even more dramatic recovery is 9 quarters. If we take this literally, investors predicted a slump of slightly more than two years – which means they underestimated the length of the deflation period by exactly one year. (It is probably not accidental that the term structure recovers at the beginning of 1930. Once the slump had visibly set in also in the international scene, it was not entirely extraneous to believe that conditions would improve within reasonable time.)

The evidence on the term structure also permits conclusions regarding the importance of international capital movements. Conventional wisdom at the end of the Golden Twenties maintains that the downturn in the European economies was caused by dwindling American capital exports, which in turn is held to have caused investment to fall. If this was the case, investment should have been choked off by rising interest rates instead of deteriorating through worsening expectations and falling domestic demand. This, in turn, should have caused long-term interest rates to rise relative to short-term rates. Evidently, the converse holds true. If investment rates were really brought down by high interest rates, we should see the term structure spread out instead of becoming more compressed. Hence, we must conclude that the transmission must have gone from falling investment demand to falling relative interest rates at the long-term end of the yield curve, not the other way round.

III. German capital imports and U.S. capital exports

We may also compare German capital imports and U.S. capital exports directly. Following Fleisig (1970), Kindleberger (1973) concluded that the upcoming stock market boom choked off U.S. foreign lending. If the German credit expansion of the 1920s was merely a passive reflection of American lending, its time profile and term structure should more or less follow the U.S. data. Data in Figure 3 provide data on German net capital imports during the decade following the end of hyperinflation. Once again, we observe a peak in 1927, followed by a collapse from 1928 to 1929. Note also that much of Germany's foreign borrowing was short-term, to be converted into long-term loans by German banks at home. It was precisely this "hot money" end of the market which collapsed first.

If we now compare this to the U.S. data on capital exports (Figure 4), we find a number of markedly contrasting features. First, U.S. capital exports peaked only in 1928, one year after German capital imports. Second, we do observe a small decline in short-term capital exports, which however is too little to explain the collapse of German short-term capital imports in the same period. Third, U.S. direct investment abroad continued to increase in 1929 and went down only in 1930, while German long-term capital imports were practically dead already in 1929 (the blip in 1930 is caused by the Young loan for German reparations, designed to postpone Germany's foreign debt crisis by one year).

Figure 3: German Capital Imports, 1924–1935

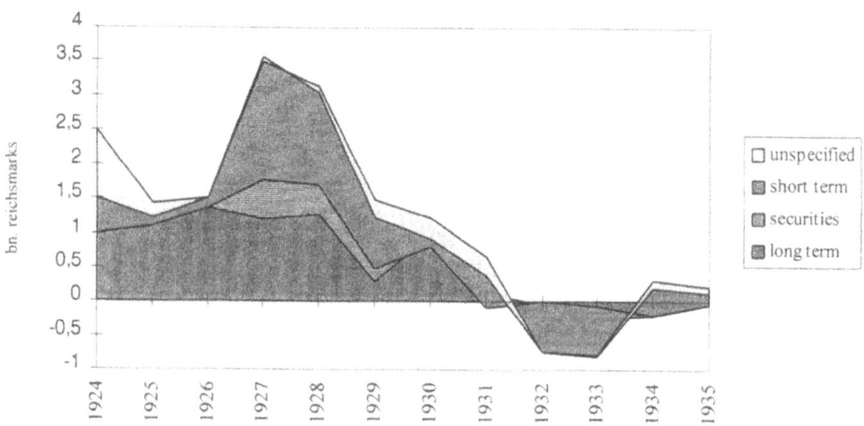

German net capital imports: Bundesbank (1976, p. 328).

Figure 4: U.S. Capital Exports (US funds only), 1924–1935

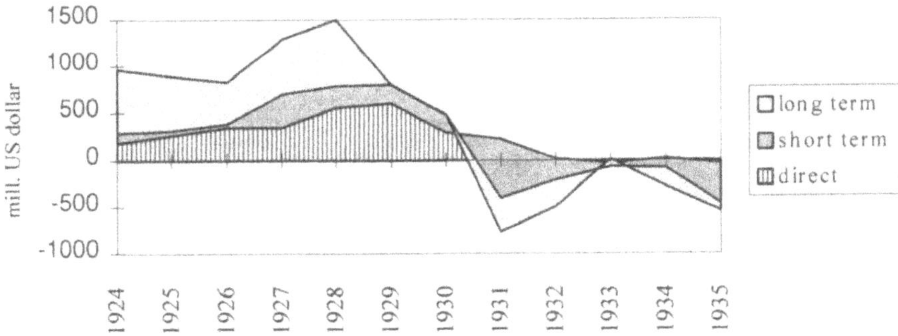

U.S. net capital exports (U.S. funds): Dept. of Commerce (1972).

It seems safe to conclude from these discrepancies that there must be more to the decline in German capital imports than just faltering U.S. capital exports: the decline in German capital imports comes too early, and it occurs at the wrong end of the term structure.

This observation squares well with the German interest data we examined in the previous section. Had there been a sudden lack of loanable funds for long-term investment projects, as Kindleberger (1973) and many others have suggested from U.S. data, we would have seen an increase in German long-term interest rates relative to short-term rates. At the same time, long-term capital flows between the U.S. and Germany would have had to go down simultaneously. Instead, in 1927 and 1928 we see a sharp decline in German short-term borrowing which has no counterpart in U.S. short-term lending, and German short-term interest rates go up while long-term rates remain stable: Germany had become an unsafe place for hot money once its stock market boom was over, even before the New York stock market really took off.

Last in this section, let the argument be carried still further. Traditionally, economic historians are educated to think of the United States as the capital-exporting giant whose cough would cause pneumonia in the rest of the world. As the above figures bear out, Germany at that time was not exactly a small economy either: its net capital imports after 1924 oscillated between 40 and 65% of America's own capital exports. They were even higher relative to U.S. figures if the movements of all funds and not just U.S. ones are included in the latter. Figure 5 provides a synopsis of German and U.S. net capital imports.

As the figure bears out, Germany's capital imports during the 1920s are actually often larger than America's capital exports. The average from 1925 to 1929 is 117% of U.S. net capital exports, including funds of foreign origin in the latter.

There is yet another observation to be made in Figure 5. With the movements of foreign funds included, the U.S. capital balance looks notably less business-cycle

Figure 5: Total Capital Imports, US and Germany, 1924–1935

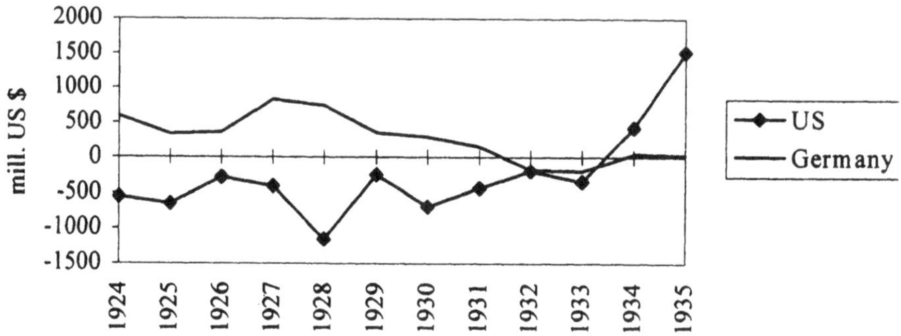

U.S. net capital exports (foreign funds): Dept. of Commerce (1972).

driven than before, and also less so than the German figures. Even in 1931, U.S. net capital exports are still larger than in 1927.

With all these elements in place, there seems to be little room for the traditional capital-flow hypothesis: apparently, Temin (1971) was right. There is much in the German data that points to a domestic-driven business downturn already by 1927, and it is hard to see how the impulse for this should have come from abroad, especially from the U.S., where lending of U.S. funds declines too late and aggregate net lending exhibits no clear trend at all.

Given the magnitudes involved in Germany's capital imports, the question of the direction of causality is not a trivial one. One may even wonder if Germany's balance-of-payments troubles could possibly have had their own international repercussions.

IV. Turning points in the business cycle in the U.S. and Britain

In the following, we do not endeavor to make a contribution to the debate about whether or not the New York stock market boom prior to October, 1929 was a bubble. We only are interested in tracing major fundamentals in the U.S. economy to find turning points and identify their timing. The obvious first candidate are corporate dividends. From a self-constructed dividend series for the Dow Jones listed companies, White (1990) concluded that from 1928 on, the index systematically outperformed dividend growth, which indeed would indicate a bubble. However, what is notable is that dividends continued to grow; there are few signs of a downturn in the data before the end of 1929. Nevertheless, White (1990) concludes from his analysis that managers apparently did not share the enthusiasm of the public, hence the discrepancy between stock market and dividend growth must have been a bubble.

Of course, dividend growth does not need to match the growth in the value of equity, at least in the short run. But if a change in dividend policies occurred between 1926 and 1927, an explanation is needed. For this, we repeat the exercise from section II above in which a suitably deflated version of the stock market index was compared to machinery output (or, in that case, new domestic orders). This way, we may determine if managers shared the expectations of the financial market. If they did, Tobin's q theory of investment would advise them to adjust their capital stock upward by the same measure. If they didn't and remained pessimistic instead, growth of machinery output should fall short of stock market performance.

We saw above that for Germany, there was indeed a tight correlation between the stock market and investment activity, and that the stock market actually predicted how much would appear in next month's order books. Data for the U.S. economy are shown in Figure 6.

Figure 6 tells us two things: first, the order of magnitude of the changes in investment demand and stock market value is the same. If there was a bubble in the late 1920s, it extended to managers' expectations as well and was not confined to financial markets. Second, in contrast to the German case, the investment climate in 1928 was consistently better than in 1927. Orders of new capital goods only stop growing in the spring of 1929; it is the very last part of the stock market boom which is no longer supported by the fundamentals of the order series.

Figure 6: Orders of US Machine Tools and Tobin's Q in the Dow Jones Stock Market Index, 1921–35

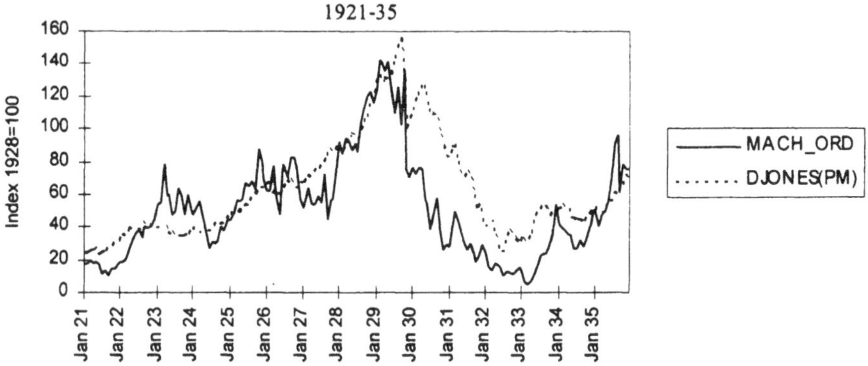

U.S. machine orders: NBER Macrohistory database, series 06029 (shipments of machine tools).
Stock market index: NBER Macrohistory database, series 11009 (Dow Jones Index), series 04066 (prices of metal products).

Note that there does not seem to be a very clear lead-lag pattern between the two series in Figure 6; however, at the onset of the depression, machinery orders fall earlier and deeper than the stock market index. In sum, there are no signs of a depression in U.S. investment and the stock market until well into 1929: by the time the investment boom came to an end, investment orders and the stock market in Germany had already fallen by some 25%.

V. Interest Rates and Term Structures: the Transatlantic Perspective

If the major European players in the pre-depression credit gamble experienced difficulties in borrowing from the U.S., this should be reflected in interest rate differentials with respect to the U.S. As data in Figure 7 below bear out, long-term interest rates in Britain were consistently higher than in the U.S. for the whole period of Britain's adherence to the gold standard. One might conclude that markets did not reward Britain's "good housekeeping" with a seal of approval, as Bordo/ Edelstein/ Rockoff (1998) would have it. On the contrary, lacking ability to sustain foreign exchange equilibrium without credit restrictions was apparently punished by international markets, if only slightly.

Figure 7: Long-Term Interest Rates Differentials vis-à-vis the US

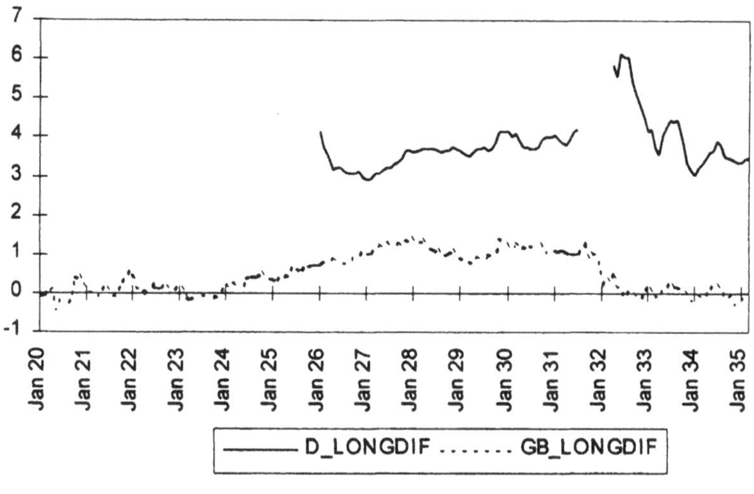

Long-term Interest Rate Differential, Germany/U.S.: NBER Macrohistory database, series 13028 (yields on gold bonds), series 13033 (yields on United States eight-year bonds). Long-term Interest Rate Differential, Britain/U.S.: NBER Macrohistory database, series 13041 (yields on UK consols), series 13033 (yields on United States eight-year bonds).

The real action is no doubt in the German data. German bonds commanded a premium over U.S. bonds that never fell below three percentage points and that increased notably during 1927. In 1928 when U.S. capital exports reached their maximum, German long-term interest rates were higher and German capital imports lower than in the previous year. During early 1929 when U.S. lending dropped dramatically from its 1928 peak (Fleisig, 1970), we see no upward response in Germany's and Britain's interest rates. Note that in contrast, Britain's interest rates went down relative to the U.S. in the same period. Only in late 1929 do interest rate differentials widen. Apparently, there was more to the transatlantic capital market than just dwindling U.S. capital exports.

The evidence obtained in this section may be complemented with data on the term structure of interest rates across major countries. In each of the three countries, we compare the interest on long-term bonds with yields on three-monthly paper (Figure 8).

Data for the years of 1927 to 1929 exhibit a striking regional pattern: the yield curve collapsed first in Germany (late 1927), half a year later in the U.S. (early 1928), and only in early 1929 did the change affect Britain. Unfortunately, data quality does not permit us to compare levels of the term structure directly across

Figure 8: The Term Structure of Interes Rates
Long-Terms Bonds vs. Three-Monthly Paper

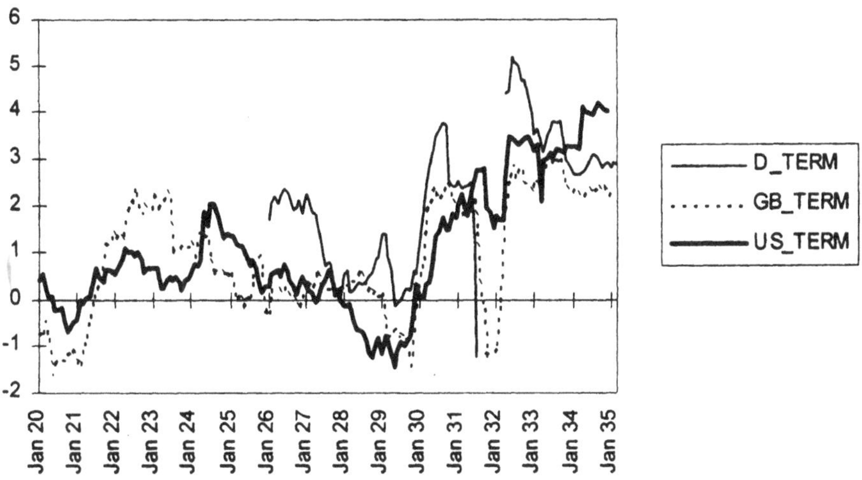

German term structure: see Figure 2.
British term structure: NBER Macrohistory database, series 13041 (yields on UK consols), series 13016 (London open market rates of discount).
U.S. term structure: NBER Macrohistory database, series 13033 (yields on United States eight-year bonds), 13029 (yields on short-term Treasury notes, certificates, and bills).

countries[5]. However, a clear temporal pattern emerges which is consistent with the findings in Section II above: the writing on the wall appeared first in Germany, not in the U.S.

We do not want to enter into the debate on whether deflation in the U.S. was anticipated at the onset of the depression[6]. Lacking more detailed information on the yield curve, little can be said about the time horizons at which investors in the bond market expected deflationary turnarounds. However, the deterioration of expectations we observe is a quick one. Already by mid-1928, a trough is reached. Thus, deflationary expectations did exist in the U.S. bond market well before the depression set in. However, if we look only at the period where the term structure is inverted, neither the extension of the deflationary period nor the depth of deflation seem to be well anticipated by the market.

We might alternatively argue that the flattening of the yield curve in 1924/25 already predicts the depression. Given that the peak occurs in 1924, the peak of activity in 1928/29 would be predicted with a lead of 4½ years. Consequently, assuming the same lead from mid-1928 to late 1929 would predict the trough of the depression to occur between early 1933 and mid-1934, with subsequent sharp recovery thereafter. This speculation may, however, be too daring. Clearly, more research on this issue is needed.

VI. Conclusions and Implications

A reexamination of international capital movements at the onset of the Great Depression leads to new results which may shed light on the causes and the spread of the slump. During the second half of the 1920s, Germany's net capital imports were on average larger than American capital exports. This paper has studied the term structure and the timing of these capital movements to draw conclusions about the possible causes of the collapse in international credit relations prior to the Great Depression. To find out whether there were domestic factors behind these credit flows, we also identified turning points in the domestic business cycles of both countries.

In Germany, domestic investment demand, the stock market, and foreign borrowing start to decline in 1927 and continue to fall almost without interruption through mid-1932. As U.S. lending continues to grow spectacularly through mid-

[5] The reason is that both the British and German short-term bills whose yields we included were risk-bearing, while in the U.S. we chose short-term treasury bonds. Repeating the exercise with risk-bearing commercial paper for the U.S., the results are basically unchanged; the collapse of the U.S. yield curve is postponed somewhat further into 1928.

[6] On this, see *Cecchetti* (1992) with evidence in favor and *Hamilton* (1992) with evidence against predictability of the deflation process. Given our results on the yield curve, we would cautiously lean toward the first position.

1928, this decline in Germany comes too early to be explained by reduced supply of U.S. credit.

Our results lend new credibility to Temin's (1971) hypothesis of an autonomous beginning of the depression in Germany in 1927. The fall in German borrowing abroad was apparently induced by factors pertaining to the domestic economy. Uncertainty over the future reparation burden and the German policy of paying reparations on credit under the Dawes Plan increased the risk of lending to domestic and international investors in that country. Buoyant export demand and the injection of fresh money under the Young Plan would postpone the hour of reckoning, but the unsustainable credit expansion of the German economy was an issue of public debate as early as 1927.

In contrast, market fundamentals in the U.S. continued to look favorable. The stock market boom was fully supported by rising investment demand up until early 1929. The only disturbing evidence we found came from the bond market. Examining the term structure of interest rates across countries, we find that expectations of a business downturn become visible in Germany already in the second half of 1927, when the German yield curve becomes compressed or even inverted. These deflationary expectations carry over to the U.S. in the first half of 1928, when the yield curve suddenly inverts itself, while the British bond market is affected only in early 1929.

These results have their possible implication for our understanding of the interwar gold standard. While traditionally, we have been led to think of a monetary transmission of deflationary shocks from the U.S. to the rest of the world, the evidence presented in this paper suggests that in the late 1920s, the main deflationary impulse originated in Germany. More research is needed to trace the interactions between bond markets and money markets prior to the Great Depression at an international level.

References

Balderston, T., The German Business Cycle in the 1920s: A Comment, in: Economic History Review 30 (1977) 159–161

Balderston, T., The Origins of Economic Instability in Germany, 1924–1930. Market Forces versus Economic Policy, in: Vierteljahrschrift für Sozial- und Wirtschaftsgeschichte 69 (1982) 488–514

Bordo, M. / Edelstein, M. / Rockoff, H., Was Adherence to the Gold Standard a 'Good Housekeeping Seal of Approval' during the Interwar Period?, mimeo (1998)

Cecchetti, S., Prices During the Great Depression: Was the Deflation of 1930–1932 Really Unanticipated?, in: American Economic Review 82 (1992) 141–56

Donner, O., Die Kursbildung am Aktienmarkt. Grundlagen zur Konjunkturbeobachtung an den Effektenmärkten, in: Vierteljahreshefte zur Konjunkturforschung, Sonderheft 34 (1934)

Eichengreen, B., Conducting the International Orchestra: Bank of England Leadership under the Classical Gold Standard, 1880–1913, in: Journal of International Money and Finance 6 (1987) 5–29

Eichengreen, B., Golden Fetters. The Gold Standard and the Great Depression, 1919–1939 (Oxford 1992)
Falkus, M. E., The German Business Cycle in the 1920s, in: Economic History Review 28 (1975) 451–65
Hamilton, J., Was the Deflation During the Great Depression Anticipated? Evidence from the Commodity Futures Market, in: American Economic Review 82 (1992) 157–78
Hayashi, F., Tobin's Marginal q and Average q: A Neoclassical Interpretation, in: Econometrica 50 (1982) 213–224
Kindleberger, C. P., The World in Depression, 1929–1939 (Berkeley 1973)
Link, W., Die amerikanische Stabilisierungspolitik in Deutschland 1921–32 (Düsseldorf 1970)
Maddison, A., Monitoring the World Economy, 1820–1992 (Paris 1995)
Schuker, S., American Reparations to Germany, 1924–1933 (Princeton Studies in International Finance 61) (Princeton 1988)
Temin, P., The Beginning of the Great Depression in Germany, in: Economic History Review 24 (1971) 240–248
VDMA, Statistisches Handbuch für die deutsche Maschinenindustrie (Berlin 1930)
Wagemann, E. (ed.), Konjunkturstatistisches Handbuch 1936 (Hamburg 1935)
White, E., The Stock Market Boom and Crash of 1929 Revisited, in: Journal of Economic Perspectives 4 (1990) 67–83

Dietmar Rothermund

Currencies, Taxes and Credit
Asian Peasants in the Great Depression, 1930–1939

Introduction

The Asian peasants would not have been affected by the Great Depression if they had been subsistence agriculturists with only minimal relations with the market. In fact, food production rather than the production of cashcrops was predominant in most Asian countries. But even the producers of wheat, rice and millets and other food crops were tied to market forces because they had to pay land revenue and other taxes, or they had to pay rent to landlords and interests to moneylenders. Many of them had become enmeshed in rural credit networks once and for all, because their creditors were eager to keep them in debt by charging high nominal interest rates, while resting content with lower effective interest rates adjusted to the living conditions of their debtors. After all, the peasant had to stay alive in order to serve his creditor.

The burden of rent or revenue had contributed to peasant indebtedness. Moneylenders were usually willing to help the peasant when the collectors of rent or revenue approached them in order to obtain possession of their land in terms of mortgages or by pre-empting their harvest in this way. Moneylenders were usually also graindealers and often financed forward trading. Some of them may have been able to conduct their business purely with their own funds. But most of them had to re-finance their operations through banks or wholesalers etc. Thus the rural credit network was interlinked with higher levels of credit management.

Governments which depended on revenue income were usually glad to rely on these credit networks, because they could be sure of collecting their revenue, as both peasants and moneylenders were eager to protect the land against compulsory sale for arrears of revenue. Moreover, the combined squeeze of revenue demand and debt service ensured that peasants would produce for the market and thus support the cities and yield an export surplus.

This system of linkages was influenced by the behaviour of currency in circulation. The velocity of circulation was slow under rural conditions and the money supply had to adjust to this. Peasants tended to distrust paper money and rather liked to handle coins. The governments concerned therefore had to see to it that such coins would be readily available. Thus, their monetary policy was affected by the relative prices of the respective metals in the world market. In conducting their monetary policy their best hope was for a mild inflation. An increase in inflation would reduce the burden of debt of the peasants but also curtail the revenue income of the government in real terms. Deflation could damage the credit system and thus impair revenue income in a different way.

Currencies, taxes and credit were thus interrelated in most Asian countries in a complex system which could be affected by the forces of the world market. The impact of the Great Depression showed this in a dramatic way. The American stock market crash of October 1929 did not affect Asia directly, but precipitated the credit contraction which soon led to a decline of the prices of agricultural produce. Cotton and wheat prices were the first to be affected. But it was only in 1930 that Asia was drawn into the vortex of the depression and therefore we shall begin our account by taking this date as a point of departure. It would be impossible to cover all Asian countries in this paper. Therefore we may present only a few case studies which highlight the complexities mentioned above and also provide studies in contrast. We shall begin with British India and China, which had very different currencies and whose peasants were subjected to different regimes of rent and revenue. A special section will be devoted to Burma which was then still a part of British India. French Indo-China, the Netherlands Indies (Indonesia) and the Philippines will be briefly compared and finally we shall turn to Japan, which experienced the depression in a rather special way as it returned to the gold standard at a most inopportune moment in 1930 and then devalued its currency in 1932 so drastically that it became a champion in the game of competitive devaluation or "exchange dumping" in which many countries at that time participated.

I. British India: The Overvalued Rupee, Peasant Indebtedness and Nationalism

India had been on a silver standard up to 1893 and this had shielded the prices of Indian produce against the fall of agrarian prices (in gold) during the depression of the late 19th century. The gradual depreciation of silver after 1876 had contributed to a slow but steady rise in Indian prices. At the same time India had absorbed a great deal of silver and had thus prevented a steeper fall in its world market price. British silver traders profited from this and they wanted the Indian mints to be kept open for the free minting of silver Rupees. But the Government of India was caught in a dilemma as it had to pay its "Home Charges" in gold and could not increase its revenue income in silver. Therefore the mints were closed in 1893 and the Rupee became a token currency pegged to the Pound at 1 s 4 d (Rothermund, 1970: 351–367). The Secretary of State for India had to manage this currency. He had reserves at his disposal for this purpose. Keynes praised this "gold exchange standard" in his first book "Indian Currency and Finance" (1913). But it was not as easy to manage as he had thought at that time. The rise of the silver price during the First World War in which India once more absorbed huge amounts of silver forced the Secretary of State to adjust the exchange rate upwards as the silver content of the Rupee surpassed its nominal value. If he had not adjusted the rate, the Rupees would have been withdrawn from circulation and been melted down.

After the war the Rupee declined once more, but now the Secretary of State tried to support it by buying Rupees. He soon exhausted his reserves and thus he had to adopt a different stratagem. Used Rupees returned to the government were not replaced. No new silver Rupees were minted after 1922, nor was paper money issued to the extent that coins were withdrawn from circulation. The silver saved by the government was sold in the world market, thus depressing the silver price. The Rupee was not affected by this as it was a token currency managed by the Secretary of State whose deflationary policy succeeded in stabilising it at 1 s 6 d in 1927. The Currency Act of that year pegged the Rupee to the gold standard at that rate which was 12.5 per cent above the pre-war rate of 1 s 4 d (Rothermund, 1992: 34). No other currency returned to the gold standard above the pre-war parity and the French demonstrated in 1928 that they could do so at one fifth of it (Rothermund, 1996: 70). But by that time India was stuck with a highly overvalued currency. For India's indebted peasants this meant an appreciation of their debts and an increasingly burdensome debt service. When the depression hit them, their incomes were halved, but debt service and the rent or revenue demands remained at the previous level. The government continued its deflationary policy with a vengeance so as to defend the exchange rate and to prevent a "Flight from the Rupee" which hung like a Sword of Damocles over the head of the British government, which feared that a bankruptcy of British India would immediately affect London as well. The Government of India was accordingly instructed to defend the overvalued Rupee (Rothermund, 1992: 41).

The Indian peasant was not only "depressed" by this deflationary policy, but also by the inflexibility of the rent and revenue demand. An economist used to the term "rent" in the context of capitalist agriculture would presume that this is a market price charged by the landlord for the use of his land by a freely contracting "farmer" who would cancel the contract if the price of his produce did not justify the amount of rent to be paid by him. Under such conditions rent charges would have had to be adjusted to the steep fall of prices. But in India "rent" was not determined by the market but by the government, because it was nothing but land revenue in a different guise. In most parts of Southern India, the government had eliminated "landlords" and collected revenue from the peasants who were considered to be "government tenants". In Northern India "landlords" paid the revenue and collected "rent" from the peasant. Originally the respective revenue system had been based on the theory that the government could claim half of the "net rental assets", but, as the government had never been able to establish a proper method of determining such "rental assets", it had simply turned the theory upside down and had empowered the settlement officer to fix the rent, half of which could then be retained by the landlord (Rothermund, 1978: 127). Settlements were normally fixed for thirty years and based on the averages of the prices of the preceding ten years. Since these calculations were supposedly based on "scientific standards", no allowances were normally made for bad harvests or other calamities, because these were supposed to be taken care of by the decennial averages. The reaction of the revenue authorities to the impact of the depression was predictable: a fall in prices, even if it was steep and sudden, did not justify any remissions of revenue. It took some time before the depth and persistence of the depression became apparent to the government, but then it was also faced with a dwindling of income from other sources and could not afford to be generous. Even the onerous salt tax which Mahatma Gandhi had made the target of his famous civil disobedience campaign in April 1930 was increased in subsequent years – not to spite him, but simply because the government desperately needed the money (Rothermund, 1992: 109).

When Gandhi had started his campaign he had not at all thought of the depression. Actually the fall in the wheat price affected India only in the summer of 1930 and then many of the peasants of the wheat growing tracts of Northern India provided added momentum to Gandhi's campaign by embarking on a no-rent campaign. For reasons explained above, the landlords were not inclined to remit rents as they themselves had to pay revenue. Furthermore, most of them were also indebted to moneylenders and had to bear the burden of debt service.

In previous years when economic conditions had been favourable, the moneylenders had lent freely to lords and peasants alike. The British laws introduced into India protected creditors fully. If the debtor was recalcitrant and did not appear in a court of law, the judge would grant an ex-parte decree to the moneylender which he could use to extort more from his debtor (Rothermund, 1978: 17). The relationship between creditor and debtor would normally last for a lifetime, because the moneylender saw to it that the peasant would never be able to redeem his debt and would thus provide him with a constant source of income. Moreover, most moneylenders were also merchants and could use their position to dictate terms to the peasant when buying up his produce. The moneylender refinanced his own credit operations with the help of larger graindealers who maintained storehouses. Such full storehouses would serve as collateral for getting loans from banks at fairly low interest rates whereas the rates charged lower down the line were often "usurious".

The depression put this whole system into reverse gear. The banks stopped providing credit for agricultural produce, the wholesalers emptied their storehouses in panic sales and, of course, did not refinance the moneylenders. Those then pounced on their debtors, asking them to pay up. This they could only do by selling land or gold. It is remarkable that Indian land prices only stagnated but did not fall in the depression years, showing that land continued to be regarded as a valuable asset. Gold was available to the peasant mostly in terms of his wife's ornaments. A man who sold his wife's ornaments lost his honour and therefore he would never force her to part with them. But if the only alternative was to sell the family's land she would herself offer her ornaments. The moneylender would carry them off triumphantly because he would get a good price for them, particularly after the price of gold increased by about 30 per cent when Great Britain abandoned the gold standard in September 1931.

The British authorities witnessed the stream of gold which poured out of India with great relief, because this unexpected boon saved their exchange rate policy, provided India with the necessary export surplus, and gave a boost to the newly created Sterling area. An independent Government of India could have imposed a gold export embargo and reflated the economy, but the British Indian government and – even more so – the Secretary of State for India were pleased with this result of their deflationary policy which squeezed the gold out of India and helped to support the overvalued Rupee (Rothermund, 1992: 47f.).

Because no attempt was made to reflate the economy, the depression lingered on in India until the Second World War led once more to an increase in prices. The peasantry resented its fate and turned against the British and towards the Indian National Congress. This was shown by the results of the elections of 1936/37. In preparation for a wider franchise for these elections the Government of India had seen to it that all substantial peasants (as defined in terms of property qualifications) would be able to vote (Rothermund, 1992: 223). There was a hope that these peasants would vote for pro-British agrarian parties. They had earlier not been touched very much by nationalist politics which were mostly urban-based. The depression had changed all this.

Interestingly enough, the moneylenders also flocked to the Congress, because they felt as much betrayed by the British as did the peasants. The law which protected the creditor had been so much taken for granted by the moneylenders that they were surprised when the British tried to impose all kinds of regulations to control rural credit, grant moratoria to indebted peasants, establish debt settlement boards etc.(Rothermund, 1992: 124–127). The nationalists could pick up all these dissatisfied elements and enlist them in the freedom struggle. The British authorities watched with alarm and tried to avoid all steps which might further aggravate rural discontent. The land revenue system was sacrificed for this reason and it did not recover. It was geared to a steady price increase but could not cope with a sudden fall in prices. So-called "revision settlements", which became due after 1930, were quietly shelved as the revenue authorities did not want to instigate political turmoil and also did not know how to fix new decennial averages under the prevailing conditions (Rothermund, 1992: 234f.).

II. Burma: The Rice Export Economy, Taxation and Peasant Rebellion

Burma, which remained a part of British India until 1936, was operating under similar conditions as described above, but its economy and its revenue system had some special features which aggravated the depression. Here we shall only deal with Lower Burma, which was the centre of a highly productive rice export economy. The fertile Burma Delta was a vulnerable monocrop region which had been reclaimed only under British rule (Adas, 1974: 58–82). The Burmese peasants who had migrated into this area participated in a modern export economy geared to the world market, but they continued their traditional methods of cultivation and remained attached to Buddhism. However, Buddhist institutions in the newly reclaimed Delta were not as strong as in the regions which the migrants had left. The Delta peasants were thus prone to articulate their cultural identity in new associations such as *Wunthanu Athin* (Own Race Association) which defended the interests of the "sons of the soil" against increasing Indian immigration (Adas, 1974: 196). The "rice frontier" of this new region was closed by the 1920s. Horizontal expansion was no longer possible. Land prices rose steeply while yields declined, peasants lost their land to landlords for whom they had to work as tenants. By 1929, 46 per cent of the land in the Delta was let out to tenants (Adas, 1974: 150). The rice export economy of the Delta was financed to a large extent by the firms of Chettiar moneylenders who had migrated to Burma from Tamil Nadu since the 1870s. They provided rural credit of nearly 500 mill. Rupees annually (Adas, 1974: 136). Much of this was channelled through local Burmese moneylenders and rice brokers who often advanced money without interest in order to pre-empt the next harvest. As long as prices were stable, there were no problems with this type of rural credit. But when prices fell, the Chettiars would be blamed. The sources of tension had thus developed before the Depression hit Burma. The Delta was like a tinderbox which could be ignited by a sudden spark.

World rice production far surpassed wheat production, but most of the rice did not enter international trade as it was grown for local consumption. Burma, which exported about 2 mill. t per year, was by far the largest rice exporter. The government profited from this in several ways. Unlike in other provinces of India, all male inhabitants between the ages of 18 and 60 had to pay a capitation (poll) tax of Rs. 5 per year if they were married, while bachelors paid half of this rate (Brown, 1999: 5). This was collected before the rice harvest and most people had to resort to the moneylenders for a loan to pay this tax. The moneylenders lent this amount gladly, because it enabled them to pre-empt the harvest. Some months after the harvest, the land revenue was due. The government also collected a rice export duty. Of course, this was of no concern to the peasants, and the government would see to it that this duty did not impede exports.

Rice prices had remained high until October 1930 when wheat prices had already fallen (Rothermund, 1992: 85). Wheat was no substitute for rice either in production or consumption, and there was no overproduction of rice of the kind which had ruined the world wheat market. Supply and demand remained fairly stable for rice throughout the depression years. But the value of rice declined so steeply that by 1933 rice was cheaper than wheat. This was entirely unprecedented. The story of the decline of the rice price is an extraordinary one. As we shall see when discussing Japan, the decline of the rice price started there in October 1930 and should have remained a domestic affair, because Japan neither exported nor imported rice at that time. But the news of this fall by 30 per cent immediately reached Liverpool, which controlled the British import market for rice. The traders there felt that the rice price would now follow the wheat price and accordingly the Liverpool price fell by 50 per cent in November. This news reached Calcutta and Rangoon very quickly and rice prices there fell even more steeply when the winter harvest reached the market (Rothermund, 1992: 86). In anticipation of this, the moneylenders refused to provide loans to the peasants when the capitation tax was due in December. The peasants petitioned the government to suspend this tax for the time being, but the Governor of Burma turned down this request (Brown, 1999: 7).

The Burmese peasants had a charismatic leader, Saya San, who had guided them in this petition campaign. He was close to the Burmese nationalists and had been active in agrarian economic enquiries before. He was well informed, but when the Governor remained adamant, Saya San projected himself as a righteous Buddhist king under whose rule there would be no taxes. The Delta with its fragile social order was ripe for a millenarian movement. The branches of the *Wunthanu Athin* provided an infrastructure for the rebellion (Adas, 1974: 196). Although Buddhism teaches non-violence, Saya San felt justified in advocating violent resistance. The peasant rebellion led by him lasted for almost two years and the government had a hard time in suppressing it.

From what has been said before about the attitude of the British Indian revenue authorities, it is clear that a similar initial intransigence could be expected in Burma. The authorities in Burma also maintained that Saya San's rebellion had absolutely nothing to do with their policy (Brown, 1999: 7). Nevertheless, when the depression persisted, they did relent to some extent. With regard to the land revenue they could do this more easily in Burma than elsewhere in British India, because in Burma this revenue was assessed annually whereas in other parts of India it was usually fixed for a period of 30 years. However, the remission of about 10 per cent in the revenue year 1931/32 and a similar reduction of the capitation tax did not match the steep decline in the income of the peasants and their loss of access to credit. Tensions between peasants and moneylenders were very acute in Lower Burma. As we have seen, rural credit was controlled by Chettiars who were regarded as rapacious strangers. In the areas affected by the rebellion, the Chettiars fled and credit dried up almost completely.

With no credit forthcoming the revenue authorities found it difficult to collect the revenue. In several districts the amounts on which peasants defaulted were quite substantial (about 10 to 15 per cent of the revenue demand) (Brown, 1999: 10–12). In normal times the law of land sale enabled the revenue authorities to auction the land of revenue defaulters immediately. But with a rebellion and with the Chettiars in flight, the government found it hard to proceed in this manner. It seems that in the years after the rebellion had been suppressed, the revenue authorities were able to recover lost ground although the prices remained depressed and the revenue remissions were not very generous. The depression greatly enhanced the alienation of land. Whereas only 31 per cent of land in the Delta was held by non-agriculturists in 1929, their share had increased to 50 per cent in 1934 (Adas, 1974: 188).

It should be stressed that the depression led to a loss of the value of the rice crop, but not to an immediate decline in the volume of exports. This implies that initially there was no glut in the Burmese rice market which could be blamed for the drastic fall of rice prices. In 1931 rice exports from Lower Burma remained at the pre-depression level (2 mill t.). They then declined to 1.6 mill t in 1932 and 1.4 mill t in 1933. In 1930 the value of rice exports stood at 220 mill. Rs, in 1933, when both volume and value had declined, it amounted to 90 mill. Rs only. By 1933 declining demand clearly affected the price level and depressed the price of rice even below that of wheat. In that year the other great rice economy, China, was also hit by the depression after having escaped its impact in 1931 and 1932.

III. China: The Silver Currency, Delayed Depression and Rural Misery

China experienced the depression in a very strange way because of its peculiar currency arrangements. While almost all other countries – by 1930 even the Japanese neighbours – had returned to the gold standard, China had retained its silver standard. The gold/silver ratio which in the 19th century had been 1/15 for a very long time stood at 1/35 in 1928; it amounted to 1/54 by 1930 and in 1931 to 1/71 (Bao-Seing Liao, 1939: 71). The silver price had fallen to the same extent as the prices of commodities such as wheat. This automatic devaluation shielded China against the impact of the depression, but the decline of the silver price also triggered off another surprising development: Chinese overseas who lived in gold standard countries converted their savings into silver and sent it to China where it fuelled an enormous boom at the same time as the rest of the world reeled under the impact of the depression (Remer, 1933: 185). Most of this money was invested in industry which benefited from a measure introduced by the Kuomintang government in 1930 for purely fiscal reasons but then turned out to be the equivalent of a protective tariff. The government relied on customs duties as a major source of its revenue income and decided to assess these duties in gold rather than in depreciating silver (Bao-Seing Liao, 1939: 96). This greatly encouraged the growth of an import substituting industry.

The stream of the savings of overseas Chinese which poured into China in the late 1920s stopped suddenly in September 1931 when the British abandoned the gold standard and silver became much more expensive in terms of British Pounds. By 1932 silver started flowing out of China, initally only in a small way, but to an ever increasing extent in subsequent years (Bao-Seing Liao, 1939: 80).

The Chinese peasants were scarcely affected by this boom, but at least they were protected against the fall of prices of agricultural produce by the inflow of depreciating silver. However, it soon became apparent that for them the depression was only delayed. The deflation caused by the outflow of silver depressed agricultural prices in 1933. Rice prices in the Yangzi Delta had averaged about 11 silver taels per *shi* from 1926 to 1929. In 1930 they had increased to 13 taels, in the subsequent two years they remained at about 9 taels, dropping to 6 taels in 1933 (Yeh-Chien Wang, 1992: 47).

The fate of the Chinese economy was sealed when the silver mining interests in the USA prevailed upon President Roosevelt to raise the world silver price through the Silver Purchase Act of June 1934. This act obliged the American government to provide one quarter of the backing for its currency in silver instead of in gold. Initially the amount required for this purpose was modest, and if Roosevelt had succeeded in limiting the purchase to that amount and fixing a reasonable price for it, China would have been able to remain on a silver standard. But more gold flowed into the USA and was absorbed in the currency reserve, and this automatically called for an increase in the amount of silver. Moreover, the silver lobby had seen to it that Roosevelt did not fix a silver purchase price and thus this price skyrocketed. It nearly doubled from February to April 1935 (Ghosh, 1976: 352–358). It seems that the silver purchase policy was not made a subject of public debate in America. Except for the silver lobby nobody was interested in it. This is why Roosevelt faced no criticism when he followed the advice of that lobby. The Chinese had no voice in this affair, and their appeals could be neglected.

In 1935 silver was sucked out of China and the country was subjected to a severe deflation. The terms of trade had turned against agriculture throughout the period of boom and depression. The inflationary pressures of the boom period from 1930 to 1932 had led to an increase of the prices of goods bought by the peasants. The prices of those goods were reduced by the severe deflation of 1933, but they were still well above the level of the late 1920s and thus were approximately 60 per cent higher than the prices which the peasants received for their produce (Eastman, 1974: 184). Rural credit in China was mostly provided by traders and landlords who pounced on the poor peasants, whose income had dwindled in the depression of 1933–34. Tenancy prevailed in most parts of China, but rents were mostly paid in terms of a fixed amount of grain. This was better than sharecropping because the tenant could enjoy the increase in the harvest due to improvements made by him. But as the grainrents demanded by the landlords were usually quite high, the tenants could get into trouble when the harvest was bad (Perkins, 1969: 102). They then had to ask for grain credits which had to be repaid at the time of the next harvest. The amount to be returned was usually twice the amount taken as a loan (Durau, 1977: 139, 162). The economic position of the landlords also deteriorated during the depression. Land prices fell almost to the same extent as those of produce. Many landlords hired poor people as minions who helped them to intimidate other poor people (Durau, 1977: 100). Law and order in the countryside deteriorated. The stage was set for the political turmoil which soon engulfed the country and made it an easy prey for Japanese aggression.

Before this happened, the Chinese finance minister, H. H. Kung, made a bold attempt at extracting his country from the abyss in which it had been pushed by the American silver purchase policy. He had implored Roosevelt in December 1934 to fix the silver price at 45 cents per ounce (Ghosh, 1976: 355). When this was of no avail, he launched a strategy which was so bold and devious that it is hard to believe that it worked. He drove all Chinese banks into bankruptcy and then subordinated them to the Bank of China. Then he abandoned the silver standard and confiscated and demonetised all silver available in China. For this he needed the support of the British ambassador, who issued a Silver Payments Prohibition Regulation which was binding on the British banks which were not under Kung's jurisdiction. Having achieved all this, Kung could issue a new paper currency and got enough notes printed so as to reflate the economy (Bao-Seing Liao, 1939: 125). Whether this would have led to a proper revival of the depressed Chinese economy is difficult to judge, because the Japanese invasion soon subjected China to wartime conditions even before the Second World War engulfed the rest of the world.

IV. Indonesia: Rural Poverty and 'Agrarian Involution'

Unlike most other colonial governments, which operated colonial currencies such as the Indian Rupee, the Piaster of Indochina or the Peso of the Philippines, the Dutch had no such currency in the Netherlands Indies, where the guilder circulated in the same way as at home. Moreover, the Dutch were the most faithful adherents to the gold standard, which they left only in 1936. This meant that global price movements were bound to affect the colony immediately, but on the other hand the Dutch did not have to follow a specific deflationary policy like the Government of India which was worried about a "flight from the Rupee". Nevertheless, the Dutch drastically reduced the circulation of the currency in Indonesia. In the period from 1925 to 1929, 542 mill. guilders were in circulation, of which 344 mill. were paper money and 183 mill. in silver coins; ten years later the total amount had dwindled to 284 mill. guilders, 117 mill. in paper money and 94 mill. in silver coins. The rest consisted in both periods of about the same amount of copper coins (ca. 14 mill.). The most severe reduction was that of the circulation of silver coins. The reason for this is evident from our discussion of the fate of the Chinese currency. The deflation was accompanied by an outflow of gold from the Netherlands Indies which amounted to 144 mill. guilders in the period from 1931 to 1935 (Boomgaard, 2000: 39). As in India, the peasants had to part with their savings, and the dehoarded gold was not used by the colonial government for reflating the colonial economy, but was permitted to flow from the periphery to the centre.

The pressure on the peasants was not only due to indebtedness but to an increasing revenue demand. "Landrent", as this revenue was called in the Netherlands Indies, was raised by about 60 per cent from 1929 to 1934 while rice prices declined by about 60 per cent in the same period (Boomgaard, 2000: 36). The government was obviously forced to fall back on "Landrent", as other sources of income such as customs duties, sales taxes etc. had dried up under the impact of the depression. It is surprising that this did not lead to a peasant rebellion, but Governor General de Jonge, who was in charge from 1931 to 1936, was a tough autocrat who enjoyed the full support of the Dutch government. Nationalist leaders like Sukarno had been arrested even before the depression. They spent the depression years in jail and could not provide leadership to the suffering peasants.

Some local institutions may have helped to tide the peasants over difficult times. There was, for instance, the village paddy bank (*desalumbung*) which was not affected by price movements as credit and repayment were in kind (Boomgaard, 2000: 51). The operations of these banks continued throughout the depression and even increased. But, of course, they were entirely geared to the rice economy and did not deal with cashcrops, which were both affected by the fall in prices and the dwindling of exports.

The most obvious casualty of the depression in the Netherlands Indies was the Javanese sugar industry. Cane cultivation was concentrated in Central and Eastern Java, where it was grown by peasants on land which would otherwise have been available for rice cultivation. Sugar refineries were processing the crop locally. In the pre-depression period 1928–30 nearly 3 mill. t of refined sugar were produced annually. Most of this was exported. About 200000 hectares were under sugar cane at that time. By 1935 this area had been reduced to 28000 hectares and the production of refined sugar had dwindled to 0.5 mill t. Moreover, the price of sugar had fallen to such an extent that export earnings from sugar in 1935 amounted to only about 10 per cent of those in 1928 (Boomgaard, 1988: 158). Much of the land devoted to sugar had reverted to rice cultivation, but with the low price of rice this was not a very profitable option either. In fact, many peasants turned to subsistence crops such as cassava or sweet potatoes.

The blow to Javanese sugar production was largely the result of the protective tariff on sugar introduced by British India, which used to import large amounts of refined sugar from the Netherlands Indies. India had few refineries at that time and produced mostly brown sugar made and consumed by the peasants. Thus the urban population depended for the most part on imported refined sugar. The protective tariff introduced on April 1, 1932 gave an enormous boost to the Indian sugar industry. Sugar imports declined from 0.5 mill t in 1931 to 0.01 mill t in 1937 while Indian sugar production increased from 0.4 mill t in 1931 to 1 mill t in 1937. Investment in sugar mills was the only line of industrial investment which progressed very rapidly in India during the depression years. The number of mills increased from 32 in 1931 to 136 in 1937 (Adarkar, 1941: 197f), whereas in the Netherlands Indies the number of mills receded from 178 in 1931 to 81 in 1937 (Boomgaard, 1988: 158).

Rice was an important element of subsistence agriculture in the Netherlands Indies. Moreover, rice cultivation responds almost to an unlimited extent to additional inputs of labour. Yields can be increased by better watering and terracing and other such measures. In strictly economic terms, there may be a problem to what extent additional labour inputs actually produce gains. But if labour is cheap and work-sharing rather than work-shedding is the order of the day, such calculations do not matter and it becomes more important how many people who would otherwise remain unemployed can be absorbed in this way. This is the logic of "agrarian involution", which Clifford Geertz has analysed in a thoughtful study of Java's economic history (Geertz, 1963). It seems that this type of "involution" was encouraged by the depression.

A peculiar feature of Dutch colonialism in Indonesia was the comparative smallness of the metropolitan power in relation to the large size of its empire. This was reflected in the rather limited share of the Dutch in Indonesia's foreign trade. In 1933 Dutch imports from this empire constituted only 19 per cent of total Dutch imports, whereas the corresponding ratios for Great Britain and France were 33 and 89 per cent respectively. The export ratio was even smaller: 12 per cent of Dutch exports were absorbed by the empire as compared to 24 per cent and 67 per cent for British and French exports to their respective colonial empires (Prince, 1989: 208). This meant that the metropolitan connection was of marginal importance for Indonesia. But as far as the "national debt" of Indonesia was concerned, more than 80 per cent were held by Dutch creditors (Prince, 1989: 215). These creditors were opposed to any proposal of debt relief or of separating the colonial currency from the metropolitan one so as to be able to devalue it. In this respect the hardening of colonial control on behalf of metropolitan creditors was as much a feature of Dutch colonialism as of the British and French ones in this period.

V. Indo-China: The Piaster and the Peasant

The currency of French Indochina was the Piaster issued by the Banque de L'Indochine. This bank operated almost like a central bank and could conduct its own monetary policy – of course, in the interest of the French rulers. The Piaster was originally a silver currency like the Indian Rupee. It seems that the authorities concerned followed a deflationary policy after 1928, in order to stabilise the Piaster and peg it firmly to the Franc and thus to the gold standard. By 1931 this was achieved and the circulation of the Piaster was further reduced (Brocheux, 2000: 257, 263). This stabilisation was intended to protect French capital in Indo-China rather than benefit the peasants. In 1931, the French government sanctioned a massive loan to the colony amounting to 1.3 billion Franc (ca. 55 mill. US $), aimed at warding off a bankruptcy of the colony which faced a budgetary deficit at that time. The French government could still afford to be generous, because the impact of the depression hit France only in 1934 when the earlier advantage of having rejoined the gold standard much below the pre-war parity in 1928 had worn off (Rothermund, 1996: 70).

In Indochina the rice price fell by about one half in 1931 and stood at about one third of the 1930 price in 1933. This was a particularly harsh blow for the Mekong rice delta, which the French had made into a rice export area very similar to that of Lower Burma. France also collected a capitation tax, and Chettiar moneylenders were in evidence here as well. The amount of land mortgaged to creditors in the delta region and in neighbouring Cambodia increased very rapidly in the depression years. Land prices were reduced by about 50 per cent in the depression years (Brocheux, 2000: 257). This was in striking contrast with India where land prices remained stable, but it was similar to the fall of land prices in China in 1933.

Unlike in Burma, the volume of rice exports did not decrease substantially. This was largely due to the fact that metropolitan France absorbed a great deal of Indochinese rice exports (Booth, 2000: 314). From 1930 to 1933 about 1 to 1.2 mill. t were exported annually. But as the value of these exports dwindled, the balance of trade deteriorated. At the same time the budget deficit of the government increased until 1934. After France went off the gold standard in 1936, the situation in Indochina became also more tolerable. The Piaster was devalued twice – 1936 and 1937. Debtors could heave a sigh of relief now (Brocheux, 2000: 265). The rice price rose after that and almost reached the 1930 level in 1938 (in Piasters).

An important feature of social change which determined the subsequent fate of the country was the increasing influence of big enterprises and big landlords in the depression years. This was due to the fact that the colonial government bailed them out at that time so as to strengthen its political base. In spite of its budget deficit the colonial government sanctioned in 1932 loans of altogether about 10 mill. Piaster to 355 landlords of one of the delta districts (Brocheux, 2000: 265). The peasants could not expect such consideration, and at the most the government showed some leniency by gradually reducing the capitation tax by about 20 per cent from 1931 to 1936. One may wonder why there was no peasant rebellion in the Mekong delta similar to that which shook Lower Burma. The explanation for this fact could be that there had been an earlier rebellion – not related to the depression – in Northern Annam in 1930, where peasants had risen in protest against the collection of the capitation tax after a drought had ruined their crops. The colonial rulers had put down this rebellion with a heavy hand, and perhaps this was enough to discourage others. The colonial police was omnipresent and was prepared to punish any offender including peasants who refused to pay the capitation tax (Scott, 1976: 105–113). Peasant insurgency was conspicuous by its absence here as well as in the Netherlands Indies and in the Philippines in the days of the Great Depression.

VI. The Philippines: Benefits of the American Connection

Compared to tough French colonial rule in Indochina, American rule in the Philippines was rather relaxed. There was a capitation tax here, too. It had been introduced by the Spanish colonial rulers and was then called *cedula personal.* Under Spanish rule it had contributed about half of the total revenue income (Doeppers,

2000: 57). The Americans relied more on other taxes such as sales taxes and customs duties, and the capitation tax made up only a quarter of their revenue income in the Philippines. Payment used to be strictly enforced, but in the depression years the authorities allowed about a fifth of the population to default on this tax (Doeppers, 2000: 58). When the first Philippine President, Manuel Quezon, assumed office in 1935, he soon introduced a legislative measure which pardoned those who were in arrears with their capitation tax payments in 1936, and then he abolished this unpopular tax altogether in the following year (Doeppers, 2000: 58). One may argue that the French in Indochina also reduced the capitation tax by about one fifth in the course of the depression years. But this was a very gradual procedure and affected all taxpayers in the same way, while the tolerance of the Philippine administration meant total and immediate relief for the peasants in the regions worst affected by the depression.

The colonial currency, the Peso, was pegged to the Dollar. It had been devalued in 1921, and subsequently a strict currency board system had managed to maintain the peg at 2 Pesos to the Dollar until 1941 (Booth, 2000: 301). The authorities reduced the money supply by about 30 per cent from 1929 to 1932 (Wolters, 2000: 88). Perhaps this was done in order to support the exchange rate, but it may also have been due to the conventional wisdom of this time that money supply should be adjusted to the level of economic activity.

A special benefit which the Philippines could derive from the American connection was access to the American market for its sugar production. This saved the sugar growers of the Philippines from the fate of their Javanese counterparts who had to reduce their output drastically. Sugar export of the Philippines even increased from an average of 0.7 mill. t in the period from 1929–31 to 1 mill. t in 1932–34. Sugar, which had contributed only about one third to total exports in 1929, made up nearly two thirds of them in 1932. More than three quarters of the foreign trade of the Philippines was with the USA at that time, while it had only been one half in 1914. The access to the American market was not quite free, but was regulated by a quota system which privileged the larger sugar mills, many of which were controlled by American companies (Yoshiko Nagano, 1988: 177). Colonial economic integration of the Philippines with the USA was thus enhanced by the depression. Products which did not quite fit into this pattern, such as the famous Manila hemp (abaca), lost much ground during the depression, and the regions producing it (Southern Luzon, Samar, Leyte) were badly affected by it. Under the immediate impact of the depression, hemp production declined by about 50 per cent. There was a recovery in 1934, but another slump in subsequent years. The peasants in the respective regions returned to subsistence agriculture, growing crops like cassava etc. normally regarded as food for the poor. The hemp region had the highest incidence of non-payment of the capitation tax (Doeppers, 2000: 63).

The rice economy of the Central Luzon plains which produced food for internal consumption, but was nevertheless affected by the global fall of the rice price, could not benefit from the US connection either (Wolters, 2000: 102f.). The colonial administration had introduced a measure, the Bonded Rice Warehouse Law of 1930, which was supposed to support rural credit and free the peasants from their dependence on the credit provided by Chinese rice traders. The licensed warehouse keeper could issue receipts for rice stored by him on behalf of the peasants who could use these receipts as collateral for obtaining loans from banks. This led to a withdrawal of the Chinese from the rural credit market. They had freely lent money to peasants without interest as long as they could pre-empt their rice harvest in this way. The warehouse scheme limited this activity. Moreover, the warehouses were mostly run by local people and not by the Chinese, who were used to buying and selling rice, but not to storing it in large quantities. The legal measure was well-meant, but it reduced the volume of rural credit at a crucial time and probably benefited the richer peasants and landlords who knew how to handle warehouse receipts and bank loans. But colonial governments were normally interested in strengthening their social base among the rural upper strata rather than among the poor. Thus in terms of politics this may have been a very shrewd move.

VII. Japan: 'Beggar-thy-neigbour' and Exploit Yourself

Of all the countries of Asia, Japan alone was both economically fairly advanced and politically fully in control of its fate. As a sovereign nation it could conduct is currency policy so as to suit its perceived national interest. But it followed the general craze for the re-establishment of the international gold standard. Great Britain had set a precedent by returning to the gold standard at the pre-war parity in 1925, and the Japanese leaders were not satisfied with less. National prestige more than anything else drove the Japanese to adopt this course (Allen, 1983: 106). The British decision of 1925, which also proved to be unwise when considered with the benefit of hindsight, could perhaps be explained in terms of the quest of London to recover its position as the world's financial centre, but Japan had no such excuse, and the timing of its return to the gold standard (January 1930) and its adamant defence of the Yen by a severely deflationary policy in the subsequent two years looked like a tragic comedy. Finance Minister Inouye played the role of a latter-day Don Quixote in this drama. He was murdered by army officers for this, and his successor Takahashi, who managed to get Japan out of the depression, eventually met with the same fate, because he resisted re-armament (Allen, 1983: 147).

The Japanese peasantry had all along been the neglected half of the nation and also suffered most under the impact of the depression. Japanese agriculture had been transformed in the nineteenth century. Old feudal ties of dependence had been relinquished under the impact of a modern market economy. Land had become concentrated in the hands of larger landholders, much of it by means of the foreclosure of mortgages. But this had not led to large-scale capitalist farming. Wage labour was expensive and landlords had increasingly let out their lands to tenants. Productivity had been enhanced by intensive family labour. Although Japanese industry had absorbed a great deal of labour, the share of the population engaged in agriculture had remained fairly stable at around 50 per cent from 1868 to 1940 (Smith, 1966: 210). The agriculturists were subjected to a land tax which usually amounted to more than 30 percent of the gross produce. Many peasants were indebted to local moneylenders who used their hold over the peasantry so as to control their land by means of mortgages and to appropriate their produce which they marketed at a profit (Smith, 1966: 158–160).

In spite of increases in agricultural productivity the cultivation of rice had in the early twentieth century lagged behind urban demand. After the First World War, the urban underclass had shocked the ruling elite by "rice riots", because the cost of living had risen due to wartime inflation (Allen, 1983: 103). As a reaction to this, the government had encouraged large-scale imports of rice so as to keep the rice price low and the urban underclass contented. This was, of course, of no benefit to the Japanese peasants. Burma, Thailand and Indochina exported rice to Japan in those years. Burmese rice, which was harvested in winter and arrived in Japan in March, was of strategic importance in keeping the rice price down, because in Japan the rice was harvested in October and most of this was consumed by March. However, the Japanese government was interested in attaining national selfsufficiency in this field. This was achieved in 1928 when a rice import embargo was introduced (Rothermund, 1996: 41).

In the meantime many peasants had also discovered another source of income: the breeding of silkworms for the Japanese silk industry which had a good market in the USA. By the late 1920s about one third of Japanese exports consisted of silk, of which more than 90 per cent was absorbed by rich Americans. The stock market crash of 1929 reduced the demand for silk all of a sudden and the deflationary policy mentioned above raised its export price. Thus from 1929 to October 1930 silk exports shrank by 60 per cent. And as we have mentioned before, the deflationary policy and a good rice harvest led in October 1930 to a fall of the rice price by 30 per cent. In this way the peasantry suffered a severe loss of income both with regard to rice and silk worms. Many peasants had to sell their daughters to brothels or hire them out to the new cotton textile mills which exploited cheap labour (Waswo, 1988: 116f., 123–131).

The Japanese army whose soldiers and young officers mostly came from peasant families now emerged as the moral advocate of the suffering peasantry. But the leaders of that army were more interested in increasing military expenditure than doing anything for the peasants (Allen, 1983: 141f.). By 1934 this expenditure amounted to 942 mill. Yen whereas only a meagre amount of 83 mill. Yen had by that time been spent on rural public works which actually did not benefit the peasants but the construction industry.

When the Yen was allowed to float in 1931 after Japan had followed British precedent in abandoning the gold standard, the Japanese currency almost immediately lost 60 per cent of its previous value and thus made Japanese exports extremely competitive in the world market. Joan Robinson in analysing competitive devaluation coined the term "beggar-thy-neighbour" (Rothermund 1996: 6). Another term referring to the same phenomenon is "exchange dumping", meaning that goods are actually sold below the cost price due to a low exchange rate. Both terms focus on the "neighbour" who is affected by this policy. But it should also be noticed that the exporter must exploit himself in order to follow this course. In fact, Japan did exploit itself by flooding the world market with cheap goods so as to earn foreign exchange which was then mainly spent on machinery and armament (Rothermund, 1996: 152f.). The Japanese elite which pursued this policy did not exploit itself, but rather the peasants and other poor people who had to pay the bill. The recovery from the depression was thus not a story of a glorious achievement, but of social injustice. This was defended in terms of the national interest which eventually produced military aggression.

Conclusions

This survey of several Asian countries has shown that the respective currencies and the monetary policies adopted to support the exchange rate and to prevent the flight of capital were crucial in transmitting the impact of the depression – often with a vengeance. The only exception was China which stuck to its silver standard, but was then caught in a delayed but even more severe depression due to the American silver purchase policy. We have also seen that governments everywhere showed great reluctance to cut taxes so as to relieve the sufferings of the peasantry. First of all, the authorities concerned initially did not see that the depression was more than a passing phenomenon, and once they noticed this, they were caught in a dilemma as other sources of revenue income dwindled and they were thrown back on the most regressive and broadly based taxes which were also most unpopular. Colonial rule thus turned out to be more oppressive at a time when it became practically superfluous. Imperialists had always argued that colonies were required so as to have access to scarce resources. Now that the depression had made all colonial commodities extremely cheap, it was hardly worth spending much on the administration and defence of colonies.

Credit relations were, of course, one good reason for holding on to colonies which were indebted to creditors in the countries at the centre of the world economy. Credit also determined financial relations all the way down to the remotest village. Many debts incurred before the onset of the depression became terribly burdensome under the double impact of deflation and the loss of income due to the steep fall in prices.

With all this, peasant protest might be expected to have been much more widespread than it actually was in the depression years. In fact, peasant solidarity was difficult to establish due to the internal differentiation of the peasantry, the variety of local conditions and the uneven incidence of the demands of the authorities. If credit was available, the peasant would normally rather pay up than defy the tax collector. It was only when credit was refused at the very moment when taxes were due that the peasant was caught with his back to the wall. Under such conditions peasant solidarity could suddenly arise, and under a charismatic leader might pose a dramatic challenge to the government. This was a rare constellation and therefore peasant protest in the years of the depression was isolated and hardly articulated at all.

References

Adarkar, B. P., The Indian Fiscal Policy (Allahabad 1941)

Adas, M., The Burma Delta: Economic Development and Social Change on an Asian Rice Frontier, 1852- 1941 (Madison 1974)

Albert, B. / Graves A. (eds.), The World Sugar Economy in War and Depression, 1914–1940 (London 1988) 157–169

Allen, G. C., A Short Economic History of Japan (London [4]1983)

Bao-Seing, Liao, Die Bedeutung des Silberproblems für die chinesischen Währungsverhältnisse (Berlin 1939)

Boomgaard, P., Treacherous Cane: The Java Sugar Industry between 1914 and 1940, in: *Albert / Graves* (eds.), (1988) 157–169

Boomgaard, P. / Brown I. (eds.), Weathering the Storm. The Economies of Southeast Asia in the 1930s Depression (Leiden 2000)

Boomgaard, P., Surviving the Slump. Development of Real Income during the Depression of the 1930s in Indonesia, in: *Boomgaard / Brown* (eds.), (2000) 23–52

Booth, A., Crisis and Response: A Study of Foreign Trade and Exchange Rate Policies in Three South East Asian Colonies in the 1930s, in: *Boomgaard / Brown* (eds.), (2000) 295–320

Brocheux, P., The state and the 1930s Depression in French Indo-China, in *Boomgaard / Brown* (eds.), (2000) 251–272

Brown, I. (ed.), The Economies of Africa and Asia in the Inter-war Depression (London 1989)

Brown, I., Material Conditions in Rural Lower Burma during the Economic Crisis of the early 1930s: What the Cotton Textile Import Figures Reveal, in: *Boomgaard / Brown* (eds.), (2000) 109–120

Brown, I., Tax Remission and Tax Burden in Rural Lower Burma during the Economy Crisis of the early 1930s, in: Modern South Asian Studies 33,2 (1999)

Doeppers, D. F., The Philippines in the Great Depression: A Geography of Pain, in: *Boomgaard / Brown* (eds.), (2000) 53–82

Dore, R. / Sinha, R.. (eds.), Japan and World Depression. Then and Now (London 1987)

Durau, J., Die Krise der chinesischen Agrarökonomie, in: *Lorenz* (ed), (1977)

Eastman, L. E., The Abortive Revolution. China under Nationalist Rule, 1927 -1937 (Cambridge, Mass. 1974)

Feuerwerker, A., The Chinese Economy, 1912–1949 (Ann Arbour 1968)

Geertz, C., Agricultural Involution. The Process of Ecological Change in Indonesia (Berkeley 1963)

Ghosh, P. S., Sino-American Economic Relations, in: International Studies 15 (1976)

Lorenz, R. (ed.), Umwälzung einer Gesellschaft. Zur Sozialgeschichte einer Revolution, 1911–1949 (Frankfurt 1977)

Maddison, A. / Prince, G. (eds.), Economic Growth in Indonesia, 1820–1940 (Dordrecht 1989)

Perkins, D. D., Agricultural Development in China (Chicago 1969)

Prince, G., Dutch Economic Policy in Indonesia, 1870–1942, in: *Maddison / Prince* (eds.), (1989) 203–226
Rawski, T. G. / Li, L. M. (eds.), Chinese History in Economic Perspective (Berkeley 1992)
Remer, C. F., Foreign Investments in China (New York 1933)
Rothermund, D., India's Silver Currency. An Aspect of the Monetary Policy of British Imperialism, in: Indian Economic and Social History Review 7,1 (1970)
Rothermund, D., Government, Landlord and Peasant in India. Agrarian Relations under British Rule, 1865–1935 (Wiesbaden 1978)
Rothermund, D., India in the Great Depression, 1929–1939 (New Delhi 1992)
Rothermund, D., The Global Impact of the Great Depression, 1929–1939 (London 1996)
Scott, J., The Moral Economy of the Peasant: Rebellion and Subsistence in Southeast Asia (New Haven 1976)
Smith, T. C., The Agrarian Origins of Modern Japan (New York 1966)
Waswo, A., Japan's Rural Economy in Crisis, in: *Brown* (ed.), (1989)
Wolters, W. G., Uneven Impact and Regional Responses: The Philippines in 1930s Depression, in: *Boomgaard / Brown* (eds.), (2000) 83–108
Yeh-Chien, Wang, Secular Trends of Rice Prices in the Yangzi Delta, 1638–1935, in: , *Rawski / Li* (eds.), (1992) 35–68
Yoshiko, Nagano, The Oligopolistic Structure of the Philippine Sugar Industry during the Great Depression, in: *Albert / Graves* (eds.), (1988) 170–181

Monika Rosengarten, Carl-Ludwig Holtfrerich

Economic Policy Positions and Influence of the International Chamber of Commerce during the Great Depression*

1. Introduction

The International Chamber of Commerce (I.C.C.) represented all parts of international business, including finance, industry, transportation, and commerce. It was founded by American, British, French, Belgian and Italian representatives in Paris in 1920. German industry and commerce could not join the organization at that time. Political reasons resulting from the First World War and the unsolved reparation question obviously prevented German participation until Germany – according to the Versailles Treaty – regained its autonomy in foreign trade policy in 1925. In contrast to the chiefly politically-dominated League of Nations, the I.C.C. quickly became the exclusive spokesman of the business world's interests during the interwar period. Thus, in the economic sphere, the I.C.C. constituted a sort of "business men's League of Nations"[1].

The organizational structure of the I.C.C. was composed of two levels: It consisted of an international level situated at the Headquarters in Paris (Presidency, General Secretary, Administrative Council, Committee Meetings) and a national level located in each member country around the world (National Committees). The difficulty of the organization lay in bringing into line both of these spheres in such a way as to make apparent a common position of the corporation, that is to say the unity of the national economic interests of each country on a common international platform. The founding fathers of the I.C.C. had seen this ambiguity and therefore installed a mechanism to solve this problem: When opinions diverged within the I.C.C., the Administrative Council should always take the

* This paper is based on preliminary results of a doctoral dissertation of Monika Rosengarten, supervised by Carl-Ludwig Holtfrerich of the Free University in Berlin. We would like to thank the post-graduate NaFöG scholarship program for generous financial support. We gratefully acknowledge the cooperation of the International Chamber of Commerce in Paris and the company Nestlé in Vevey in pursuing this research.

[1] *George L. Ridgeway,* Merchants of Peace. Twenty Years of Business Diplomacy Through the International Chamber of Commerce 1919–1938 (New York 1938) 15.

"final decision" with regard to the public[2]. With this internal regulation mechanism the business world was given the opportunity to speak with one voice in the face of the economic problems emerging during the Great Depression.

In studying the economic policy positions of the I.C.C. during the interwar period, the following questions arise: Did the economic policy advice of the I.C.C. represent a real alternative to the policy actually pursued by the U.S.A., Great Britain, France and Germany during the Great Depression? Furthermore, could the economic policy program recommended by the I.C.C. have contributed to a mitigation of the Great Depression from 1929 to 1939?

We will start out with the foreign economic policy positions taken by the I.C.C. during the interwar period on monetary/financial matters, on the one hand, and commercial policy, on the other. Then, we will compare these recommendations with the economic policies actually pursued by the U.S.A., France, Great Britain and Germany. The subsequent section is devoted to measuring the actual extent of the influence taken by the I.C.C. using its different channels of influence. In conclusion, we will analyze the possible effects of the I.C.C.'s economic policy advice on the fight against the Great Depression.

2. Foreign Economic Policy Positions of the I.C.C. During the Interwar Period

Within the I.C.C. there were conflicting views as to what should be given priority in mitigating the Great Depression: monetary stabilization or commercial stabilization. Frederick Fentener van Vlissingen, President of the I.C.C., obviously gave first priority to the restoration of a stable monetary system and second to the abolishment of the multitude of trade barriers in the world[3]. However, there was also a growing number of members calling for the opposite priorities, but without any success[4]. In our opinion, the majority of the I.C.C. was right in presuming that no government would agree to give up its trade-protection measures, so long as monetary stability had not been restored in a definite way[5]. The two foreign economic policy spheres were intertwined and could not be detached from each other in pursuing a solution for the interwar depression problems.

[2] Archives of the I.C.C. in Saint Denis (=ASD): Document No. 4294, International Economic Relations Group. Committee on Commercial Policy and Trade Barriers, Report of the Meeting held on October 23rd, 1930, 4.

[3] Bundesarchiv Dahlwitz-Hoppegarten: Reichswirtschaftskammer R 11/1354, 75.

[4] For example Owen Jones from the British National Committee. ASD: BIB 44 Document No. 5426, Comité Monétaire, Procès-verbal de la réunion tenue les 7, 8 et 9 Mars 1934, 3–5.

[5] Cf. *René Duchemin*, Headquarters of the I.C.C. in Paris (=HP): Document No. 5373, 35th Meeting of the Executive Committee, January 12th, 1934, 2.

2.1. Monetary and Financial Policy Positions

During the Great Depression the I.C.C. pleaded for an immediate return to the gold standard. For the I.C.C., gold constituted an important basis for the guaranteeing of stable exchange rates in a world where the financial and monetary system had been totally disrupted. Actually, the Chamber regarded its recommendation to return to gold more as a compromise, a necessary rather than a sufficient condition or a real remedy to cope with the crisis[6]. Further devaluation would have been prevented by the realization of this pro-gold monetary advice on the part of the I.C.C. But could it really have contributed to a mitigation of the Great Depression 1929–1939? Quite the reverse: Since 1985 economic historians have published evidence that the countries which clung to the gold standard were at a relative disadvantage because they had to pursue restricted monetary policies, which meant deflation rather than devaluation[7]. They showed that for countries that had devalued their currencies early on, the depression was milder and shorter. From this perspective, the recommendation of the I.C.C. to reinstate the gold standard was bad policy advice. Because the United States were unwilling to stabilize the non-functioning gold standard system by means of an expansionary monetary policy, only the renunciation of a fixed exchange rate, as the British did in September 1931, or exchange controls, as in the German case, provided the monetary leeway to surmount the crisis.

As far as monetary policy is concerned, the I.C.C. showed a certain ambiguity with respect to state intervention: In the documents submitted to the World Monetary and Economic Conference in 1933, the Chamber emphasized the necessity of keeping the Central Banks free from all political influence[8]. Nevertheless, the government's entry into the lending field was sometimes welcomed, not only by borrowers, but by the bankers as well[9]. For that reason President Franklin D. Roosevelt founded state agencies as a sort of stopgap measure until private banks would have recovered from depression. But, in general, the U.S. Treasury favored a restrictive monetary policy. It exercised a great influence on the Federal Reserve

[6] HP: Document No. 5242, Projet de Rapport de la Chambre de Commerce Internationale à la Conférence Monétaire et Économique présenté par M. Owen Jones, Rapporteur, au "Comité Spécial" en sa session du 21 Mars 1933, 1.

[7] Cf. *Barry Eichengreen, Jeffrey Sachs*, Exchange Rates and Economic Recovery in the 1930s, in: Journal of Economic History 45 (1985) 925–946; *Peter Temin*, Lessons from the Great Depression (Cambridge Mass. 1989) 33; *Harold James, Ben Bernanke*, The Gold Standard, Deflation, and Financial Crisis in the Great Depression. An International Comparison (National Bureau of Economic Research Working Paper No. 3488) (Cambridge Mass. 1991) 1; *Barry Eichengreen*, Golden Fetters. The Gold Standard and the Great Depression, 1919–1939 (Oxford 1992) 28.

[8] HP: Document No. 5100, Special Committee for the Preparation of the Documents to be Submitted to the World Monetary and Economic Conference, Meeting of January 13th, 1933, 7.

[9] ASD: BIB 50, The Effect of the Economic Depression on the American Banking System. Address delivered by R. S. Hecht before the International Bankers Conference, Paris June 27th, 1936, 5.

Board's decisions with respect to the fixing of discount rates. In sum, one can say that central banks which were politically independent could have helped to carry out a policy of monetary expansion, even if it had been temporarily painful for those governments that aimed at stabilizing the exchange rate and at defending the gold parities. But, during the post-World-War-I period, neither the central banks of Great Britain and France nor those of Germany until May 1922 and of the U.S. were absolutely free from political influence; governments pushed for deflation rather than inflation. Even though the central banks did not fully share the views of their respective governments on this matter, they bowed to the official policy line as to a restrictive monetary policy[10]. Like the governments, the Council of the I.C.C. did not approve of an "easy" allocation of credit in October 1931. It even appealed to the members of the I.C.C. to help shunning "the illusory benefits of credit inflation"[11].

The severity of the Great Depression was evident in and partly caused by the falling prices for commodities. For this reason the I.C.C. recommended the increase of the wholesale price level. Pure monetary measures would never lead to such a recovery, declared the I.C.C. Council on October 19th, 1932[12]. Even an intervention on the part of the state to maintain prices would aggravate rather than alleviate the crisis. Instead, the I.C.C. propagated the application of a self-imposed limitation of production, wherever the supply exceeded demand. In short: price-diminishing overproduction should be regulated by restricting output rather than prices be lifted by monetary measures. For this reason, the I.C.C. intended to promote the creation of cartels and of trusts to exercise a greater pressure on the producers of industrial goods. To be sure, this would have served the interest of the business world much better than monetary expansion. While the latter would, in principle, have lifted the general price level, self-imposed limitations of production would have improved the terms of trade of products of cartellized industries vis-à-vis other products. This would have increased their relative profits. Only one representative of the I.C.C. contradicted the official view of the Chamber. W. H. Coates, from the British National Committee, attached great importance to monetary remedies in fighting the sudden fall in prices. In his speech before the I.C.C. Council on June 24th, 1932, he established a negative correlation between the discount rate and the price index[13]. Thus, in the 1930s he was already propagating far-reaching ideas which only became popular with the writings of Milton Friedman and Anna J. Schwartz after the Second World War[14]. Coates' monetary

[10] *Stephen V. O. Clarke*, Central Bank Cooperation: 1924–31 (New York 1967) 29f.
[11] Cited after: New York Herald-Tribune October 24th 1931, in: National Archives Maryland (=NA), Correspondence of the Office of the Treasury/Central File of the Office of the Secretary of the Treasury 1917–32. I.C.C. 1931–32, Box 93.
[12] ASD: BIB 43, Document No. 4940, Projet de Declaration du Conseil de la Chambre de Commerce Internationale, 19 Octobre 1932, 3.
[13] HP: Document No. 4897, XXXVIIIth Meeting of the Council, 24th June 1932, 4.
[14] *Milton Friedman, Anna Jacobson Schwartz*, A Monetary History of the United States 1867–1960 (Princeton 1963).

advice was rejected by the majority of the I.C.C. The honorary president of the organization, Georges Theunis, expressed his utter disagreement with Coates' remarks in a harsh reply[15].

The official recommendation of the I.C.C. to restrict output and thus to shorten supply, conflicted with a critical view of U.S. monetary policy during the Great Depression advanced in the sixties. Friedman and Schwartz considered the money supply as the key factor that had caused and could have prevented the severity of the crisis[16]. Their thesis was later on supported by the economist Allan H. Meltzer: "A more expansive monetary policy in the Fall of 1929, after the recession was recognized, and in 1930, would have limited the decline."[17] But the Friedman/Schwartz analysis also contains some deficits. The authors did not mention, for example, that changes in the quantity of money always affect the real economy only with a certain time lag. Furthermore, they omit to analyze – in contrast to the I.C.C. – the influence of the protectionist tariff policy of the U.S., especially of the Smoot-Hawley Act, on sales and prices during the interwar period.

How little importance the Chamber attached not only to monetary but also to fiscal expansion to solve the crisis could also be seen in the following recommendation of the I.C.C.: to balance the public budget in each country[18]. Governments should achieve this end by reducing expenditures rather than by increasing taxes, declared the business organization. Therefore, the I.C.C. came in opposition to the "deficit spending" theory of John Maynard Keynes, already explained in some articles before having published his book "The General Theory of Employment, Interest and Money" in 1936. Keynes obviously supported various forms of economic stimulation by public investment financed by central bank credit creation. The I.C.C., however, preferred supply-side policy, like reduction of taxes and wages, rather than the demand-side policy advocated by Keynes. Despite the excitement among the younger economists created by the General Theory and their subsequent influx into Washington – especially the Federal Reserve Board under Marriner Eccles from late 1934 became the chief centre of Keynesian influence –, conservatives were firmly opposed to any expansion of the public sector. The fear of additional public debt was so deeply ingrained that the U.S. government hesitated to advocate a policy which would openly increase deficits[19]. Finally, in the field of budgetary policy the Americans acted exactly as the I.C.C. had recommended. At present we can say that the leeway of the public sector to boost

[15] HP: Document No. 4897, XXXVIIIth Meeting of the Council, 24th June 1932, 5.

[16] *Friedman*, *Schwartz*, Monetary History 301.

[17] *Allan H. Meltzer*, Comments on "Monetarist Interpretations of the Great Depression", in: *Karl Brunner* (ed.), The Great Depression Revisited (Boston 1981) 149–152.

[18] Internationale Handelskammer (ed.), Entwurf des Berichts der Internationalen Handelskammer für die Weltwirtschafts- und Finanzkonferenz, Drucksache Nr. 1 (Paris 1933) 8.

[19] *John Kenneth Galbraith*, How Keynes Came to America, in: *John Kenneth Galbraith* (ed.), Economics, Peace and Laughter (New York 1972) 44–56; *Alan Sweezy*, The Keynesians and Government Policy, 1933–1939, in: American Economic Review 62 (1972) 116–125.

demand and thus counteract the crisis was underestimated in the United States. Even though it was an inhibition to some degree, the budget balancing principle actually left considerable room for manoeuvre[20]. More acceptance of anticyclical spending during the Great Depression could have accelerated the pace of recovery more effectively than financial restraint by the state[21]. "Yet deficit financing had an important part to play, in 'priming the pump'", summarizes W. Arthur Lewis[22]. It did not automatically require the governments to recommend a tax increase, explained Herbert Stein[23]. The opinion of the I.C.C. that taxes and wages were too high for an economic revival during the interwar period has been tested empirically by economic historians during the eighties and nineties and is not generally accepted[24].

[20] *Herbert Stein*, The Fiscal Revolution in America. Policy in Pursuit of Reality (Washington D.C. [2]1996) 16.

[21] Cf. *Carl-Ludwig Holtfrerich*, Vernachlässigte Perspektiven der wirtschaftlichen Probleme der Weimarer Republik, in: *Heinrich August Winkler* (ed.), Die deutsche Staatskrise 1930–1933. Handlungsspielräume und Alternativen (München 1992) 137.

[22] *W. Arthur Lewis*, Economic Survey 1919–1939 (London [7]1970) 113.

[23] *Stein*, Fiscal Revolution 28.

[24] For Germany *Knut Borchardt*, Zwangslagen und Handlungsspielräume in der großen Wirtschaftskrise der frühen dreißiger Jahre: Zur Revision des überlieferten Geschichtsbildes, in: Bayerische Akademie der Wissenschaften, Jahrbuch (München 1979) 1–47; *Carl-Ludwig Holtfrerich*, Zu hohe Löhne in der Weimarer Republik? Anmerkungen zur Borchardt-These, in: Geschichte und Gesellschaft 10 (1983) 122–141; *Carl-Ludwig Holtfrerich*, Was the Policy of Deflation in Germany Unavoidable?, in: *Jürgen Baron von Kruedener* (ed.), Economic Crisis and Political Collapse. The Weimar Republic 1924–1933 (German Historical Perspectives V) (Oxford 1990) 81–98. *Hans-Joachim Voth*, Did High Wages or High Interest Rates Bring Down the Weimar Republic? A Cointegration Model of Investment in Germany 1925–1930, in: Vierteljahrschrift für Sozial- und Wirtschaftsgeschichte 83 (1996) 801–819; *Hans-Joachim Voth*, Much Ado About Nothing? A Note on Investment and Wage Pressure in Weimar Germany, 1925–29, in: Historical Research 19 (1994), 124–139; *Richard Tilly, Norbert Huck*, Die deutsche Wirtschaft in der Krise, 1925 bis 1934. Ein makroökonomischer Ansatz, in: *Christoph Buchheim, Michael Hutter, Harold James* (ed.), Zerrissene Zwischenkriegszeit. Wirtschaftshistorische Beiträge. Knut Borchardt zum 65. Geburtstag (Baden-Baden 1994) 45–95. For the opposite view see: *Knut Borchardt*, A Decade of Debate About Brüning's Economic Policy, in: *Kruedener*, Economic Crisis 99–152. *Stephen N. Broadberry, Albrecht O. Ritschl*, The Iron Twenties: Real Wages, Productivity and the Lack of Prosperity in Britain and Germany Before the Great Depression, in: *Buchheim, Hutter, James* (ed.), Zerrissene Zwischenkriegszeit 15–43; *Knut Borchardt, Albrecht Ritschl*, Could Brüning Have Done It? A Keynesian Model of Interwar Germany, 1925–1938, in: European Economic Review 36 (1992) 395–701; *Albrecht Ritschl*, Zu hohe Löhne in der Weimarer Republik? Eine Auseinandersetzung mit Holtfrerichs Berechnungen zur Lohnposition der Arbeiterschaft 1925–1932, in: Geschichte und Gesellschaft 16 (1990) 375–402; For a differentiated view: *Mark Spoerer*, German Net Investment and the Cumulative Real Wage Position 1925–1929. On a Premature Burial of the Borchardt Debate, in: Historical Social Research 19 (1994) 26–41; *Barry Eichengreen*, Wages and the Gold Standard. Perspectives on the Borchardt Debate, in: *Buchheim, Hutter, James* (ed.), Zerrissene Zwischenkriegszeit, 177–203; for the United States of America, cf. *Herbert Stein*, Presidential Economics. The Making of Economic Policy from Roosevelt to Reagan and Beyond (New York 1984) 385 f.

During the Great Depression the I.C.C. wanted to ensure an expansion of capital exports by creditor nations – especially the United States – with the aim of facilitating a speedy recovery in all countries[25]. In our opinion, an increase of international capital transactions alone could not have contributed to a recovery during the interwar period. The dismantling of customs barriers would have contributed more effectively to breaking the spiral of falling world demand and export activity. With regard to the United States of America this meant: "Variation in U.S. import activity generally seems to have been of greater importance [for the supply of U.S. dollars] than variation in capital outflows."[26] But a free and comparatively unhampered flow of credit was in a certain sense a precondition for the revival of world commerce. That is why Silas H. Strawn, member of the American National Committee of the I.C.C., advised in 1932 that nations should revive and foster international trade – apart from reducing tariffs – by granting loans and extending credits for sound and productive projects[27]. It is interesting that this recommendation came from a member nation of the I.C.C., which had already been asked by other countries to expand its capital export to a certain extent. The most intense pressure for a laxer U.S. lending policy came from the British National Committee: Arthur R. Guinness pleaded for an expanded credit supply of the U.S. to other countries at moderate interest rates. That strategy could have helped Germany, above all, to abandon its foreign exchange controls during the Great Depression[28]. Nevertheless, there had been some voices within the I.C.C., like those of Maurice Golay from Switzerland and Benjamin M. Anderson from the U.S., warning of artificially cheap money. It is no coincidence that these voices came from countries of whom more capital exports were expected. But their opinion did not represent the view of the I.C.C. Council[29]. We share the I.C.C.'s official view. Of course, cheap money and abundant credit alone might not have overcome the depression, as the case of Japan has demonstrated in recent years. For example, when businessmen's profit expectations remain depressed, cheap credit may have little effect in inducing investment and recovery. Expectations for

[25] *Bernhard Dernburg*, Das Niveau der Preise und die Ursachen, die es beeinflussen, Drucksache Nr. 11, Washingtoner Kongreß 1931, 4.

[26] *Carl-Ludwig Holtfrerich* , U. S. Economic (Policy) Development and World Trade During the Interwar Period Compared to the Last Twenty Years, in: *Ivan T. Berend, Knut Borchardt* (eds.), The Impact of the Depression of the 1930's and Its Relevance for the Contemporary World. Comparative Studies Prepared for the A/5 Session of the 9th International Economic History Congress, 24–29 August, 1986, Bern, Switzerland (Budapest 1986) 73. This reflects one of the main results of the classic study by *Hal B. Lary*, The United States in the World Economy: The International Transactions of the United States During the Interwar Period (Washington D.C. 1943).

[27] HP: Document No. 4785, XXXVIIth Session of the Council, Statement presented by Mr. Silas H. Strawn on behalf of the American National Committee of the International Chamber of Commerce, March 9th 1932, 3.

[28] Offizieller Sitzungsbericht des Neunten Kongresses der Internationalen Handelskammer in Berlin vom 28. Juni – 3. Juli 1937, in: Internationale Wirtschaft 7/8 (1937) 46f.

[29] ASD: BIB 44, Document No. 6685, Committee on Monetary Policy and Credit. Minutes of the Meeting of October 19th and 20th, 1938, 11.

more demand seem to play an important part in promoting investment. But international lending at reasonably low interest rates from capital-rich countries to countries in distress and anticyclical capital exports generally have been shown by Charles P. Kindleberger to be essential conditions of stability in the world economy[30].

The transfer problem of the reparation and interallied-debt payments attracted the attention of the I.C.C. since its founding. For that reason, the I.C.C. had actively participated in the formulation of the Dawes plan[31]. Finally, during its Congress in Brussels in May/June 1925, the I.C.C. set up a Committee of International Settlements which looked for solutions for the reparation and the international debt problems. The realization of the Committee's recommendations would have been an important basis for the restoration of monetary stability in the debtor countries and the stimulation of world trade. In the course of the Amsterdam Congress in July 1929 the I.C.C. approved the Young plan as an important step to settle the difficult matter of reparation payments. The founding father of this plan, Owen D. Young, worked as a banker and was himself actually a representative of the American National Committee[32]. So, implicitly, the international agreement to fix and reduce the reparation payments during the Great Depression goes back to proposals by a member of the I.C.C. itself. More concrete efforts of the I.C.C. in this field had been presented by the Committee on International Settlements. Sir Alan G. Anderson even worked out a concrete draft for a ten-year moratorium for all reparation and interallied-debt payments. He proposed to integrate the Young plan into this new form of debt settlement[33].

Wolfram Fischer has played down the real significance of the reparation problem for the German economy[34]. We share his view and that of Joseph A. Schumpeter "that, looked at as a business proposition, the Dawes tribute would have been nothing else but a 'commission' paid by Germany for the industrial conquest of the better half of the world"[35]. But in our opinion, Fischer assigned too little importance to the burden of all the other private debt payments, which also weighed heavily on Germany's shoulders. Businessmen were interested in securing priority for private international credit over intergovernmental debt. There-

[30] *Charles P. Kindleberger*, The World in Depression 1929–1939 (Berkeley ^{2}1986) 292.

[31] *Jean Meynaud*, Les Groupes de Pression Internationaux (Études de Science Politique 3, Lausanne 1961) 369f.

[32] Minutes, Executive Committee of the American Section, International Chamber of Commerce, February 13th, 1934, in: Franklin D. Roosevelt Library (=FDR) in New York, President's Official File 273. Young was also member of the Dawes Commission.

[33] Draft Resolution Proposed to the Committee on International Settlements, 13. 1. 1931 in: NA: Correspondence of the Office of the Treasury/Central File of the Office of the Secretary of the Treasury 1917–32. I.C.C. 1931–32, Box 93, 2.

[34] *Wolfram Fischer*, Die Weimarer Republik unter den weltwirtschaftlichen Bedingungen der Zwischenkriegszeit, in: *H. Mommsen, D. Petzina, B. Weisbrod* (eds.), Industrielles System und politische Entwicklung in der Weimarer Republik 1 (Düsseldorf 1977) 336.

[35] *Joseph A. Schumpeter*, Business Cycles. A Theoretical, Historical, and Statistical Analysis of the Capitalist Process 2 (New York 1939) 704, note 1.

fore, the reparation and interallied-debt question became one of the central points during the discussion in the course of the I.C.C. Congress in Washington in 1931. It was the opinion of I.C.C. President Abraham Frowein that the reparation question could hardly be separated from the interallied-debt problem. He pleaded for a complete cancellation of payments on both accounts[36]. For that reason, the contribution of Herbert Hoover during the Washington Congress of the I.C.C. on May 4th, 1931, was understandable: In his opening address he did not raise the interallied-debt problem at all[37]. In our opinion, the cancellation or, at least, considerable reduction of the reparation and interallied-debt payments early on could have played an important part in mitigating the Great Depression, especially so as the real burden of the nominally fixed payment obligations had increased enormously since 1929 due to the decline in prices during the course of the Depression. The idea presented, on January 13th, 1933, by the I.C.C.'s Special Committee for the Preparation of the Documents to be submitted to the World Monetary and Economic Conference, to create a kind of international organization to which the question of the fulfillment of obligations could be submitted, would have been worth implementing[38]. Appeal to this institution was to be made possible for both: debtors and creditors. Furthermore, a central fund for the allocation of credit was proposed by Felix Mlynarski from the Hungarian National Committee in 1939[39]. Economic historians in the 1990s generally approve of an international organization, as it was suggested by the I.C.C. during the Great Depression for the following reason: The absence of established procedures and the politicization of the intergovernmental process enormously hindered the necessary extension of the credit in the thirties[40].

2.2. *Commercial Policy Positions*

During the interwar period, the I.C.C. made tireless efforts to lower the artificial barriers erected by nations to international trade. The protectionist tariff policy pursued by many governments after the war had been seen by the Chamber as a

[36] Zur Wiederherstellung der Weltwirtschaft, in: Mitteilungen der Deutschen Gruppe der Internationalen Handelskammer 1 (1932) 3. As against that, the government of the United States insisted on a different handling of these two types of debt. *Dietmar Rothermund*, The Global Impact of the Great Depression 1929–1939 (London 1996) 32.
[37] Internationale Handelskammer (ed.), Sitzungsberichte des Washington-Kongresses Mai 1931, Drucksache Nr. 78, 10f.
[38] HP: Document No. 5100, Special Committee for the Preparation of the Documents to be Submitted to the World Monetary and Economic Conference, Meeting of January 13th, 1933, 5.
[39] Internationale Wirtschaft 4 (1939) 66.
[40] *Michael D. Bordo, Barry Eichengreen*, Implications of the Great Depression for the Development of the International Monetary System, in: *Michael D. Bordo, Claudia Goldin, Eugene N. White* (eds.), The Defining Moment: The Great Depression and the American Economy in the Twentieth Century (Chicago 1998) 444. Ralph G. Hawtrey already pleaded for a less restrictive credit policy during the interwar period. *Ralph G. Hawtrey*, Trade Depression and the Way Out (London 1931) 74.

major contributor for the outbreak of the Great Depression. Therefore, Georges Theunis, president of the I.C.C. from 1929 to 1931, concluded that common action in this sphere might be effective[41]. The I.C.C. demanded substantial reductions in the level of existing tariffs, unreasonable customs regulations, and restrictions on transportation so that the tide of international exchange would be able to flow again with a substantially increased volume. Actually, collective action in this field would have aided in overcoming the depression in world trade. Walter Leaf, President of the I.C.C. from 1925 to 1926, emphasized the independence and non-political character of his organization in achieving this aim. He asserted: "We speak for trade alone, and have no need to think of votes."[42]

Nevertheless, within the corporation there was considerable disagreement between member firms of the I.C.C. as to which tariff policy should be pursued by their respective governments. In March 1934 at a meeting of the I.C.C.'s Council, one participant described the ambiguity of the organization when he said that there was a perceptible demand on the part of the industry in the United States to urge additional protection for domestic production, on the one hand, and certain producers of export manufactures, who in the interest of an expansion of foreign trade favored governmental action to reduce tariffs, on the other[43]. The same observation could be made for other countries. In sum, the I.C.C. tried to play the leading role in the field of reduction of trade barriers, but at the same time the forces of protection were to be found in its own ranks. Therefore, it was very significant that a member of the American Section of the I.C.C. pronounced that the key for solving the Great Depression did not lie in the political sphere. "Government co-operation was imperative but leadership must come from business", said Melvin A. Traylor during the Washington Conference of the Chamber in May 1931[44].

There had also been differences between certain National Committees about the way to remove import restrictions. While the Americans approved of a tariff truce, even if it were limited to the European Continent, it was rejected by the British. The latter regarded the customs truce recommended by the Assembly of the League of Nations in 1929 as a hindrance to the abolition of tariffs and the expansion of their imperial trade. The French took a moderate position in that controversy: After having stopped the world-wide decline in production, they would support a tariff truce, with the exception of the colonies[45]. In its report to the World Economic and Finance Conference in 1933, the I.C.C. finally recom-

[41] Internationale Handelskammer (ed.), Ansprache des Präsidenten der Internationalen Handelskammer Herrn Georges Theunis, Drucksache Nr. 16, Washingtoner Kongreß 1931, 2.
[42] Cited from: Ridgeway, Merchants 235.
[43] HP: Document No. 5420, XLVème Session du Conseil, 9 Mars 1934, 6.
[44] International Chamber of Commerce (ed.), Proceedings of the Washington Congress May 1931, Brochure No. 78, 20.
[45] HP: Document No. 3978, Groupe des Relations Économiques Internationales. Trêve douanière. Analyse des résponses des comités nationaux au questionnaire de la C.C.I. (par le Service Industrie et Commerce), Février 1930, 2, 5, 7f.

mended the conclusion of the customs truce[46]. In sum, one can say that such a commercial disarmament, if it had been implemented by the governments, could have been only a temporary measure to prevent the worsening of the Great Depression. Steps of greater scope would have been necessary to contribute to a mitigation of the crisis. One of these could have been the I.C.C.'s ambitious program to organize industry into cartels, syndicates, or trusts on a world-wide scale. "By reducing costs of production and so adjusting output to consumption"[47], cartels might indeed have contributed to a mitigation of the Great Depression. In addition to that, the Chamber wanted to use cartels as a means of monetary stabilization "because they are quickly able to make themselves independent of the oscillations of the currency in the individual countries either through the fixing of flexible prices or only directing the exchanges towards countries with similar monetary condition"[48]. The I.C.C. also understood cartels as an instrument to prevent a further decline of the price level. For the interwar period this assertion was empirically proven: In Germany, for example, the cartellized prices fell less, only one percent, than the non-cartellized prices, with 24 percent[49].

The I.C.C. recognized the instability of international tariff treaties. In 1929 and 1930 all the existing agreements which were valid only for a limited time expired. From this time on, contracts which were terminable in the short term dominated international business relations. The duration of treaties diminished because some nations wanted to keep open the possibility of adapting their tariff levels to changed circumstances in the world. Therefore, the I.C.C. recommended the conclusion of long-term trade agreements. Between certain National Committees there nevertheless existed differences of opinion about their character: Some preferred multilateral treaties with the unconditional most-favored-nation (M.F.N.) clause; others gave priority to bilateral agreements with a restricted M.F.N. clause[50]. This divergence became obvious in the statements given by the American and British National Committees. While the first rejected the multilateral approach, the latter approved of this sort of agreement[51]. All in all, three possible options for tariff reform were seen by the I.C.C. – autonomous reductions as well as bilateral and multilateral agreements. The members of the Chamber obviously disagreed as to what policy approach should be favored. That the I.C.C. finally took refuge to bilateral agreements can be explained by the fact that the multilat-

46 Internationale Handelskammer (ed.), Die Weltwirtschafts- und Finanzkonferenz, Drucksache Nr. 84 (Paris 1933) 9.

47 *Pierre Vasseur*, General Secretary of the I.C.C., in: HP: Document No. 4580, 29th Session of the Executive Committee, July 30th 1931, 6.

48 HP: Document No. 4597, Committee on International Ententes, Meeting of October 5th, 1931, 1.

49 League of Nations (ed.), The Course and Phases of the World Economic Depression. Report Presented to the Assembly of the League of Nations (Geneva 1931) 167.

50 Deutsche Gruppe der Internationalen Handelskammer (ed.), Bericht über die Tagung des Beirats der Deutschen Gruppe der Internationalen Handelskammer (Berlin 1934) 24.

51 HP: Document No. 5420, XLVème Session du Conseil, 9 Mars 1934, 7.

eral approach had not the slightest prospect of succeeding[52]. Bilaterialism became a sort of stopgap measure of the I.C.C. after the failure of certain collective actions, also on the part of the League of Nations (cf. World Economic Conferences of 1927 and 1933). Finally, in the course of the Paris Conference of 1935, the I.C.C. recommended the conclusion of bilateral agreements on a M.F.N. basis. This approach was supposed to be the first step on the way to a world-wide abolition of tariff and non-tariff barriers[53]. The success of the Reciprocal Trade Agreements Policy, which had been initiated by the Secretary of State Cordell Hull and was taken up by the U.S. in 1934, showed that the I.C.C. advice on the course of trade policy contributed to mitigating the Great Depression.

The I.C.C.'s recommendation to apply the M.F.N. clause when concluding commercial treaties was another attempt by the organization to approach the goal of free trade during the Great Depression. The Chamber saw the application of this commercial principle as an important instrument to abolish discriminatory practices among the nations and to check retaliation measures on the part of the European Continent resulting from the Smoot-Hawley Tariff Act in the U.S.A. Moreover, the M.F.N. clause could pave the way for new tariff agreements in the world, which would contribute to a mitigation of the crisis. The I.C.C. even formulated a kind of draft-clause which was supposed to be integrated word for word in various trade agreements. But not all National Committees supported the M.F.N. clause as an important basis for trade negotiations. Above all, the British and the French refused to adopt this principle because of their special relationship to certain overseas territories[54]. In short, neither nation wanted to share the economic advantages they held in their colonies. Finally, in working out a common platform, the Chamber could not disregard the different national positions represented by its members. For this reason, the Committee of Ten of the I.C.C., which had been created during the crisis for the special purpose of advising on trade questions, recommended the exclusion of the colonies from every sort of trade agreement: "The question of the international exploitation of colonies touches on singularly delicate and essentially political problem of mandates – a question in which it is preferable that the Chamber should not interfere."[55] The position of the League of Nations toward an M.F.N. clause was contrary to that of the I.C.C. In the opinion of Arthur Salter, the M.F.N. clauses would impede tariff reductions along the only practicable path of progress – that of agreements between pairs or groups of countries with complementary production and comparable tariff and

[52] Cf. *Owen Jones*, in: Bundesarchiv Dahlwitz-Hoppegarten, Reichswirtschaftskammer R 11/1354, 58.
[53] Der VIII. Kongreß der Internationalen Handelskammer, in: Mitteilungen der Deutschen Gruppe der Internationalen Handelskammer 5 (1935) 8.
[54] HP: Document No. 5142, Projet de Rapport de la Chambre de Commerce Internationale à la Conférence Monétaire et Économique présenté par M. Owen Jones, Rapporteur, au "Comité Spécial" en sa session du 21 Mars 1933, 10.
[55] ASD: BIB 43, Document No. 4593, Committee of Ten, October 5th, 1931, 6.

currency system[56]. That was why Richard Riedl from the Austrian National Committee asked for certain exceptions from the clause in the course of creating regional organizations in the world. This idea was finally rejected by the Americans and the British, but strongly supported by the Germans and French. The latter gave their support to certain exceptions from the application of the M.F.N. clause with regard to the creation of a European Economic Union. Therefore, it was not without reason that the General Agreement on Tariffs and Trade (GATT) exempted customs unions, free trade areas and Commonwealth preferences from the M.F.N. obligation upon its founding in 1948.

In the eyes of the I.C.C. the creation of a European Economic Community seemed to be a necessary condition for mitigating the Great Depression in the interwar period. It is interesting to see the great differences which existed between the I.C.C. and the League of Nations in achieving the aim of a closer union of Europe: While the Chamber attached great importance to the economic aspects of European Unity, the League gave priority to political aims. The goal of the I.C.C. was to create a common market through the realization of more freedom for the international movement of goods, of persons, of capital and of services which became popular only after the Second World War[57]. Nevertheless, differences also existed between some National Committees about the character of a closer co-operation in Europe in the discussion of Aristide Briand's proposal for a European Federation in May 1930: "As regards the essential point, the subordination of economic to political problems, certain national committees were for this principle, other against it."[58] There were even some members of the I.C.C. who seemed to be opposed to the creation of a European Customs Union. Above all, the British National Committee declined to participate in this project because of its special attachment to the "imperial preferences". Furthermore, the English members of the I.C.C. feared the reinforcement of commercial antagonism vis-à-vis the U.S.[59]. But ultimately the Americans were also interested in strengthening Europe in its development by encouraging the I.C.C. plan for a closer union of Europe. During the Conference of the I.C.C. in Washington in 1931, Abraham Frowein, president of the I.C.C., recalled the recommendations which had been formulated in America itself in favor of a closer integration of European national economic units[60]. During the interwar period it would have been easier, in our opinion, to achieve European integration by an economic union corresponding to

[56] *Arthur Salter*, World Trade and Its Future (London 1936) 95.
[57] ASD: BIB 44, Document No. 4613, "Comité des Dix". Recommendations faites par la Commission réunie à Berlin le 17 Octobre 1931 en vue de la conclusion de Fédérations économiques en Europe, 2.
[58] HP: Document No. 42014, Thirty-Third Meeting of the Council, 9.
[59] International Chamber of Commerce/British National Committee (ed.), Some Considerations of the United Staates of Europe and other possible Economic Groups. An Independent Study prepared for the Information and Consideration of the British National Committee (London 1930) 4, 6.
[60] International Chamber of Commerce (ed.), Proceedings of the Washington Congress May 1931, Brochure No. 78, 67.

the recommendations of the commercial representatives than by an attempt at political union between national governments. For that reason, the I.C.C. plan for the creation of a European Economic Community would have been easier to realize than political union and could have been an important contribution to alleviating the Great Depression. It would have smoothed the path for trade liberalization and for controlling production, at least in a certain region. But without England the continent of Europe alone could not have been a world economic power comparable to the one which had built up in America[61]. But political developments, especially in Germany in 1933, precluded all options of European integration anyway.

3. The Extent of the Influence of the I.C.C.

3.1. Channels of Influence

The interwar period revealed different channels which could have been taken by the I.C.C. to influence governments. First of all, there was the option of direct contact with politicians responsible for shaping policies. Several times the I.C.C. in Paris energetically appealed to the National Committees to urge their respective governments to favor the reduction of customs barriers for the benefit of increasing international commercial exchange. For this reason, some countries assembled a delegation of qualified representatives who not only filed a complaint with their government but also tried to convince policy makers with their economic know-how[62].

The I.C.C. also used the distribution of specialized publications. Various books and brochures were meant to inform a broader public by analyzing causes of and remedies for the Great Depression[63]. For this aim the I.C.C. also widely distributed the proceedings of its Conferences. Each National Committee tried to obtain the attention of its respective government by sending a copy of the Conferences' final resolutions with individual recommendations demanding their implementation. The influence of the I.C.C. grew indirectly due to the fact that a large number of its members had already occupied leading positions in government.

[61] Cf. *André Siegfried*, European Reactions to American Tariff Proposals, in: Foreign Affairs 1 (1929) 18. Siegfried gave important advice to the French National Committee during the interwar period.

[62] There are only two minutes of meetings between members of the British Government and representatives of the British National Committee left in the Public Record Office in Kew (PRO). One I.C.C. delegation met Prime Minister Stanley Baldwin on June 5th, 1923 (PRO/T171/1315). Another went to John Simon, the Chancellor of Exchequer, on June 5th, 1938 (PRO/T172/1889).

[63] Joint Committee Carnegie Endowment-International Chamber of Commerce (ed.), Separate Memoranda from the Economists Consulted by the Joint Committee on the Improvement of Commercial Relations between Nations and the Problems of Monetary Stabilization (Paris ^{2}1936).

Their contacts with the old guard had not been disrupted and could be seen as an important channel of influence in the political sphere. For example, Georges Theunis, the President of the I.C.C. from 1929 to 1931, had once been the Prime Minister of Belgium.

Generally speaking, in the United States of America the I.C.C. could exercise a somewhat greater influence on policy than in Europe. The Chamber did not regularly participate in the hearings of the U.S. Congress but often undertook various efforts at establishing direct contact with the President himself. For that reason, Herbert Hoover had also been invited to inaugurate the I.C.C. Congress, which took place in Washington in May 1931. His final refusal to address the reparation and interallied-debt question had been a rejection of the Chamber's principal plan. Hoover was at least present, which enhanced the status of the business organization in the media. The fact that the delegates of the Conference discussed the reparation and interallied-debt problem in spite of the disapproval of the U.S. President and of the American Section of the I.C.C. finally exerted great pressure on the Hoover administration in this matter.

There was also close cooperation between the League of Nations' Economic Committee and the I.C.C., initiated in 1921 under the special guidance of Alberto Pirelli, at the same time I.C.C. vice president and member of the Economic Committee. The Council of the League accordingly invited the I.C.C. to take part in the work of its international economic conferences in an advisory capacity. Gustave L. Gérard of the I.C.C. frankly described the intention of his organization to influence the most precious tool of the governments, the League of Nations, according to the economic wishes of the business world[64]. With regard to the field of trade barriers, the I.C.C. pursued a double objective: The influencing of the public, on the one hand, and changes in national legislation on the other.

3.2. Successes and Failures

The I.C.C. exercised a kind of influence which is not easily measurable, for it was often implicit rather than explicit. The recommendations of the I.C.C. were not only realized in the economy but also in the political sphere. Its actions were sometimes concentrated on developing the guiding principles to be aimed at on international conferences, afterwards often shaped by the League of Nations into concrete policy proposals (cf. World Monetary and Economic Conferences of 1927 and of 1933). The different National Committees of the I.C.C. finally adapted the principals to diverging national cirumstances. With regard to the reparation and interallied-debt problem, a certain success can be attributed to I.C.C.'s work. It was in fact the discussions at the Washington Conference of the Chamber in May 1931 which prompted President Hoover to elaborate the famous moratorium for all reparation and interallied-debt payments. This, however, did not

[64] Sitzungen und Arbeiten, in: Ergänzungsheft 2 zur Internationalen Wirtschaft (Oktober 1929) 76.

actually contribute quickly to a mitigation of the crisis. During a meeting of the British National Committee on June 28th, 1932, the I.C.C.'s influence on the Hoover proposals of June 1931 had been explicitly summarized as follows: "It was not generally known at the time that the Hoover Moratorium initiated last summer was in fact an interesting consequence of our Congress [in Washington], but Mr Castle, the United States Assistant Secretary of State for Foreign Affairs, made a public admission that it was the discussions at our Congress in Washington which first caused President Hoover to consider the necessity for courageous action."[65] The Hoover Moratorium was, in fact, an interesting result of the I.C.C. Congress in Washington concerning the reparation and interallied-debt problem at the same time. To sum up, the I.C.C. played a leading role in solving the reparation and interallied-debt questions thanks to the broad coverage of the I.C.C. Washington Congress in the U.S. media. They strongly supported the work of the Chamber and exerted a great pressure on the attitude of the American government: Journalists wrote many articles about the final position taken by the I.C.C. in its resolutions in 1931 and obviously disapproved of the refusal of the U.S. government and the American Section of the I.C.C. to tackle the interallied-debt question. In contrast to the Hoover Moratorium, the Conference in Lausanne in July 1932 only dealt with Germany's reparation payments – not the interallied-debt problem[66]. This was the reason why the Americans did not take part in its negotiations[67].

The intervention of the Chamber would have been particularly useful in the domain of collective action against tariff policy, but this did not take place on a great scale until the Second World War had ended the Great Depression and had triggered a new orientation of U.S. foreign economic policies[68]. It manifested itself in the multilateral agreements on tariff reduction within the framework of the GATT. Despite the commercial policy positions of the I.C.C. during the Great Depression, the interwar period was characterized by rising tariffs and an increase in other import barriers around the world. In enacting the Smoot-Hawley Tariff Act in June 1930[69], the U.S.A. triggered a wave of retaliatory measures, above all in

[65] Unpublished document of the British National Committee in the British Library in London. Annual Meeting of the British National Committee, June 28th, 1932, 2. Cf. Edward W. Bennett: "The conference of the International Chamber of Commerce, held in Washington from May 4 to 7, must have given further impetus and direction to Hoover's thoughts." *Edward W. Bennett*, Germany and the Diplomacy of the Financial Crisis (Harvard 1962) 132.
[66] *Gian Trepp*, Die Bank für Internationalen Zahlungsausgleich im Zweiten Weltkrieg: Bankgeschäfte mit dem Feind. Von Hitlers Europabank zum Instrument des Marshallplans (Zürich 1993) 21; *Wolfram Fischer*, Die wirtschaftspolitische Situation der Weimarer Republik (Schriftenreihe der Niedersächsischen Landeszentrale für Politische Bildung 9) (Celle 1960) 53.
[67] *Herbert Hoover*, Memoiren, Die große Wirtschaftskrise 1929–1941, Bd. 3 (Mainz o. J.) 171 f.
[68] *Lutz Frühbrodt, Carl-Ludwig Holtfrerich*, Die Neugestaltung der US-Wirtschaftspolitik nach 1945. Die Erfahrungen der Zwischenkriegszeit als Argument, in: Jahrbuch für Wirtschaftsgeschichte 1 (1998) 85–123.
[69] For a detailed description cf.: *Carl-Ludwig Holtfrerich*, The Grown-up in Infant's Cloth-

Europe[70]. While in 1931 the British increased duties for certain commodities up to 50 percent and in 1932, with the Ottawa Agreement, erected a special trading system of imperial preferences, the French imposed a more severe quota system. The Germans joined in this prohibitive development by raising agricultural tariffs and establishing foreign exchange restrictions. As a result, world trade continued to shrink. No recovery was in sight. Finally, a change in the course of U.S. tariff policy emerged in 1934 when the United States, departing from Republican protectionism, with the Democrats in control of the Congress and the Presidency, embarked upon a program of reform in tariff-making which represented a belated attempt to follow the commercial policy advice given by the I.C.C. in the interwar period. The methods adopted by the U.S. Department of State in the formation of this tariff policy marked an essential departure from the notorious Smoot-Hawley Tariff Act. Thus, export interests which had lacked influence in preparing the tariff bill in 1929 were, five years later, granted the right to a full hearing in Washington. Nevertheless, there was a flaw in the new trade policy of the U.S. under Secretary of State Cordell Hull: Commercial treaties were not concluded with all important trading nations, for example Germany and Japan, because trade policy was used as a sort of containment policy against totalitarian and militaristic nations.

The influence of the I.C.C. during the Great Depression can, however, be ascertained in the 1934 Reciprocal Trade Agreements Act, if we are to believe the statement of Frederick Fentener van Vlissingen, former president of the I.C.C.[71]. Nevertheless, the members of the I.C.C. did not always act consistently with one another with regard to commercial policy recommendations. In the thirties, voices even emerged within the I.C.C. speaking out for more protectionism. A member of the British National Committee remarked in June 1932: "In France the demand for these quotas comes largely from the leading industrial organizations which constitute the French National Committee."[72] In short, the ambiguity of policy positions of I.C.C. members revealed the greatest weakness of the Chamber in its attempts to bring governments to cut back on trade barriers rather than increase them during the Great Depression.

The I.C.C. periodically discussed economic policy questions and issued recommendations, but it was not successful in convincing all the respective governments of the necessity of a powerful and comprehensive united action to reduce trade impediments. Apart from the Hull program, the organization failed to extend the system of commercial treaties throughout the world. But in this failure the

ing. The U.S. Protectionist Relapse in the Interwar Period, (J. F. Kennedy-Institut für Nordamerikastudien. Abteilung für Wirtschaft, Working Paper No. 19) (Berlin 1989) 30–49.

[70] See the classic study: *Joseph M. Jones, Jr.*, Tariff Retaliation. Repercussions of the Hawley-Smoot Bill (Philadelphia 1934).

[71] *Frederick Fentener van Vlissingen*, Das amerikanische Handelsvertragsprogramm. Ein wirksamer Angriff gegen die Handelshemmnisse, in: Internationale Wirtschaft 3/4 (1937) 8, and *idem*, Die Förderung des internationalen Güteraustausches, in: Internationale Wirtschaft 2 (1939) 13.

[72] International Chamber of Commerce (ed.), British National Committee, Annual Meeting of the British National Committee June 26th, 1932, Report of Proceedings 3.

Chamber did not stand alone. The World Monetary and Economic Conferences of 1927 and 1933, organized by the League of Nations, and their recommendations in favor of liberalizing trade were also clearly failures. Even though American and European business leaders failed in their attempt at a combined League and I.C.C. tariff offensive, the I.C.C., at least, was effective in providing the impetus which helped to place trade problems in the hands of experts drawn largely from its own ranks. Furthermore, the I.C.C. sometimes exerted influence on national legislatures; this happened, for example, in the case of Congressional hearings on the Reciprocal Trade Agreements Bill[73]. All in all, the shaping of a fair and equitable partnership between government and business conceived in terms of national interests broadly instead of narrowly defined, i.e. taking into account the repercussions of protectionism on other nations' trade policy and import demand, had slowly taken shape. Its effectiveness was considerably improved after the Second World War.

Progress could be observed during the interwar period in the attitude of the governments toward the most-favored-nation treatment. The Americans had changed their position from strong opponents of the unconditional M.F.N. clause to real advocates of this foreign-trade principle already in connection with the Fordney-McCumber Tariff Act of 1922[74]. But it grew to importance only after the Reciprocal Trade Agreements Act of 1934, when the M.F.N. clause became part of the bilateral trade agreements. In November 1939 twenty parties already held contracts with the U.S.A. on an M.F.N. basis. Nearly 60 percent of American foreign trade was affected by this clause. The British, in contrast, mostly denied the most-favored-nation treatment, mainly on account of their imperial preferences. They pursued a policy of "bilateral balancing", which reinforced trade at the expense of third parties. His Majesty's Government had decided to make concessions only on the basis of reciprocity[75]. The same attitude could be observed in Germany. In France, however, a certain willingness to realize the M.F.N. clause emerged in 1931, but it had little practical bearing due to the prevailing quota system.

The advice of the I.C.C. to create a European Economic Community found the greatest approval in France, where Aristide Briand proposed the formation of a European Federation in May 1930. While the French Foreign Minister put the main emphasis on the political side of a European Unity, the I.C.C. exclusively stressed the economic advantages of a Common Market. The French efforts also had a certain anti-American thrust[76]. Nevertheless, the American government was

[73] *Ridgeway*, Merchants 390.

[74] For details cf.: *William B. Kelly, Jr.*, Antecedents of Present Commercial Policy, 1922–1934, in: *W. B. Kelly, Jr.* (ed.), Studies in United States Commercial Policy (Chapel Hill 1963) 38f.

[75] House of Commons, Parliamentary Debates 1932–33, Vol. 275 (London 1933) 2024. Cf.: *Margaret S. Gordon*, Barriers to World Trade. A Study of Recent Commercial Policy (New York ^{2}1983) 409f.

[76] *Hans-Jürgen Schröder*, Widerstände der USA gegen europäische Integrationsbestre-

not principally opposed to the plans for the unification of Europe. Quite the reverse: the U.S.A. supported the idea of abolishing the inner-European customs barriers to a certain extent[77]. The responsibility for the failure of the Briand plan for a European Federation has to be attributed to the German and British politicians. In Germany, the Brüning government obviously prevented actual steps for the creation of a European Union[78]. Also, the British government expressed doubts about the I.C.C.'s plans for Europe. Because of their "special relationship" with the Commonwealth and the United States of America, the British remained sceptical of every sort of European regionalism. They obviously gave priority to their colonies over the European Continent[79].

During the interwar period, the monetary-policy decisions of the central banks in the U.S., Great Britain, France and Germany contributed to deepening rather than mitigating the Depression. By means of high discount rates the Federal Reserve System, the Banque de France and the Bank of England were responsible for a severe monetary contraction, even though the I.C.C. pleaded for more relaxation. Similar charges have been made against the Reichsbank, which permitted an overvaluation of German currency and a dramatic monetary deflation as measured by the monetary aggregates M1, M2, or M3[80]. Restrictions on Reichsbank lending by increasing bank rates were maintained during the depression until the summer of 1931. When thereafter the discount rates were lowered, the finance sector in Germany made serious mistakes in the distribution of credit: Bank lending was concentrated not in dynamic branches of the economy but rather in stagnant ones with few technical innovations[81].

After 1931, the Banque de France held firmly to the prestige of the Franc Poincaré and resisted a devaluation and the creation of new credits. Also, the Bank of England first dealt a severe blow to Britain's international competitive position by bringing the pound back to the gold standard at the prewar parity of $ 4.86. Later on, England was one of the first countries to abandon the gold standard on September 21st, 1931[82]. In contrast, the other currencies were detached from gold much later than the pound: the dollar in 1933 and the franc in 1936. The Germans

bungen in der Weltwirtschaftskrise, in: *Helmut Berding* (ed.), Wirtschaftliche und politische Integration in Europa im 19. und 20. Jahrhundert (Göttingen 1984) 171.

77 *Walter Lipgens*, Europäische Einigungsidee 1923–1930 und Briands Europaplan im Urteil der Deutschen Akten, in: Historische Zeitschrift 203 (1966) 75. Other opinions cf. *Schröder*, Widerstände der USA 169–184.

78 Akten zur Deutschen Auswärtigen Politik 1918–45. Aus dem Archiv des Auswärtigen Amts, Serie B 1925–1933, Bd. XV, 1. Mai bis 30. September 1930 (Göttingen 1980) Nr. 123/127/136.

79 *Karl Dietrich Erdmann*, Der Europaplan Briands im Licht der englischen Akten, in: Geschichte in Wissenschaft und Unterricht 1 (1950) 28.

80 For data on the large reduction of the money supply in Germany after 1929 see: *Tilly, Huck*, Die deutsche Wirtschaft in der Krise 62, 77–80.

81 *Harold James*, Did the Reichsbank draw the Right Conclusions from the Great Inflation, in: *Gerald Feldman* (ed.), Die Nachwirkungen der Inflation auf die deutsche Geschichte 1924–1933 (München 1985) 227.

82 *James*, Reichsbank 211.

implemented their deflation policy as a sort of "Ersatzabwertung" [substitute devaluation] which did not have the same economic effects as a real devaluation, for example the one in Great Britain[83]. In sum, the countries that defended their gold parities experienced a markedly further deterioration in their economic activity. It became evident that they suffered from a relative disadvantage as to their international competitive position[84]. In some respects, the failure of the I.C.C. to influence all governments to hold on to gold finally turned out as an advantage for countries with freely floating exchange rates. These experienced early recoveries. Above all, the British economy profited from its improved international competitive position after having devalued the pound.

With regard to price policy, the U.S., Great Britain, France and Germany made serious efforts to stabilize the price index. Cartels were created to achieve this aim by restricting output. For this reason the Americans and Germans even revised their legislation during the Great Depression. The French government openly approved the creation of cartels as a remedy against the fall in prices[85]. This attitude corresponded to the economic policy advice given by the I.C.C. in May 1933[86]. In Germany, however, state intervention was aimed at fixing prices at lower levels. Cartels were ordered to reduce their prices. In November 1936, after full employment had been reached and inflationary pressure had been built up, this development ended in an officially dictated price stop. None of the countries mentioned adopted monetary policies as a means to increase the price level. They all clung to an economic policy basically oriented at the supply side. In this respect, their economic policies can be seen as having been largely in line with the economic policy positions taken by the I.C.C. during the Great Depression. Furthermore, accordance between the governments' actions and the I.C.C.'s policy proposals can also be observed in some other fields: The U.S.A., Germany, Great Britain and France all aimed at achieving a balanced budget during the Great Depression. But finally, this goal was abandoned in the first-mentioned two states: in Germany with the formation of a National Socialist government, and in the U.S.A. with the introduction of the New Deal.

4. Conclusion

In conclusion, the economic policy positions of the I.C.C. during the Great Depression represented a real alternative to the actual policies pursued only in the field of commercial policy advice: The reduction of trade barriers, the conclusion of multilateral trade agreements on the basis of the unconditional M.F.N. clause and the creation of a European Economic Community constituted an effective

83 *Holtfrerich,* Vernachlässigte Perspektiven 150.

84 *Lary,* United States 185. See also footnote 7.

85 Cf. Report of *Philippe Berthelot* from January 6th, 1932, in: Archive Diplomatique in Paris (=AD), B-Information Economique 34, 3.

86 Offizieller Sitzungsbericht des Siebten Kongresses der Internationalen Handelskammer, Wien 29. Mai-3. Juni 1933, in: Internationale Wirtschaft 7 (1933) 10.

program for mitigating the Great Depression. But the I.C.C. lacked concrete influence on the governments' policies in these fields, with the exception of the 1934 Reciprocal Trade Agreements Act.

However, not all of the I.C.C.'s monetary and financial policy recommendations would have been equally effective in alleviating the crisis. For example, the countries which clung to the gold standard – as the I.C.C. recommended – suffered more under the depression than those which abandoned it early on. Furthermore, the raising of prices could have been better attained by monetary remedies than by restricting output; the latter policy device had been recommended by the I.C.C. and was generally applied in the U.S.A., Germany, France and Great Britain. However, an extension of capital exports by creditor nations, especially the United States, and a solution of the interallied and reparation debt problem – as recommended by the I.C.C. – could have presented a real alternative to the policies actually pursued by the governments. But, ultimately, they were not adopted by the creditor nations due to a narrow view of their national interests. During the Great Depression the world suffered from a dollar gap: Not only did the U.S.A. stop exporting capital to Europe, but it also put heavy restrictions upon imports. The dollar supply in the world thus diminished by about 68 percent between 1929 and 1932[87]. Nevertheless, the U.S. government and, above all, the public was not prepared to make further concessions in the interallied-debt question. U.S. trade protectionism gave debtor countries no other chance than trade protectionism of their own, devaluation or exchange controls to cope with their external deficits. Domestic credit shortages were reinforced by rising discount rates; the concomitant increase in interest rates contributed to the deep fall of investment activity. In Germany the interest rates continued to increase while they were already at the point of decreasing in the other countries. The Reichsbank's discount rate was hiked to 15 percent shortly after the banking crisis broke out in July 1931[88]. The failure of the U.S.A. to fill the dollar gap abroad was a symptom of its unwillingness to embark upon a policy of "easy money" which would have contributed to supplying capital and credit at reasonably low interest-rates for the debtor nations already at the beginning of the Great Depression. The U.S. government also aggravated the Great Depression in that it was adamant, against the advice of the I.C.C., that war-related international debts should be collected. Their alleviation early on could have provided an essential basis for keeping up international liquidity and improving world economic conditions during the Great Depression.

In sum, the economic policy positions of the I.C.C. during the Great Depression often contrasted with the actual policies chosen. The governments pursued their short-term national interests. This beggar-my-neighbour policy course contributed substantially to the weakening of the economic situation not only abroad

[87] *Lary*, United States 5f.

[88] *Heinrich Irmler*, Bankenkrise und Vollbeschäftigungspolitik (1931–1936), in: Deutsche Bundesbank (ed.), Währung und Wirtschaft in Deutschland 1876–1975 (Frankfurt a.M. [2]1976) 292.

but also domestically. In addition to that, the I.C.C. itself gave monetary advice which – insofar as it was heeded by central banks and governments – contributed to an aggravation of the Great Depression, while the International Chamber of Commerce remained unaware of the detrimental consequences of its recommendations in this field.

Gerald D. Feldman

Insurance Company Collapses in the World Economic Crisis
The Frankfurter Allgemeine Versicherungs-AG (Favag) and the Austrian Phönix

While considerable attention has been paid to the national and international significance of the great Central European banking collapses in the World Economic Crisis, especially those of the Austrian Credit Anstalt in May 1931 and the Darmstädter- und Nationalbank (Danat) in July 1931, similar disasters in the insurance field have received very little historical consideration. This is understandable for a number of reasons. The banking disasters occurred at the height of the Depression and contributed significantly to the deepening and broadening of the Depression in the countries where they took place and in transmitting their evil consequences abroad. They were a very visible result of the financial and economic disorders of the postwar world economy. They called forth national and international regulatory efforts in the form of standstill agreements, foreign exchange controls, and currency and banking regulations that were important constituent elements of the financial and economic "regime changes" that took place in the wake of the Great Depression. The banking crises have also been the object of extensive commentary and study by contemporaries and historians[1].

While the insurance company collapses discussed in this paper, the Favag in August 1929 and the Austrian Phönix in March 1936, were great shocks at the time and provoked much commentary in the national and international press, they have received little if any attention from business historians and scholars of the Great Depression. An important reason certainly is that the insurance industry itself has received very little scholarly study. In these specific instances, however, two other factors certainly have promoted such neglect. First, they occurred

[1] On "regime changes", see *Douglas J. Forsyth, Ton Notermans* (eds.), Regime Changes. Macroeconomic Policy and Financial Regulation in Europe from the 1930s to the 1990s (Providence, Oxford 1997). For the literature on the banking crises, see *Gerald D. Feldman*, Current Problems in the Study of Banking Crisis, in: *Philipp Cottrell, J. Reis, C.E. Nuñez* (eds.), Finance and the Making of the Modern Capitalist World, B 9 Proceedings of the Twelfth International Economic History Congress, Madrid, August 1998 (Seville 1998) 53–62.

at the temporal peripheries of the Great Depression, the Favag collapse on the eve of the Depression, the Phönix debacle at a time when Central Europe seemed to be pulling out of the Great Slump. Second, the insurance company crises were contained and successfully terminated, in the case of the Favag through its absorption by its chief competitor, the Allianz Insurance Company, in the case of the Phönix, by government and insurance industry intervention to protect policyholders and redistribute liabilities and assets. For these reasons, the full significance and relevance of these collapses for the history of the Great Depression have been veiled but, as I hope to show, they certainly deserve more study than they have received.

I. The Fall of the Favag

On December 11, 1928, Deutsche Bank Director Paul Bonn wrote to the Director of the Frankfurt branch, E. Rothschild, about a recent conversation with Director Georg Solmssen of the Disconto Gesellschaft concerning a major business engagement for which the Favag was supposed to give a guarantee: "Herr Dr. Solmssen asked me on this occasion whether I took the guarantee to be of full value and explained his question by pointing out that the business methods of the Frankfurter Allgemeinen have been extraordinarily displeasing to the Disconto of late; they have the impression that engagements are being undertaken which have very little transparency and whose uncovered risks could amount to very significant sums. One does not to be sure have a definite conception at the Disconto about what is going on, but one has an uncomfortable feeling. These remarks were made very casually. But they were all the more interesting to me since I have already for some time spelled out for you my impression that neither the large-scale guarantee business of the Frankfurter Allgemeinen, nor especially the transactions conducted by interlocking companies, which as far as one can tell have the character of being practically business in goods, could be considered acceptable. Also the apparently very extensive business with automobile purchase financing, as is the case with the Automobile Bank, cannot be seen as an especially promising line for such an insurance concern."[2]

Bonn was worried about the leadership of the company. He had the impression that the General Director, Paul Dumcke, "has become very old" and feared that one of the directors, Dr. Kirschbaum, to whom he attributed the character traits of "a certain recklessness and lack of concern" as well as "other elements" in the company had gained the upper hand. Bonn confessed that he had been worrying about the situation at the Favag for some time and thought it was necessary for the bankers serving on the Supervisory Board of the Favag, one of whom was Direc-

[2] Paul Bonn to E. Rothschild, Dec. 11, 1928, Historisches Archiv der Deutschen Bank (HADB), S233.

tor Rothschild, "to get into touch with one another about this question cautiously, inconspicuously, and without taking any special action".

Unfortunately, the bell was already tolling for the Favag. It tolled first, however, for Dumcke, who died unexpectedly but perhaps fortunately from an operation on February 14, 1929 with his reputation still very much intact and widely praised in obituaries for his contributions to the development of large scale enterprise in the insurance field. While the hymn of praise was to have a rather ironic quality a few months later, it is important to recognize that Dumcke was indeed one of the great leaders in the field, becoming a director of the company in 1892 and then Chairman of the Board of Directors in 1897[3]. He had built up the company before the war through communities of interest with various reinsurance companies and then fusion with the important Preussische Rückversicherungs-AG, which was renamed Helios Allgemeine Rückversicherungs-AG. At the same time, Dumcke expanded into multi-branch direct insurance as well. War and inflation provided him with the opportunity to expand still further. Foreign business was particularly important, since the Favag's participations in Southeast Europe and in Switzerland and its extensive international transportation insurance activities provided the company with the hard currency needed to use the inflation to expand at home. Favag took the whole or substantial portions of the Karlsruher Lebensversicherungsbank AG, the Vereinigte Berlinische und Preußische Lebens-Versicherungs-AG, and the "Hammonia" Allgemeine Versicherungs-AG, Hamburg under its wing. Thus, by the end of the 1920s it was second only to Allianz in the German insurance business and was a major national and international player in both direct insurance and reinsurance. At its shareholders meeting on June 18, 1929 the directors reported a 14 million mark increase in premiums over the previous year, assets amounting to 73.8 million RM, a net profit just short of 3.1 million RM, and a 12½% dividend totally 2.3 million RM[4].

The Allianz Concern had also been engaging in a systematic but much more careful policy of expansion under the leadership of General Director Kurt Schmitt, who considered a fusion with the Favag a potentially promising acquisition. While Schmitt was aware that the Favag had been doing business with a considerable amount of borrowed money and had told Dumcke that he believed this to be a mistaken policy whether it was proving profitable or not, he also thought Dumcke hard to replace and thus only broached the subject of Allianz-Favag collaboration in a conversation with Director Bodenheimer of the Danat Bank, a Favag super-

[3] The roots of the company go back to 1865, when it concentrated on glass insurance. It then moved into transportation insurance and was called the Frankfurter Transport- und Glasversicherungs-Gesellschaft until its takeover of the Frankfurter Lebensversicherungs-AG in 1911 led to its change of name to Frankfurter Allgemeine Versicherungs-AG. See *Ludwig Arps*, Durch Unruhige Zeiten. Deutsche Versicherungswirtschaft seit 1914. I. Teil (Karlsruhe 1970) 424–427.

[4] Bericht der in der General-Versammlung vom 30. September 1929 gewählten Revisions-Kommission der Frankfurter Allgemeinen Versicherungs-Aktien-Gesellschaft zu Frankfurt am Main, p. 17, Firmenhistorisches Archiv der Allianz AG, München (FHA), B-2, Nr. 601 (Hereinafter cited as Revisions-Commission).

visory board member, after Dumcke's death. This seemed all the more opportune since the leading personage in the concern, Director Philipp Becker, was a "finance man" rather than "insurance man" and none of the "insurance men" were of Dumcke's alleged caliber. There were reports of conflicts among the directors, and one of the Favag directors had actually approached Director Hans Hess of the Allianz in 1928 and suggested a fusion and buying out of the contracts of some of the leading Favag directors. There were also rumors going around about the investments of the directors. Schmitt pointed out that a careful audit of the Favag's finances would be required before any consolidation could take place. Bodenheimer thanked Schmitt for the suggestion, but responded that "he knows the situation exactly, and that the financial business of the Frankfurter has run profitably. Even if the banks are not in agreement with all the engagements, there is still no doubt that the Frankfurter was a first-class corporation that is making good earnings and progressing. He saw no place for a collaboration with Allianz at the moment."[5]

This was quite optimistic given the rumors that had been circulating, and the passivity of Bodenheimer and the other bankers on the Favag supervisory board is no less remarkable in the face of the newspaper articles that began to appear in the "Frankfurter Zeitung" in the spring of 1929. These articles were the work of Artur Lauinger, a pioneer in investigative journalism who had a special interest in insurance questions. A diligent reader of company reports and balances and careful observer of shareholder meetings, Lauinger was also a regular visitor at the Frankfurt exchanges and had heard all sorts of rumors about banking activities by the Favag through the Südwestdeutsche Bank A.G. Indeed, one branch bank director who had a seat on the Favag supervisory board and who probably was Rothschild of the Deutsche Bank, showed Lauinger a bill of exchange with Dumcke's signature and raised the question as to whether it was properly discountable. For Lauinger, the even more important question was whether an insurance company had any business discounting bills of the type shown to him and engaging in banking business of this kind.

Be this as it may, Lauinger visited Dumcke shortly before the latter's death and insisted on knowing more about the Favag's activities in the guarantee and lending fields. Dumcke referred him to Finance Director Becker. Lauinger saw Becker sometime in late March or early April 1929. He found Becker as reluctant to provide concrete information as the late Dumcke, whereupon Lauinger told him that he considered the credit operations of the Favag totally inappropriate for an insurance company and that he intended to attack the Favag openly if he were not provided with accurate balances and if a halt was not put to the credit operations in question. Becker then promised to gather the information and to keep Lauinger abreast of developments, but Lauinger soon launched a press campaign against the Favag's way of doing business. Also, Lauinger began informing members of the supervisory board and the Reich Supervisory Agency for Insurance of serious problems at the Favag.

[5] Aktennotiz Schmitt, Nov. 26, 1929, Bundesarchiv Berlin (BAB), 80 Ba 2, P5785.

The supervisory board of the Favag did decide to take some action in May by setting up an auditing committee, but Becker and Director Kirschbaum continued to maintain that the company was sound and only slowly and reluctantly provided the required information. Finally, however, enough facts were out to make impossible any further unwillingness on the part of the supervisory board to at least discuss the problem. Sometime in the summer of 1929, Lauinger was summoned home from vacation for a special meeting of the supervisory board of the Favag, which was in a state of despair over the mounting evidence of irregularities in the Favag's balances. Lauinger advised them to insist on the production of an accurate balance and to determine who was responsible for the losses, advice toward which the bankers on the board showed little enthusiasm since they feared that the Favag would close its accounts with banks which pressed them too hard and give its business to competing banks instead. Needless to say, the supervisory board members were also rather nervous about revelations that would make matters worse and cast a shadow over their performance as supervisors. The trouble was that the Reich Supervisory Agency was also responding to the news it was getting from Lauinger and began to launch an investigation of its own[6]. On August 17, the Favag announced the cessation of payment to its creditors. Three days later, Allianz took over its direct insurance business, thus guaranteeing that policyholders would be protected. The satisfaction of other creditors, however, both national and international was to become the subject of tedious negotiations for half a year and civil law suits, a few of which dragged on into the mid-1930s, while the criminal trials of the leading directors lasted into 1932 when they received jail sentences and fines. The Favag affair thus blended in nicely with the other bankruptcies and scandals of the depression period and public perceptions that there was something rotten in the world of capitalism.

As was so often the case with such failures in Central Europe, the roots of the difficulties lay in the inflationary period and in the gold mark opening balances following the hyperinflation. In the case of the Favag, the gold mark opening balance was considered five million gold marks in excess of what it should have been and was attributed to the desire of Dumcke to increase the company's prestige and attraction to investors. As the General Director of Allianz and chief beneficiary of Dumcke's folly Kurt Schmitt, who later attributed Allianz's survival in the depression to the modesty of its 1924 gold mark opening balance and the purposefulness of its expansion policy, explained: "The excessively high demands on the capital resources of the company necessarily arose from the exaggerated conver-

[6] *Artur Lauinger*, Das öffentliche Gewissen. Erfahrungen und Erlebnisse eines Redakteurs der Frankfurter Zeitung (Frankfurt 1958) 18–22. Lauinger's account telescopes some of the events between late 1928 and August 1929 since he leaves the impression that his interviews with Dumcke and Becker and the supervisory board meeting took place within a short space of time, which could not have been possible since Dumcke died in February. Fortunately, a memorandum of Münchener Rück General Director Wilhelm Kisskalt of January 25, 1930, who spoke with Lauinger in April 1929 about the interview with Becker, helps clarify the sequence of events. The memorandum is in BAB, 80 Ba 2, P5785.

sion to gold of the Frankfurter Allgemeinen. The decision to enter into dangerous financial engagements also arose from the effort to master these difficulties, which in the last analysis led to the collapse of the Frankfurter."[7] Even as Schmitt swallowed up the best and most profitable parts of the Favag's business, he warned against excessive optimism and risky engagements. Indeed, the analysis of the Favag's situation revealed a Panglossian approach to the economic situation that was uncommon in the industry. Thus, the company did a great deal of indirect business in transport insurance which produced a stream of high premiums but constant losses. The premiums provided the liquidity to pay for the past year's losses, presumably in the expectation that at some time or other the premium income would overtake the liquidity problem. Even more risky was the Favag's engagement in credit insurance, a dangerous business in times of economic instability, but most adventuresome was its extension of guarantees and credits not only for transactions with goods but also for purely financial transactions. These activities had very little or nothing to do with insurance; the premiums, such as they were, were not properly booked; reserves were not held for them; they were not reinsured. Most serious, however, was that many of these transactions never showed up in the balances. The business was conducted by the directors personally, and they accounted to no one but themselves for what they were doing. Not only did the concern operate through a series of interlocking directorates in which accountability was tossed to the winds, but the concern included some enterprises in which the directors played shareholders using false names or in which they gave credits to enterprises which did not even exist. The most notorious instance was the Deutsche Keramik-Gesellschaft mbH in Vienna which was run, with no success whatever, by Paul Dumcke's son Ernst and to which the Favag gave considerable credits. The credit granting of Südwestdeutsche Bank, which was run and supervised by Favag directors, was often simply criminal. The Favag thus collapsed because of spectacular mix of bad decisions in the field of indirect insurance, banking activities inappropriate for an insurance company, an inorganic concern structure, and the mixing of the concern's interests with the personal enterprises of the directors. In the process, the concern had accumulated very high debts, including short-term debts in Switzerland, England, and Holland for the financing of long-term projects[8].

Obviously, the directors of the Favag had every interest in veiling these activities, but the fact that they could do so with such "success" reflected the failures of the agencies created to supervise the concern. In the case of the Reich Supervisory Agency for Insurance, this manifested itself in a willingness to accept minimal reporting and satisfaction of the technical requirements connected with the actual insurance business of the Favag, a willingness to overlook many activities inappropriate for an insurance company, and a failure to follow up on activities which it did protest. In the case of the Favag supervisory board, the chief problem lay, as

[7] Vorstandssitzung am 5. und 6. November 1929, FHA 17, 2/4.
[8] The details are to be found in the Revisions Commission report 18–124.

was and is so often the case with such scandals, in the blind confidence placed in the directors and the failure to demand information even when, as has been shown, there was considerable suspicion that all was not well with its financial management. This led to the peculiar consequence that the culprits on the board of directors not only created the crisis but also dictated the solution. Thus, when Director Becker, after much pressure, finally came through with an account of the Favag's debts, he also declared: "Now I must honestly give you my view as a member of the board of directors so that you can deal with the situation: the 'Frankfurter' is finished, since the confidence that has been upset can only be won again with great difficulty. It is in the interest of the German economy that a collapse not be allowed to take place. The bank consortium must immediately declare that the consortium stands behind the Frankurter. Toward this end the consortium must place 30 million at the disposal of the Frankfurter, half in cash, half by guarantee."[9] This would make possible the liquidation of the debts and the survival of the insurance side of the business. He went on to urge that they let Allianz take over the insurance business, but he also mentioned the Schweizerische Rück, Prudential-London, and two American companies as possible future owners of the insurance assets. Becker provided not only revelations and advice but also the confession that the directors had known about the debts for years, but claimed that this had been the only way to build up the business after the inflation.

Becker, like his boss Dumcke, escaped punishment, in his case by falling victim to incurable heart and kidney problems, but five of his colleagues received prison sentences and fines in February 1932, the judge severely condemning the dead and dying and expressing regret that he could not pronounce harsher sentences on the living. Press coverage had been extensive, and the courtroom was full. All this reflected the great public interest in such scandals, the concern over the decline of business morality to which it bore witness, the inadequacy of government regulation in the past, presumably now corrected by a new insurance law with much tougher provisions that was passed in March 1931, and the failure of the supervisory board, above all the bankers, to supervise. By the time the trial came to an end, of course, the banking crisis had taken place, triggered by the failure of the Nordwolle concern and the failure of the Danat bank as a result in July 1931. As in the case of the Favag, the allegedly supervising bankers, especially Jakob Goldschmidt of the Danat, had failed to stop the speculations of the Lahusen brothers, who ran the Nordwolle, until it was too late. The analogies between the Favag and the Nordwolle were not lost on the public and worried the government, which feared that the cases "would have the consequence of producing a further sharpening of the mistrust of the capitalist form of economy"[10]. This mistrust was expressed already by the Social Democratic jurist Hugo Sinzheimer shortly after

[9] Ibid. 144.

[10] State Secretary Trendelenburg at the Ministerialbesprechung vom 7. September 1931, Akten der Reichskanzlei. Weimarer Republik, Die Kabinette Brüning I u. II (Boppard am Rhein 1982) vol. 2, p. 1663. For the trial judgements, see "Nach 4 Monaten Verhandlung: Gestern Favag-Urteil," Frankfurter General-Anzeiger, Feb. 26, 1932, in FHA, B-2/601.

the Favag scandal broke: "In this connection, the collapse ... has a special significance. It shows clearly that the private personal responsibility of the entrepreneur in no way offers a guarantee for rational economic management. It further shows that the great 'private' large enterprises of our age can only be regarded as private enterprises on the basis of an unsustainable fiction ..."[11].

Another problem was the danger of international distrust of German financial institutions and the German private economy in general. After the banking crisis, this was a reality, and the major concern was increasing it still further. At the outset of the Favag scandal, however, there was more reputation to save. In this respect, the management of the Favag collapse shows some interesting contrasts and similarities with the Danat debacle. Where in the latter case the other big banks, above all the Deutsche Bank, showed a remarkable lack of solidarity with the Danat. While prepared to take over some of its most lucrative accounts, the Deutsche Bank leadership was quite willing to see the Danat liquidated. The role of the Allianz in the case of the Favag was quite different. While there can be no question that the Allianz wished to take over its chief competitor, or at least take over the best parts of its business, the rapid intervention of Allianz meant that the investment of policyholders was secure and that the private sector managed to contain the most dangerous potential element in the catastrophe without dramatic government intervention. As General Director Schmitt somewhat cynically but still very hopefully told his board of directors: "One cannot deny that the events at the 'Frankfurter' have led to a general crisis of confidence in the private insurance business; but it is to be hoped that this crisis will be overcome soon. In working against a migration of business, especially of life insurance to foreign companies, it is useful to point out that collapses similar to the 'Frankfurter' are not unknown in America and England."[12]

Indeed, it is important to note that there had been some genuine resistance against Allianz's self-interested but salutary intervention in the Favag affair that was of international significance. As has been shown, Schmitt had broached the possibility of fusion with Allianz in his talks with Bodenheimer and other discussions had taken place at a time when the problems of the company had not been revealed. Even after they were, the basic insurance business remained very attractive, which explains the rapidity of Schmitt's intervention. It was attractive to others as well, especially the group of insurance companies connected with Director F. Nordhoff of the Berlinischen Feuer-Versicherungs-Anstalt. The latter was closely allied to the Schweizer Rückversicherungs-Gesellschaft in Zürich, which was a competitor of the Allianz-associated Münchener Rückversicherungs-Gesellschaft and which did 50–60% of its life insurance business in Germany. It was anxious to expand its operations in Germany, not by acquiring portions of the

[11] *Thilo Ramm* (Hrsg.), Hugo Sinzheimer. Ernst Fraenkel. Die Justiz in der Weimarer Republik. Eine Chronik (Neuwied, Berlin 1968) 200. I am grateful to Carl-Ludwig Holtfrerich for bringing this somment of September 1929 to my attention.

[12] Vorstandssitzung am 5. und 6. November 1929, FHA 17, 2/4.

Favag itself, from which it expected more "surprises", but rather by gaining control of two old, solid, and well respected companies in the Favag concern, the Karlsruher Lebensversicherungsbank AG in Karlsruhe and the Vereinigten Berlinischen und Preussischen Lebensversicherungs AG in Berlin. Nordhoff complained to his friends in the Disconto-Gesellschaft that the Allianz takeover would upset the balance in the insurance business and would also bring about a further economic concentration in Berlin at the expense of Frankfurt and South Germany[13].

Yet another scheme was urged by the Victoria Versicherungs-Gesellschaft which, using Jakob Goldschmidt of the Danat Bank as its spokesman, proposed common action on the part of all the large German insurance companies to deal with the problem. In the last analysis, however, the leading banks represented on the Favag supervisory board found the Allianz takeover most acceptable and welcome despite the power shift it carried with it. On the one hand, the alternatives were all being proposed in August 1929 while the full scope of the disaster was gradually coming into focus, for example, that the "silent reserves" of the Favag were really its own shares which it had purchased and was holding in the portfolios of member companies of the concern. On the other, Allianz had the distinct advantages of operating in all the various insurance fields in which the Favag operated, having a superior apparatus and organization for the management of the Favag policies, and being willing to put up guarantees for these right away while negotiating about the final purchase price. Time was of the essence if a widening crisis were to be averted and unwelcome interventions by the State avoided. As the bankers concluded: "Finally, in view of the fact that it is impossible in the time available to wait for the coming together of the big insurance companies, which would take a very long time, and that one under no circumstances should allow the Reich Supervisory Agency for Private Insurance to mix in, it was decided to ask Herren Dr. Schmitt and Hilgard from the Allianz as well as Dr. Herzfelder of the Hermes Kreditversicherungsbank AG to discuss the matter with us."[14] Furthermore, Allianz had considerable influence with the Reich Supervisory Agency, thus making its role even more advantageous.

Indeed, the Reich Supervisory Agency had to approve the contracts between Allianz and the Favag, which it did on August 20, 1929. This involved the immediate separating out and acquisition by Allianz of the most intact and lucrative portion of Favag's business without the summoning of a meeting of the shareholders. Furthermore, the Reich Supervisory Agency thereby issued an effective ban on payment to other creditors until the price Allianz would pay could be decided and until the assets and liabilities of the rump Favag could be determined. While the Reich Supervisory Agency had the right and power to give primary protection to the policyholders, it also involved a bypassing of shareholders and other creditors

[13] Aktenvermerk Frank (Disconto), Aug. 16, 1929 and other relevant correspondence in HADB, S236, and Schweizer-Rückversicherungs-Gesellschaft Ausschuss Sitzung, August 1929, Ausschuss-Sitzungen 10, Schweizer-Rückversicherungs-Archiv Zürich.

[14] Sitzung der Berliner Hauptbeteiligten des Bankkonsortiums, Aug.17, 1929, HADB, S245. Hermes was a part of the Allianz concern, and Herzfelder was a specialist in credit insurance.

that the Reich Supervisory Agency could only justify with the argument that the value of what Allianz was getting would diminish if insurance customers turned elsewhere and that this would not be to the interest of anyone. While Allianz certainly stood to gain substantially and could determine what it would and what it would not take over, it was willing to pay some heed to South German sensibilities as well as to anxieties about its increased power. Thus, the Favag would neither be formally annexed nor allowed to disappear but would rather be reestablished as the Neue Frankfurter Versicherungs-Gesellschaft, albeit as a company within the Allianz concern. Also, the major insurance companies in the Favag concern, the "Hammonia," which was taken over jointly by the Allianz and Münchener-Rückversicherungs-Gesellschaft, and the Karlsruher Leben and Vereinigte Berlinisch-Preussische were to retain their formal independence and not be externally designated as belonging to the Allianz concern. Nevertheless, despite a general recognition that Allianz, and particularly Schmitt, had acted to prevent the Favag collapse from turning into a major disaster for the German insurance business and the German economy, there was also considerable feeling that the Allianz had taken whatever was worth taking, not only in the German insurance circles, but also by the Schweizer Rück[15].

There was also a great deal of sentiment at home and abroad that Allianz, which paid the Favag 36,897,301 RM for the assets it had acquired, had paid too little in the end for the advantages thus received[16]. The view of Allianz was that it had prevented a catastrophe for the German insurance industry and for the German economy in general. While both arguments were probably correct, the debate itself was highly relevant to the second and far less soluble aspect of the Favag collapse, namely paying off as much as possible of the domestic and international debts the concern had contracted. These amounted to 63,9 million RM to domestic creditors and 35,6 million RM to foreign creditors[17]. The obvious solution was to form a standstill syndicate of the creditors, while the banking committee of the Favag supervisory board provided some guarantees and the time was taken to determine the actual status of the Favag and what Allianz was willing to work out with Favag to pay for its acquisitions.

These problems were to reappear in the banking crisis and reflected the deeper economic and financial difficulties that plagued the Weimar Republic. One important issue was whether the Reichsbank would back up the effort with its

[15] Aktenvermerk Moesler, Aug. 19, 1929, HABD, S236 and Vorstandssitzung am 5. und 6. November 1929, FHA 17, 2/4. Little credence seems to have been given to the charges of the indicted directors that Allianz had been plotting to take over the Favag all along and that it had even been responsible for the Lauinger articles. See the responses by Schmitt, Hess, Hilgard, and Kisskalt and their valuable accounts of their dealings with the Favag in BAB, 80 Ba 2, P5785. For the Reich Supervisory Agency decision and justification of its actions, see its formal decision of Nov. 16, 1929 in the Protokoll über die Gläubigerversammlung, Jan. 15, 1930, HABD, S244, 1f.

[16] See Favag an das Finanzamt Frankfurt am Main, Dec. 17, 1932, Bundesarchiv Koblenz (BAK) B 280/13283.

[17] Favag an Waller, Aug. 27, 1929, HABD, S234.

authority and also provide rediscounts and guarantee funds. At an initial meeting with Reichsbank Vice-President Dreyse on August 20, the banks were quite sour about the burdens being imposed upon them. They considered it insupportable "that foreign bankers give money to business without our collaboration and ... then count on the German banks springing into the breach every time"[18]. The Favag case and the mini-League of Nations of foreign creditors who had given the Favag money showed the extent to which short-term foreign lending to Germany had gotten out of control. Furthermore, one could not force Favag creditors to agree to a standstill, and the only solution the banks could suggest, and one which Dreyse found very unsatisfactory, was that those who could afford to take the losses join the standstill syndicate while those who could not afford to wait be satisfied first. This in effect placed a premium on taking the Favag to court and made those who cooperated look foolish. The Reichsbank was willing to put pressure on domestic banks and creditors unwilling to cooperate, but Dreyse was very wary of promising Reichsbank guarantee funds after it had just turned down such requests from the agricultural cooperatives.

By November 1929 the situation had worsened considerably since some foreign and domestic creditors were refusing to cooperate and demanding payment so that there was a renewed danger that the Favag would have to declare bankruptcy. Ten days of negotiations in London and Paris failed to bring agreement. As the liquidator appointed by the supervisory board of the Favag reported: "The chief reason for this attitude is the view abroad that the German banks represented in the supervisory board of the Favag are in some form or other obligated to step in for the obligations of the corporation. The difference between the organization of German and foreign joint stock companies is not taken into account. Taking the French or English perspective, one equates the German supervisory board with the administrative board in the French and English sense and views the members as representatives of their firms who are participating in the administration of the corporation under their company's responsibility. One cannot and perhaps does not want to understand that the differently structured organization of the German corporation in no way places obligations on the members of the supervisory board and the firms with which they are associated in the manner in which such obligations are assumed in an English or French administrative board. The joint stock corporation has for a long time become an instrument of credit in international business and as such has been used and misused extensively by the previous management of the Favag. Its collapse demonstrated how disadvantageous it is for international business and financial relations that the legal foundations of the organization of joint stock companies in the European nations are so different and that the business views about the obligations of the firms and persons participating in such a corporation are so different in the individual countries. On the other side one cannot dismiss the fact that foreign creditors in some cases have not operated with the necessary caution and have given credit in large amounts to unhealthy en-

[18] Aktenvermerk, Aug. 20, 1927, ibid.

terprises simply on the basis of the credit guarantees of the Favag, the granting of which the Frankfurt banks certainly would have discouraged if they had been asked. The false business methods of the Favag enticed foreign banks to undertake business in Germany without the collaboration of knowledgeable correspondents working on the scene and thereby also to disregard tried and true principles."[19]

The situation was very worrisome to Economics Minister Curtius, who summoned Directors Oscar Wassermann of the Deutsche Bank and Jakob Goldschmidt of the Danat and told them that "the banks must make large payments to prevent a cessation of payment by the Favag. The German economy cannot bear a collapse". They all agreed, however, that the Reichsbank had to intervene and assist and went to see Reichsbank President Schacht. Schacht, however, refused to do any such thing and also warned against the Reich Supervisory Agency issuing a payment ban "because the outside world would view this as demonstrating the possibility of intervention from above with respect to the fulfillment of payment obligations ... intervention from above would create fear that the same could also happen with respect to the numerous municipal credits taken abroad"[20]. The great vulnerability created by the private and public borrowing in Germany was thus apparent. The reality of the Favag case, however, was that a Reich Supervisory Agency payment ban had been created under the terms of the grant of permission to Allianz to take over the direct insurance business of Favag. This automatically protected policyholders. The Reich Supervisory Agency also mandated a payment ban for what remained of the Favag until its financial status was established and Allianz and the Favag had settled on what the former would pay the latter for the assets it had taken over. Schacht apparently raised no objections to this. Also, the Favag bankers seem to have used his good offices and influence to bring recalcitrant English banks into accepting the standstill arrangement[21].

By the turn of 1929–1930 some progress had been made in determining the status the Favag, and the liquidator was able to issue an interim report. Impatience was increasing, however, with the slowness of the process, which sought to avoid formal declaration of bankruptcy while carrying out the liquidation through the employment of bankruptcy methods[22]. The Reich Economics Ministry desperately warned against declaration of bankruptcy, which would have serious political consequences and lead to unwanted changes in the impending reform of the corporation law. Both the banks and Allianz, however, claimed that they had done a great deal already and that the burdens should be more widely distributed in the business community. Goldschmidt was particularly outspoken, pointing out "that he always has been for an action by means of which one would finally permit the curtain to be drawn over this matter so agitating to the public". He also pointed out "one cannot wait for a final status report because in cases like the Favag a

19 Bericht über die Liquidation der Frankfurter Allgemeinen Versicherungs-Aktien-Gesellschaft in der Zeit vom 20. Aug. bis 30. Nov. 1929 v. Dr. Waller, p. 3, HADB, S240.
20 Aktenvermerk Moesler, Nov. 1, 1929, HABD, S239.
21 See Moesler to Schacht, Sept. 4, 1929, HADB, S238.
22 See the report of the Liquidator, Dr. Waller of Dec. 28, 1929 in HADB, S239.

status report is, so to speak, never final"[23]. Whether all the interested groups, that is, the insurance industry, the banks, and the government would be willing to contribute, however, remained open and, since the creditors were scheduled to meet on January 15, their representative proposed that the banks offer 20% to the creditors and agree to hold back on getting payment for their Favag credits until the other creditors had received at least 40% of their claims. This was based on the proposition that the banks in the supervisory board had a special responsibility because of their failure to detect the malfeasance of the Favag directors but also that the Allianz payment to the Favag, when finally determined, would make possible more than the 20% determined to be available at the beginning of 1930.

This was, indeed, to be the foundation on which the final liquidation of the Favag rested, and it should come as no surprise that representatives of the creditors bitterly resented the way in which the banks on the Favag supervisory board had behaved between August 1929 and when they finally met in mid-January 1930: "The first thing that the administration did in the 'protection' of the interests of the creditors was to take the most valuable assets which this enterprise had as its basis and sell them to the Allianz. They should have been all the more cautious in doing so since the Allianz concern is a concern in which the majority of the administration banks are just as much represented as in the Favag concern. Represented in the Allianz are: Deutsche Bank, Disconto-Gesellschaft, Darmstädter Bank, Commerz- und Privatbank. One had, without setting a purchase price first, shifted over this valuable set of assets from a concern that was in distress to a concern that was not and one had removed what had previously been the most dangerous competitor of the firm that was not in distress and turned it into the single most decisive insurance concern in Germany ... One had more or less skimmed the cream off the cake and left behind an unpalatable, spoiled dough for the creditors, without there being any security as to what is still to be saved from the Allianz concern for the creditors of the Favag concern."[24]

This was probably a self-interested exaggeration under the circumstances. From a longer term perspective, however, the solution to the Favag crisis must be understood in terms of the need "to draw a veil" over the very tenuous economic and financial circumstances in which the Weimar Republic was functioning. Whatever the aftershocks in the law courts, the agreements made between the Favag and Allianz and between the Favag banking committee and the creditor committee in February 1930 laid the basic issues to rest and permitted the liquidation of the Favag with some satisfaction of the creditors[25]. They did not, of course, eliminate the underlying structural and financial difficulties of which the Favag was an important symptom. It remained for the events of July 1931 to tear that veil asunder and to make the kind of highly privatized crisis management that characterized the handling of the Favag collapse impossible.

[23] Aktenvermerk, Jan. 10, 1930, HADB, S241.
[24] Justizrat Heilbrunn at the Creditors meeting on Jan. 15, 1930, HADB, S244, p. 15.
[25] The agreements are to be found in HADB, S233.

II. The Fall of the Austrian Phönix

Almost seven years separated the Favag collapse from the Phönix debacle, which took place in March 1936, and between them lay the worst years of the Great Depression and the demise of much of the liberal economic system and environment under whose auspices the Favag crisis had been settled. Nevertheless, there were significant similarities between the two cases. Like the Favag, the Phönix was a very large company, the third largest on the European continent in fact, and one that did business in no less than twenty-two countries. Some of the conditions that led to its collapse were very similar to those that had caused the Favag to go under. Just as the Favag owed its rise and fall to Paul Dumcke, so the Phönix's fate was intimately bound up with its General Director, Dr Wilhelm Berliner, by all accounts a remarkable personality with extraordinary talents as a linguist, mathematician, financial expert, and lawyer. He had entered the company, which had been founded in 1882, in 1900 and assumed effective leadership of Phönix by 1914 even though he never took the General Director title himself. He was an imaginative risk taker, greatly increasing the Phönix's insurance portfolio during the war by offering insurance for military dependents actuarially based on the experience of the Russo-Japanese war and investing heavily in war bonds. These activities gave him a high rating at least with the government authorities and led, among other things, to his appointment as a member of the Austrian delegation in St. Germain. He has also played an important role as an adviser to the Austrian Government in the negotiation of the Geneva loans in 1922 and at the Hague Conference following the collapse of the Creditanstalt in 1931[26].

The Phönix rode out the postwar crisis by selling some of its assets in the successor states and then began a policy of expansion, first by investing in the insurance portfolios of some small foreign insurance companies and also acquiring some small companies that were operating at a deficit or were illiquid. It also took over a very large portfolio of policies in Czechoslovakia at a very unfavorable exchange rate and became active in Germany as well. Indeed, it did business in practically every country in Europe and in the Near East as well. The motives for such expansion were not dissimilar to those of the Favag. In order to handle existing obligations, one had to take on new ones, obviously an expensive and dangerous way of doing business. These methods could hardly escape notice. Wilhelm Kisskalt, the General Director of the Münchener Rückversicherungs-Gesellschaft became increasingly troubled in 1929–1930 by the high administrative costs of the Phönix and its lack of profitability. At the time, the Münchener Rück was a major reinsurer of Phönix and Kisskalt was a member of its administrative council.

[26] In this account, I follow closely the very useful article of *Isabella Ackerl*, Der Phönix-Skandal, in: Das Juliabkommen von 1936. Vorgeschichte, Hintergründe und Folgen. Protokoll des Symposiums in Wien am 10. und 11. Juni 1976 (Wien 1977) 241–279. See also the very informative discussion in *Marita Roloff* and *Alois Mosser*, Wiener Allianz Gegründet 1860 (Vienna 1991) 135–155.

When Kisskalt expressed his concerns to Berliner at a meeting in March 1930, "Herr Dr. Berliner responded that the remarks of Herr General Director Dr. Kisskalt were accurate. The business of the Phönix was very large and he could not administer the apparatus more cheaply. A significant reduction of production would be suicide, since a reduction of administrative costs could only be attained by equal or somewhat increased production. A significant reduction of production would, in absolute terms, not moderate the administrative costs and would drive the percentage up."[27] Berliner expressed the hope that he could reduce the costs from 20,4% to 10% in four or five years, which Kisskalt, for all his admiration for Berliner, did not find very reassuring. He was even less happy with the fact that the Phönix was keeping afloat by speculative activities in connection with exchange rate profits. Thus, the Münchener Rück significantly reduced its business with Phönix while Kisskalt retired from its administrative board. Nevertheless, Berliner's methods were favored by certain circumstances peculiar to Austria. One of these was the loss of confidence in the banks, so that the public was more willing to invest in insurance and in insurance companies which had not yet been discredited. The other was that one was able to make a considerable amount of money speculating in shares and securities in the 1920s, and Berliner had genuine talent in this area.

While Berliner himself lived in an extremely modest manner and was extraordinarily generous to his employees and to others needing his help, his business practices nevertheless became increasingly dubious. The securities market in the Great Depression no longer offered the profits of the preceding period, and Berliner increasingly borrowed on the securities from the banks. Thus, when the Creditanstalt collapsed in May 1931, the Phönix had major financial difficulties because its Lombard account was so large. Another major problem lay in his response to the sharp competition during the Great Depression and the inability to move assets from more profitable activities in one country to less profitable activities in another because of the strict exchange controls. The Phönix became notorious for what in effect were dumping practices. It did everything possible to increase its short-term liquidity, offering rates that were unjustifiably low and imaginative combination policies that were uneconomic. Similarly, it offered a one-time premium life insurance policy to a public that had become fearful of putting its money into banks and considered such investment very promising. Indeed, Phönix's guaranteed yearly 5½% interest policies were especially attractive. Berliner also took advantage of the government's home construction program to offer mortgage insurance that guaranteed full coverage in the event of sudden death with a guaranteed declining premium. He also went into the business of guaranteeing returns on domestic and foreign government bonds and was able to circum-

[27] Aktennote. Besprechung mit dem "Phönix" wegen des Abschlusses 1929 und des Rückversicherungsvertrages, March 12/13, 1930, FHA, Münchener Rück Akten, A 2.13/42. This volume contains a great deal of material on the Phönix and its operations as well as its relations with the Münchener Rück in the 1920s and 1930s.

vent foreign exchange regulations in various countries because of the multinational network of companies in the Phönix concern.

At the same time, Berliner also engaged in a variety of business activities that had nothing whatever to do with the insurance business, and like Dumcke he became involved with a bank, the Kompass Allgemeine Kredit- und Garantiebank, which was closely associated with the Phönix and was used for various investments and activities that had very little or nothing to do with insurance. Some of these activities, to be sure, were very pleasing to the government. In 1933, for example, when the new National Socialist Government in Germany created all kinds of difficulties for the Austrian tourist business, Berliner proceeded to set up a tourist information bureau at the Phönix which organized cheap tourist trips to Austria, propagandized tourism in Austria, and even increased vacation pay for those of his employees who chose to take their vacations in Austria.

Indeed, Berliner's generosity extended far and wide. He not only gave free insurance to important government officials and other influential persons, but also gave money to causes both good and bad. He never tried to cover up his Jewish identity and gave considerable sums to Zionist causes and also helped Jews trying to leave Germany to rescue their assets. At the same time, however, he gave money to the Austrian Heimwehr and, much to its later embarrassment, also to the National Socialist Party. He showed particular generosity to journalists and seems to have done very well with the Austrian media. He did not, however, do very well with Artur Lauinger who, although a Jew, continued to work at the Frankfurter Zeitung in the early 1930s until he was sent to Buchenwald and then emigrated in 1938. When Lauinger began to report on the Phönix's banking activities, Berliner paid him a visit and asked how much he wanted, whereupon Lauinger showed him the door[28].

Despite his growing vulnerability to exposure, however, Berliner, like Dumcke, did not live to see his own disgrace and died as the result of an operation on February 17, 1936. His funeral was attended by the leading lights of the international insurance business as well as high government personages, and he was much praised for his works. The revelations came shortly afterward. On the one hand, a list was found naming the recipients of his bribes, and the head of the Austrian Supervisory Office, Oechsner, for whom Berliner had done many kindnesses and whose office had not done an audit on the Phönix since 1921, committed suicide. On the other hand, the true balances were handed over to Berliner's successor, Dr. Eberhard von Reininghaus by the chief accountant of the concern. The accountant, along with some other directors, was to end up in jail. The result of the exposures, needless to say, was a major international scandal and economic difficulties of very serious proportions. This was in fact a much larger collapse than that of the Favag, involving many more countries and policyholders.

By this time, however, one had plenty of experiences with failures and bankruptcies and the mechanisms for dealing with them had changed considerably

[28] *Lauinger*, Das öffentliche Gewissen 23–24.

since the days of the Favag debacle. In Austria, where memories of the Creditanstalt were very fresh, government intervention was immediate. Chancellor Schuschnigg himself discussed the affair in a major speech in the Bundestag on April 1 that stressed the primary importance of protecting policyholders, and the need for legislation increasing supervision and eliminating speculation by insurance companies. In fact, legislation had already been issued creating an insurance fund to be based on contributions from all the Austrian insurance companies as well as from foreign companies operating in Austria. The goal here was to avoid government guarantees and, instead, to implement the ideology of the Austrian "Ständestaat" or corporatist state and force the private interests to take collective responsibility for guaranteeing that the policyholders would be protected. As can be imagined, foreign companies were not enthralled to be forced into such participation. As Arnoldo Frigessi di Rattalma, the General Director of the Riunione adriatica di sicurtà (RAS), which had important interests in Austria, pointed out, however, "even if it is outrageous that the other corporations active in Austria should be drawn in to reconstruct Phönix, it is nevertheless unconditionally necessary from the perspective of general higher business interests to reduce the disquiet among the public concerning Phönix to a minimum in order not to provoke state interventions in the insurance business throughout Central Europe that could have unforseeable consequences"[29]. Frigessi, to be sure, was no supporter of generosity in this regard, pointing out that those who had taken out insurance with Phönix-Life had benefitted from irresponsibly low premiums, especially the one-time premium policies which Frigessi thought had ruined the concern. Nevertheless, solidarity was important if State interference was to be minimized, and he certainly believed the State had a responsibility to protect the companies called in to assist by preventing abuses in the future. Subsequently, the Austrian Government did in fact issue special legislation requiring adequate premiums and forcing reduction of costs for insurance companies by reducing salaries and pensions.

A special law of April 8, 1936 divided the Phönix-Life into two parts with the purpose of separating the insurance from the finance business of the firm. The latter was to be liquidated, while the former was lodged in a new company, the Österreichische Versicherungs-AG (ÖVAG), participation in which was made attractive by the aforementioned collective guarantee of the Austrian insurance business and various restrictions on repurchase of insurance policies by their holders. At the same time, the property insurance portion of Phönix, Elementar-Phönix, which remained basically sound, was taken over by an international consortium of companies. Among its most important shareholders were the Wiener Städtische, the Italian Generali, and the Münchener Rück. Indeed, the last named company considered it a matter of prestige to participate and requested special dispensation from the foreign exchange regulations from Schacht in order to do

[29] Frigessi to General Director Reismann, March 30, 1936 Banca Commerciale Italiana, Archivio di Arnoldo Frigessi di Rattalma, cart. 103, fasc. 1.

so. The entire affair intensified competition between German and Italian companies for the Austrian market, a competition resolved after the Anschluss in March 1938 in favor of Allianz, which at last was able to realize its ambitions in Austria, and the Münchener Rück[30].

The Austrian government also sought to protect the interests of its own companies and policyholders against demands of foreign creditors, and this intensified the nationalization of the European insurance business before the war that was a byproduct of the depression and its problems. Phönix-Life had taken advantage wherever it could of situations where insurance oversight was minimal, and there were heavy losses in Egypt. Countries that could protect themselves did so. In Hungary, for example, the government ordered that the assets of the Phönix-Life branches had to be used to satisfy Hungarian nationals and could not be tapped to solve the difficulties of the headquarters in Vienna. A similar position was taken by the Czech government, where Phönix-Life had been particularly active. Generally, because of government coverage requirements, the Phönix-Life branches in West European countries, but also in Poland did not constitute a danger to policyholders and were soon transferred to other companies. In Poland, for example, the Phönix-Life insurance stock was taken over by Generali.

In Germany, where Phönix-Life had been extremely active, there had been, as has been shown, considerable anxiety about the concern's solidity, and the Supervisory Agency had tried to get an increased bond from Phönix-Life and was worried about it having sufficient coverage. This was in fact an issue despite all the regulations, and while the public was told that there was nothing to worry about, there was a genuine danger that the German branch of the Phönix-Life could go bankrupt if negotiations for its liquidation and the assumption of its policies failed. Thus, in May 1936, the Economics Ministry summoned the insurance industry organization leaders to discuss the situation. While one could make arguments that the German insurers had no obligation to save the branch of a foreign company from a bankruptcy which it had brought upon itself, the insurance industry organization leaders dismissed such notions because "they overlook the heart of the matter, which is that the existence of many German families are at play and on the other side that the bankruptcy of the German branch of the Phönix would be a heavy blow to the entire German life insurance business". The conclusion was that a common action by the insurers to prevent such a bankruptcy was necessary in the form of a guarantee for such losses as had been incurred. This was warmly supported by Kisskalt of the Münchener Rück, who pointed out that his company had bowed out of the Phönix long before, but that he felt an obligation nevertheless. The Hungarian insurance companies had put up a 3 million pengö guarantee for their Phönix-Life branch, and "what the Hungarian insurance business can do is easily possible for the German enterprises which are much

[30] There is an excellent and informative collection of newspaper clippings and reports, including some by Ambassador von Papen from Vienna, dealing with the crisis in BAB, R 31.01/17324–17325.

stronger in capital ... One has to avoid everything that is likely to promote the view that the German insurance business is not healthy."[31] There was only one negative voice, General Director Tiedke of the Alt Leipziger, who argued that Phönix-Life had done nothing but ruin their business and that the policyholders had gone to Phönix-Life primarily for speculative reasons and thus deserved no protection. The prevailing mood, however, was that the reputation of the German private insurance business depended upon them all acting as a collectivity. In the end, the guarantee was given and a new company, the Isar, was established to take over the Phönix-Life policies.

Thus, in contrast to the Favag case, where the Allianz had saved the day and left shareholders and financial creditors to pay the bill, the Phönix-Life liquidation, in both Austria and Germany, involved a great deal more direct government action as well as collective action to cover the losses and protect the policyholders. The much more regulative regime introduced in Germany after the Favag affair was now introduced in Austria as well and, indeed, Austria was soon to have the "blessings" of the German system once the Anschluss took place. It is significant that the Phönix issue in Germany was solved under the auspices of the Reich Supervisory Agency for Insurance, whose powers had been greatly increased. There were some who even argued that the Supervisory Office should in effect run the peak association of the private insurance business, and the voluntary collective action of the private insurers undoubtedly reflected their desire to show that they knew how to keep their own house in order. Also, there were important forces in the National Socialist regime arguing for the socialization of the insurance business. It was thus important to be able to argue that "the events in Vienna give no cause for a strengthening of the tendencies which run in the direction of a nationalization of the private insurance industry, and certainly not among us, where the National Socialist economic policy by aiming at a spirit of community and securing the necessary state influence has made the means of socialization superfluous"[32]. State authority and regulation had indeed increased greatly, especially under the aegis of the authoritarian regimes that had taken over in the 1930s. The Favag and Phönix cases are significant illustrations of the international business conditions and practices that had played so important a role in producing and providing the scenario for the international economic crisis. They are also suggestive of the changes on the international business scene between 1929 and 1936, that is, at the beginning and the end of the Great Depression in Central Europe.

[31] Meeting of May 12, 1936, BAB, R 31.01/17325, Bl. 120–127.
[32] *Joseph Winschuh*, "Phönix-Gedanken", Deutsche Allgemeine Zeitung, April 6, 1936, BAB, R 31.01/1734, Bl. 164.

Patricia Clavin

Explaining the Failure of the London World Economic Conference

In June 1933 the World Economic Conference, which brought together 65 nations and representatives from six international organisations, convened in London's new Geological Museum[1]. The conference was unprecedented in both its size and expressed ambition. Unlike the World Economic Conference of 1927, politicians as well as experts were in attendance and the agenda embraced a large variety of economic and monetary issues, including the agenda of the Stresa Conference of September 1932 intended to assist the countries of Central and Eastern Europe. The Conference collapsed in undignified recrimination among the major powers barely two weeks later. Its failure marked the end of attempts at international economic co-operation in the interwar period.

From the late 1930s until the early 1980s published accounts of the World Economic Conference placed the blame for the failure of the World Economic Conference squarely on the shoulders of the United States. The case is made no where better than in Charles Kindleberger's magisterial study of The World in Depression, 1929–1939 which emphasised the failure of America to provide the leadership vital to light the way out of the crisis, regardless of whether others were prepared to follow[2]. Roosevelt's "bombshell message", as his telegram to the World Conference denouncing the temporary stabilisation agreement was known, became emblematic of America's failure to take up its hegemonic responsibilities to stabilise global economic and diplomatic relations in the interwar period that resulted in unprecedented depression and war.

More recent studies of the World Economic Conference by economic historians, however, have moved away from accounts of hegemonic failure. Indeed, the episode has taken on renewed significance because, as the work of Barry Eichen-

[1] The exhibits were yet to be installed.
[2] The most enduring examples remain: *C. P. Kindleberger*, The World in Depression, 1929–1939 (London 1987); *A. Schlesinger*, The Age of Roosevelt: the Coming of the New Deal, vol.2 (Boston 1961); *H. V. Hobson*, Slump and Recovery. A Survey of World Affairs, 1929–1937 (London 1938) 204–205; *S. V. O. Clarke*, The Reconstruction of the International Monetary System: the Attempts of 1922 and 1933 (Princeton Studies of International Finance 33, 1973); *J. R. Moore*, Sources of New Deal Economic Policy: the International Dimension, in: The Journal of American History 41 (1974) 728–44.

green has made clear, one of the best policy responses to break the stranglehold of the Great Depression on the world economy would have been for the world's leading economies to undertake a strategy of co-ordinated devaluation (coupled with deflationary measures) to reflate the world economy. Such a strategy was considered and might have been favourably employed at the World Economic Conference in 1933, but was rejected by countries determined to pursue nationally orientated policies[3]. This conclusion, coupled with research that emphasises that the smooth functioning of the gold standard was far more dependent on international cooperation than the apparent automatism of the mechanism suggested, has also served to underline how far the failure of international cooperation explains the depth and duration of the depression and that the failure to pursue international co-operation was a multilateral one[4].

Diplomatic historians, however, have been slower to exonerate the "irresponsible" Roosevelt. Although they are now in broad agreement that Roosevelt took an active interest in foreign affairs from the outset of his presidency, the "bombshell message" is the one aspect of Roosevelt's relations with Europe which diplomatic historians have found difficult to reconcile with the President's internationalist credentials. Even Robert Dallek has struggled to absolve Roosevelt from the charge of "irresponsibility" in London[5]. The message is still seen to mark the end of Europe's short-lived expectations of future collaboration with America raised by Roosevelt's election campaign and the interregnum[6].

This paper will attempt to draw the history of Roosevelt's economic foreign policy towards Europe onto a broad canvas to reflect the multilateral character of economic and diplomatic relations in the depression. The key to understanding the failure of international economic co-operation in this period lies not in the deficiencies of American leadership, nor in the lack of viable policies, but through the lack of political will for co-operation demonstrated by all the world's leading powers. True, in Roosevelt's first term of office, forays into foreign policy were shaped strongly, and sometimes constrained, by the President's determination to secure a national economic revival. The scale of the crisis, coupled with America's "exceptional" history and constitutional "safeguards", meant that neither the American administration nor the American people were inclined to take the lead in economic diplomacy. But when it came to more political questions, like those embedded in trade protectionism or war debts and reparations, the shortcomings of American internationalism was only part of the problem. As this paper seeks to

[3] *B. Eichengreen*, The Origins and Nature of the Great Slump, in: Economic History Review 45,2 (May 1992) 13–39; *P. Clavin*, The Failure of Economic Diplomacy. Britain, Germany, France and the United States, 1931–36 (London 1995) chapter six.
[4] *B. Eichengreen*, Golden Fetters. The Gold Standard and the Great Depression, 1919–1939 (Oxford 1992) passim.
[5] *R. Dallek*, Franklin D. Roosevelt and American Foreign Policy, 1929–1945 (Oxford 1979) 41–58.
[6] *T. Ginsburg*, The Triumph of Isolationism, in: *G. Martel*, American Foreign Relations Reconsidered, 1898–1993 (London 1994) 90–102.

demonstrate, the ability of other countries to demonstrate genuine political will to co-operate was equally important. Political change in Europe since 1929, for example, introduced a number of new actors, some of whom were strongly hostile to international co-operation, into the diplomatic mix. By highlighting the foreign economic policies of Europe's leading economic powers on international indebtedness, trade and monetary stabilisation, the paper underlines the external constraints on Roosevelt's foreign policy and how, in turn, the European response to America's overtures for international co-operation to tackle protectionism only worked to sour America's appetite for further co-operation with Europe.

Achieving international co-operation in 1933 was not just about the world's largest economy's ability to demonstrate leadership. International expectations were also shaped by diplomatic experience, political will, historical precedence and a perception of who was strong and who was weak in the context of the depression[7]. The see-sawing economic fortunes of the world's leading diplomatic actors further confused the picture. In particular, Britain's early recovery from the depression, coupled with its long history of international involvement, led to misplaced expectations of British leadership in 1932 and 1933[8].

The final portion of the paper touches on the continued value of the World Economic Conference as a "lesson of history". When the World Economic Conference failed in 1933, the United States at first was in little doubt that it had done so because all the major participants in London had refused to co-operate. Indeed, if the Americans charged any single nation for sabotaging the conference, then it was Britain. They had expected better of a nation with a history of economic internationalism and who had promoted the World Economic Conference since June 1932. As Herbert Feis, Economic Advisor to the State Department complained at the time, although American statesmen "were no angels", the British were behaving with a "diminished sense of international responsibility" which was "very likely to stand in the way of any about turn in the whole course of international relations"[9]. The United States was also angered at, in particular, Euro-

[7] For most participants the political will to co-operate was constrained by the primacy of domestic economic recovery. For a theoretical and historical perspective see: *B. Simons*, Who Adjusts? Domestic Sources of Economic Foreign Policy during the Interwar Years (Princeton 1994) passim.

[8] On the role of historical precedent in policy formulation see: *C. Maier*, In Search of Stability. Explorations in Historical Political Economy (Cambridge 1987) passim; for expectations of British leadership see: *P. Clavin*, The World Economic Conference 1933: the Failure of British Internationalism, in: The Journal of European Economic History 20 (Winter 1991) 490–497; for the American tendency to overestimate British power in all aspects of its foreign relations see: *B. McKercher*, Wealth, Power and the International Order: Britain and the American Challenge, in: Diplomatic History 12 (1988).

[9] Private papers of Herbert Feis, Library of Congress, Washington DC (Hereafter LC Feis), LC Feis:123, Feis to Frankfurter, 8 Nov. 1933; Franklin D. Roosevelt, Presidential Library, Hyde Park, New York (hereafter FDR), FDR:PPF 744, Kent to Roosevelt, 19 Jan. 1934. Feis' assessment focused, in particular, on British protectionism and reflected a view which was widespread in the State Department. It echoes the more recent findings of international relations theorist David Lake that Britain now acted as a "spoiler" in international trading

pean attempts to lay the entire blame for the conference's collapse at Washington's door[10]. Yet by the end of the 1930s, the United States had evolved a much more critical view of its contemporary history. In effect, the American account of the failure of the World Economic Conference had adopted the narrative presented by the European powers in 1933. The reasons for this change are complex and beyond the scope of this paper. However, the final part of the paper will sketch out the value of America's new historical narrative of events in 1933[11]. The history of the conference and in particular the "bombshell message" played a central role in American propaganda efforts designed to educate the public as to America's new responsibilities on the international stage.

The External Constraints

War debts and reparations

This is not the place to explore the imbroglio of German-American debt relations, however, Brüning's decision to pursue a vigorous foreign policy for the abandonment of German reparation payments in 1930 set in train developments which were to have important implications for American relations with Europe in the Depression in general and the World Economic Conference in particular. The banking crises which swept across Europe like a bush fire in the late spring and summer of 1931 triggered the Hoover administration's only international initiative to deal with the economic crisis, the debt moratorium of June 1931. This postponed all payments of intergovernmental debts, reparations and debt relief, both principal and interest, for a year. Most important from the perspective of America's future diplomatic relations with Europe was the mistaken interpretation placed on it by the British government who believed that the White House finally had recognised the inter-connection between reparations and war debts. This interpretation, reinforced by repeated American urging that the banking collapse was a "patently European crisis", was also shaped by talks between Hoover and the French Prime Minister, Pierre Laval in October 1931. The American administration had appeared to endorse the notion that Europe should resolve reparations before turning to the United States for talks about war debts and demanded the "initiative on this matter should be taken early by the European

relations, *D. Lake*, International Economic Structures and American Foreign Policy, in: World Politics 35 (1983) 540.

10 *Clavin*, Failure of Economic Diplomacy 168.

11 A very limited attempt to answer Emily Rosenberg's call to ask "new questions about the structures, plots, authors, and performativity of historical stories": *E. Rosenberg*, Presidential Address. Revisiting Dollar Diplomacy: Narratives of Money and Manliness, in: Diplomatic History 22,2 (Spring 1998) 165.

powers"[12]. Britain's determination to see the end of reparations in the expectation that the United States would then reciprocate by absolving its former allies of their war debts laid a false trail which was to lead British and French policy on debts into direct confrontation with the United States.

Although both Britain and the United States recognised that they were not, for the most part, responsible for the German financial crisis, they were persuaded that removing the burden of reparations would be of great benefit to the German economy. The calculation was motivated by political and economic considerations. Co-operation on the "German Question" seemed to be one of the few remaining routes to international collaboration. By concentrating its diplomatic efforts on Germany, the British government, like that of the United States, was able to side-step any detailed reflection of the implications of its own economic nationalism on the global economic and diplomatic crisis. Hammering on about the need for reparation and war debt revision was appealing to the European powers because it offered an accessible medium for translating the dire economic crisis into terms which politicians and their electorates could understand. Moreover, the extension of American commercial credits under the Dawes and Young plan loans and British short-term credits extended during the financial crisis in the summer of 1931 had tied the major powers, and more specifically the interest of powerful financiers, to Germany's economic and political future. This was especially true of Britain which, after revelations that the volume of British credit frozen inside Germany was estimated at some $70 million, experienced a drain on its gold reserves, culminating in a sterling crisis that forced the pound from the gold standard. As James has demonstrated, after 1931, the debt crisis and the convertibility crisis were linked in the minds of British policy-makers, a conviction shared by their counterparts in Central Europe and Latin America[13].

Most important from the perspective of future Anglo-American relations was the fact that British concern for German financial stability was equated increasingly with its own. In August and September 1931 Weimar's creditors voluntarily had agreed to freeze their credits inside Germany in the "Standstill Agreements". The agreements had important consequences for the future course of the German domestic economy, enabling it to sustain its foreign trade and, in theory, to borrow more on existing credit lines. The agreements also liberated Germany from the "rules" of gold standard membership, offering increased independence to formulate economic and monetary policy which official circles in Germany soon exploited to facilitate rearmament. The Standstill Agreements also had important consequences for future diplomatic relations between Britain and the United States[14]. Accepted at first by British and American financiers as a short-term

[12] Text of Hoover Laval communiqué, 25 Oct. 1931, Papers Relating to the Foreign Relations of the United States, 1931, vol.2, 252–53.

[13] *H. James*, Financial Flows Across Frontiers in the Great Depression, in: Economic History Review 45 (August 1992) 280.

[14] The standstill agreements' implications for Anglo-German relations has been explored but generally neglect to mention the implications for Anglo-American relations. See, for

necessity, the agreements were to become a long-term hardship. They were renewed in January and again in June 1932 when an agreement was signed for a further 12 months period.

In the months after the Hoover Moratorium and the Standstill Agreements were secured, both Britain and the United States grew increasingly anxious to safeguard their frozen credits inside Germany, but their policies differed in important respects. While American economic foreign policy succumbed to paralysis in the face of the domestic crisis, the new National Government in Britain, invigorated by electoral success and the apparent success of its move to protectionism and a loosening of monetary policy, was determined to take "a big bold lead in the world"[15]. London noted with increasingly alarm how many in Germany had begun to blur the distinction between commercial and political debts. Britain was very anxious to nip the trend in the bud and increasingly adopted the view that commercial credits extended by Britain to Germany would be safeguarded best by the complete abolition of political debts. In other words, both war debts and reparations should be abolished. As is well known, this conviction, coupled with fortuitous political developments in France, culminated in the effective abolition of German reparations at the Lausanne Conference in June 1932. In order to secure French agreement at Lausanne, Britain and France signed a "Gentleman's Agreement" which made French ratification of the Lausanne settlement conditional on an Anglo-French war debt agreement with the American government. In Whitehall, the Foreign Office alone feared that Britain's decision to present the incoming Democrat Administration with a *fait accompli* on reparations and war debts posed a serious threat to Anglo-American relations given the Americans often stated hostility to a "united European front of debtors"[16].

In order to lure the United States into war debt negotiations it did not want, the British government proposed a World Economic Conference to address the growing crisis in monetary and trading relations. Enshrined in the fifth article of the Lausanne Conference, Britain sought to exploit preparations for the World Economic Conference to secure an Anglo-French agreement on war debts. It was a risky strategy for the issues which secured American participation in the conference (alongside that of sixty-four other countries), were the floatation of sterling and Britain's move to protectionism – the very topics Britain did not want to open up to American scrutiny. The timing of the World Economic Conference was exploited very deliberately by the British who time-tabled the preparatory meetings for the conference to coincide with the December 1932 war debt payment due to the United States, with the 12 June payment falling three days before the opening

example: *S. Newton*, Profits of Peace. The Political Economy of Anglo-German Appeasement (Oxford 1996) passim.

[15] Record of conversation between Harrison and Mills reflecting on recent comments by *Ramsay MacDonald*, 17 July 1931, Harrison Papers, Records of the Federal Reserve Board New York, New York.

[16] Letter from Runciman to Baldwin, 24 June 1932, vol.119, Baldwin Papers, University Library, Cambridge.

of the conference proper on 15 June 1933. So, too, was the conference agenda with the western Europeans arguing that problems like currency depreciation, trade protectionism and widespread unemployment made an immediate reduction of war debts to the United States imperative. The stakes were raised further when France failed to make its December 1932 war payment to the United States and was judged to be in default.

In January and April 1933 Roosevelt spoke of Britain and the United States working together to improve the global economic climate and, encouraged by European rhetoric at the preparatory sessions for the World Economic Conference, repeatedly urged their governments to widen the parameters of debt negotiations to include issues of tariff protection and disarmament. But just as domestic considerations set limits on the war debt concessions FDR could offer Europe, regardless of any desire that FDR might have had to see the end of war debts, so the primacy of British and French domestic recovery, in particular, determined that the European powers were unable to do as the new President asked. Of course, the development of the President's domestic programme made the context of international monetary and trade negotiations more complex (more on this below), but the fact that the British government tenaciously clung to the primacy of a war debt over monetary or trade negotiations greatly soured Anglo-American relations. Rather than marking the end of war debt payments to the United States, the deadlock grew only more profound when British Prime Minister Ramsay MacDonald, in his presidential opening address to the World Economic Conference, made an explicit reference to the need, above all other co-operative measures, to resolve the war debt dispute. In his diary, the United States' Ambassador to Britain, Robert Worth Bingham, reflected the sentiment, widespread among supporters of FDR's internationalism, that MacDonald's incursion into the question of war debts was "inexcusable and unwise", serving only to weaken further the appeal of European involvement back home[17]. The conference's first "bombshell message" had come, not from the pen of Roosevelt, but the mouth of MacDonald. The following year the debt issue grew even more acrimonious with the passage of the Johnson Act in the United States. Much to Britain's chagrin, the Act branded her as a defaulter in the same class as the French and the Act prohibited all further loans to defaulting nations.

Much less public, but no less damaging to the prospects for co-operation among the leading European powers, were American negotiations with Nazi Germany over the commercial debt frozen inside Germany under the standstill agreements. While Britain's "co-operative" stance on reparations helped to secure assurances from the German government that its commercial credits inside Germany would be safeguarded, in May and June 1933 the Nazi government attempted to default on its commercial obligations to American bondholders. After his May 1933 meeting with the new German Finance Minister and Director of the

[17] Diary entry in Bingham Diary, entry 15 June 1933, Manuscripts Division, Library of Congress, Washington D.C.

Reichsbank, Hjalmar Schacht, FDR complained "this is terrible. I am in an awful mess with Europe ... European statesmen are a bunch of bastards."[18] The reference to Europeans, as opposed to Germans, was not a slip of the tongue. A number of historians rightly have pointed out that Roosevelt was not very sympathetic to the interests of American bondholders, but his anger was fuelled by reports from London and Berlin which claimed that Schacht and his old friend at the Bank of England, Sir Montagu Norman, had concluded a commercial debt agreement which largely protected the investments of British bondholders in Germany. American annoyance at an Anglo-German commercial debt agreement, formalised into a long term arrangement in 1934, was no accident. It was part of a deliberate German strategy to sow suspicion in Anglo-American relations to forestall a united "Anglo-Saxon" front which would threaten Nazi ambitions overseas at a time when the Reich was still vulnerable[19]. The American conviction that "British banking authorities are working closely with German authorities to develop further plans satisfactory to themselves" also undermined Presidential support for an initiative to encourage co-operation on international trade which the administration had hoped would strengthen its relations with Europe in general and Britain in particular[20].

An American initiative on trade

There is now a considerable body of scholarship detailing how the structural changes within the American economy, coupled with the new constellation of interest group politics and the profound desire to avert another Great Depression, generated policies to fundamentally reform international economic relations in order to restore world trade. By 1932 many, both inside the Commerce and State Departments and with-out, began to argue that the United States should move away from the inconsistent, "double-edged" Open Door and adopt a reciprocal trading policy. The State Department, in particular, was stung by repeated European criticism that American protectionism compromised its investments in Europe, that it had prompted Britain and France to abandon the collection of reparations, and was forcing countries like Germany from the international economy. The shift in official sentiment was supported by the increasingly free trade position of the largely capital intensive industries like banking, and the oil and electricity companies which had fared rather better than most in the depression. Once

[18] Entry in Diary of Henry Morgenthau Jnr., 9 May 1933, Farm Credit Diary, Book 0, Franklin D. Roosevelt Presidential Library, Hyde Park, New York.
[19] *P. Clavin*, Failure of Economic Diplomacy 103–109, 138–141.
[20] Communiqué from Hull to Phillips, 11 June 1933, SD 862.51/3168, Records of the State Department, National Archives II, Washington D.C.

Republican supporters, they were now increasingly drawn toward the professed low-tariff position of the Democratic party[21].

In the new Democratic administration Cordell Hull was the undoubted champion of such a strategy, intent on liberating world trade as "the fundamental basis of all peace"[22]. Once dismissed by scholars, Hull's contribution to successive Roosevelt administrations has been re-appraised to stress his long-term influence on American economic diplomacy and Roosevelt's internationalism[23]. After his appointment as Secretary of State in March 1933, he took every opportunity to publicise the administration's resolve to secure Congressional authority to negotiate Reciprocal Tariff Agreement Act (RTA) agreements based on a flat rate reduction of 10 per cent of existing barriers, a corresponding percentage enlargement of quotas, and bilateral agreements with unconditional MFN treatment.

The State Department's competition with the nationalist orientated "bright, young things" responsible for devising and implementing the New Deal, is well known and certainly worked to delay Roosevelt's support for the RTA until 1934, where upon the United States concluded reciprocal agreements with countries in Central and South America – the region where they were most successfully implemented (by 1945, 29 RTA treaties had been secured), reducing the United States tariff by almost three quarters[24]. Hull's initiative had important consequences for Pan-American commerce and diplomacy which have been well documented. Less well known is the fact that Hull sought to conclude his very first reciprocal tariff agreement with Britain.

From December 1932 (the initiative is more typically dated from 1934 or 1936), Hull's overtures for an agreement to halt the escalation of trade barriers were directed, in particular, at the British government. By January 1933, three months before he was fully installed as Secretary of State, Hull already had adopted the Republican sponsored tariff truce for the World Economic Conference and planned to use it to secure the first reciprocal tariff act with the British government[25]. The State and Commerce departments even harboured hopes that an Anglo-American RTA would provide the basis for initiating multilateral tariff

21 *T. Ferguson*, Industrial Conflict and the Coming of the New Deal: The Triumph of Multinational Liberalism in America, in: *G. Gerstle, S. Fraser*, The Rise and Fall of the New Deal Order, 1930–1980 (Princeton 1989) 17–18.

22 Hull's speech to the World Economic Conference, 13 June, 1933, Papers relating to the Foreign Relations of the United States, 1933, vol.1, 636–640.

23 *I. Gellman*, Secret Affairs. Franklin D. Roosevelt, Cordell Hull, and Sumner Welles (Baltimore 1995) passim.

24 *D. Steward*, Trade and Hemisphere: The Good Neighbour Policy and Reciprocal Trade (Columbia 1975) 208–220.

25 Significantly, the idea for the truce originated with Norman Davis, US Ambassador in Geneva under the Republicans, but a long time Democrat who had been widely tipped as a future Democrat Secretary of State. He corresponded with FDR about the truce and helped to shape FDR's first impressions of Neville Chamberlain. See Private Papers of Norman Davis, Library of Congress (hereafter LC Davis), LC Davis:51, Davis to Roosevelt, 15 November 1932.

reductions throughout the world through the operation of unconditional most-favoured-nation treatment. American hopes were supported by the conviction that British power was founded on free trade and that Britain would, with American support, return to free trade. The determination of men like Hull, and of like-minded advisers William Phillips, Herbert Feis, Leo Pasvolsky and later Dean Acheson, came from the lessons of history as they perceived them. History demonstrated the dependence of the British economy on the world export market and, moreover, Britain's reputation and experience in the field of trade negotiations would enhance that of the United States. As one American official put it, "the idea for a bilateral trade treaty with the British" arose because: "they would probably be the easiest person [sic] to do it with ... and then see what kind of animal that would be and how wide its application would be to others."[26] American aspirations for an agreement certainly made an impact on National Socialist Germany. From February until early June 1933 both the German Foreign and Finance Ministries repeatedly expressed a profound concern that Britain and the United States were "very likely to sign a trade agreement in the near future" heralding a new era in Anglo-American co-operation[27].

It is exercising the historians' privilege of hindsight which makes the first two years of Roosevelt's presidency seem like a lost opportunity in Anglo-American relations. Back in 1933 the timing of Secretary Hull's tariff overture appeared particularly poor – Britain's Abnormal, General and Imperial tariffs had only just passed into law and it remained unclear how far Hull enjoyed the support of a president apparently torn between the nationalist and internationalist elements in his government. Equally unconvincing from the British perspective was the way that the State Department skirted over the sticky question of whether Congressional support for the RTA could be secured[28]. On a more fundamental level, however, the problem was one of competition. Britain's £70 million trading deficit to the United States was a genuine obstacle to the conclusion of an Anglo-American trading agreement, as well as a source of great embarrassment; so, too, was British determination to strengthen its imperial power base and to meet protectionist promises made to its electorate[29]. In the short term, there was also the practical difficulty that without at least a temporary stabilisation agreement, any attempt to negotiate a reduction of tariffs was likely to be futile.

[26] James Warburg diary entry of 7 April 1933, Diaries and Papers of James Warburg, vol. 3, Butler Library, Columbia University, New York.

[27] Memorandum from Neurath to Ritter, 3 April 1933, GFM 33:1231, 3177/D684107, Records of the German Foreign Ministry, microfilm held in Public Record Office, London.

[28] *R. N. Gardner*, Sterling-Dollar Diplomacy (New York, McGraw-Hill [2]1969) 39–47; NA SD 611.0031, Exec Cttee/40, memorandum by the drafting committee, 18 November 1933. The Germans were delighted by the public display of antagonism amongst the remaining democratic powers. See records of the German Finance Ministry, Bundesarchiv, Koblenz (hereafter BA R2), BA R2/21674, Deutsche Führerbriefe, No.58, 28 July 1933.

[29] Britain earned £31 million from its exports to US in 1936 while importing £114 million. *I. Drummond, N. Hillmer*, Negotiating Freer Trade: The United Kingdom, the United States, Canada and the Free Trade Agreements of 1938 (Waterloo 1989) 42–43.

The British change of heart came in 1936 when Neville Chamberlain, then still Chancellor of the Exchequer, signalled Britain's new determination to open trade negotiations with the United States. Politics now took precedence over economics for Chamberlain was determined to secure an Anglo-American trade agreement to present Europe's dictators with "the possibility of these two great powers working together"[30]. But the missed opportunity for agreement in 1933 cost Britain dear. Since 1932 inter-imperial trade had grown stronger and American farmers more vociferous in their demands for access to the British market. London's new willingness to explore the possibility of an agreement could disguise neither the incompatibility of British and American tariff structures which had grown more acute since 1933, nor the cumbersome machinery of the RTA. The agreement, finally signed on 17 November 1938, did little to liberalise Anglo-American trade, impress the German aggressors of "Anglo-Saxon" solidarity or trigger a global move to reduce international protectionism[31].

The "bombshell" message

Of course, the drama over the issue of monetary co-operation in 1933 also served to deflect attention away from Hull's initiative and to show American policy in its most uncooperative light. As is well known, it was the clash between nationalist and international elements in the early New Deal, both in terms of policy and personalities, which pulled the rug from under Hull's feet in London. In June 1933 the Presidential support needed to get the RTA legislation through Congress evaporated, and Roosevelt embarked on a superficially radical policy of dollar devaluation which soured the climate of international co-operation. Roosevelt's famous "bombshell message", in which he rejected a planned temporary stabilisation agreement to provide a stable monetary foundation for the talks, became the ostensible cause for the collapse the conference and the basis for persistent European suspicions of Roosevelt's foreign policy thereafter. This is not the place to unpick the intricacies of the stabilisation negotiations, although the continued notoriety of the "bombshell message" is surprising given the twist and turns in international economic relations since 1931 and the renewed emphasis by economists on the benefits of currency depreciation (coupled with a commensurate loosening of orthodox policies) for national and international recovery.

30 *A. W. Schatz*, The Anglo-American Trade Agreement and Cordell Hull's Search for Peace, in: Journal of American History 57 (June 1970) 100.

31 The Treasury did its best to assure the Germans of the RTA's insignificance. In October 1938 Leith-Ross told a visiting German trade delegation that the European economy "would be in serious danger if the European Great Powers worked against one another instead of cooperating" as they were "confronted with the ever-growing strength of the economy of the United States"; *B.-J. Wendt*, Economic Appeasement: Handel und Finanzen der britischen Deutschland-Politik (Düsseldorf 1971) 526.

Much has been made of the strong language and various explanations for Roosevelt's diplomatic naiveté have been offered by historians[32]. For those seeking to defend Roosevelt's action, one of the most interesting documentary leads comes from Roosevelt's private files when Alexander Sachs, an economist of the Lehman Corporation wrote advising FDR to take a "tough stand" on the gold standard. A clear indication of American hostility to gold – it is hard to imagine one clearer than the "bombshell message" - would "force the remaining gold-linked economies into some form of inflation"[33]. In diplomatic terms, however, the President's choice of language was ill-advised as his strong condemnation of the fetishism "of so-called international bankers" for the gold standard left his representatives in London isolated and made him easy prey for British and French politicians, neither of whom were willing to co-operate with the American initiative of trade and tariffs and both of whom had made repeated demands for concessions on war debts since Roosevelt had come to power. Roosevelt had further reason to feel frustrated by developments in London, for on the very day that the London conference opened, the British and German press published news of an Anglo-German deal on commercial debts renewing the standstill machinery that sustained German imports and exports. At the same time, Schacht announced that Germany would no longer honour debts to nations who had a trading surplus with Germany, namely the United States, thereby reneging on German assurances given since 1924 that Germany would not discriminate between its debtors. Changes in French policy, too, had irritated FDR. In April 1933 France, though determined to uphold the sanctity of the gold standard, rejected an American proposal for a *temporary* stabilisation agreement to cover the forthcoming conference in the hope the Americans would offer them something better. Instead, when in May 1933 American policy took on a more radical flavour, the French were forced to revive the American proposal in the face of mounting pressure on the French franc and a weakening domestic economy. Their request was taken up by the Federal Reserve Board of New York who worked hard to revive Presidential support. At the same time, however, the French Prime Minister, Edouard Daladier and

[32] For a summary see: *Clavin*, Failure of Economic Diplomacy 129–138.

[33] FDR Sachs: box 99, memorandum by Alexander Sachs, 25 June 1933. The dollar's floatation has been described by historians of the New Deal as the president's first nationalist act. Yet it could have been an internationalist act of tremendous import. There are further memoranda that reflect what might have been. First, in late November 1932, came a proposal from Herbert Feis, international economic advisor to the State Department, for an American-led co-ordinated devaluation of all currencies within the gold standard system. His comment at the time, that the proposal belonged "to the world of HG Well's", demonstrated quite how far the idea seemed beyond the pale. Then, in April and May 1933, came wide-spread rumours in both the British Treasury and the Foreign Office– so far it has not been possible to trace their provenance – that Britain and other members of the sterling bloc were to join Roosevelt in a new currency bloc of floating currencies. See, inter alia, NA SD 550.S1/9, memorandum by Feis, 9 Sept. 1932, and papers of 1933 Ministerial Committee for the World Economic Conference, Public Record Office, Kew (hereafter PRO Cab 29/140–146), PRO Cab29/142, meetings of the British delegation, 3 and 4 July 1933.

Finance Minister George Bonnet, in part to secure renewed political support within the Chamber of Deputies, began to demand that a new, *permanent* stabilisation agreement should come out of the conference, this despite previous assurances to Roosevelt that the topic would be excluded from conference deliberations[34].

Equally frustrating for the American administration was the position adopted by the British government. Roosevelt and his advisers were only too aware that, since the floatation of the dollar there was, in real terms, little difference between American and British monetary policy. Both had abandoned the gold standard (whether they elected to do so or were "forced" off gold was a moot point), in order to raise prices, stimulate demand and investment through the fall in interest rates and to loosen the hold of orthodox policy on their economies. It is the failure to take this strategy further that explains the slow down in the national economies of Britain and America by the mid-1930s. Indeed, from September 1931 until April 1933 British monetary policy was a much greater source of international division than that of the United States. With the majority of the world's countries still on gold, it was often argued that Britain should demonstrate "responsibility" and "leadership" by returning to the gold standard[35].

After April 1933 British monetary policy was much closer to that of the Democrat Administration than to many European powers. In public, the British government rejected speculation regarding possible Anglo-American co-operation to revive the world economy because Roosevelt's intentions on monetary policy remained unclear in the summer of 1933. In private, the British government were quietly relieved that the dollar floatation had diverted international attention away from the floating pound, but were also concerned that the depreciating dollar threatened the advantages Britain had accrued since the floatation of sterling[36]. British monetary policy, too, was governed by the primacy of domestic recovery. Equally important was the fact that the imperial dimension to British policy which had evolved, partly by accident, partly by design since 1931, led by the City of London and Treasury's determination to rebuild British power by "giving sterling a new force in the world", was conceived as a means to compete with

[34] *K. Mouré*, Managing the Franc Poincaré. Economic Understanding and Political Constraint in French Monetary Policy, 1928–1936 (Cambridge 1991) 95 ; *P. Clavin*, The Fetishes of So-Called International Bankers: Central Bank Co-operation for the World Economic Conference, 1932–33, in: Contemporary European History 1 (November 1992) 296–303.

[35] In 1933 the French government were as hostile to the floating pound as the floating US dollar. (A 15% surtax was imposed on British, but not American, imports to France, for example.) There were repeated complaints of the "vulgarisation" of sterling and London's repeated failure, despite the comparative recovery and strength of its economy, to take any steps towards restabilizing sterling. See Archives Ministère des Affaires Étrangères (hereafter FFM), FFM Z/Grande-Bretange/324, Rueff to Paul-Boncour, 16 May 1933; FFM Z/Grande-Bretagne/324, Rueff to Paul-Boncour, 26 July 1933.

[36] Memorandum by Henry Clay, 12 May 1933, OV31/22, Country files in Records of the Bank of England, Bank of England, London.

America[37]. Roosevelt was right to suspect that Britain and, to a lesser extent France, exploited his unwillingness to co-operate on monetary matters "deliberately to discredit us for certain clear objectives"[38].

By exploring the relationship between different areas of policy and the diplomatic context as a whole, it is possible to conclude that Roosevelt alone was not responsible for the failure of the World Economic Conference. There were opportunities during FDR's first year in office to improve American relations with Europe, in general, and Britain, in particular, and that the failure of co-operative efforts was as much to do with the political and economic priorities of the European powers as with the primacy of domestic recovery for America. Indeed, with the floatation of the US dollar in April 1933, the first hope was that Anglo-American relations would improve, not deteriorate further, as membership of the gold standard was no longer a source of tension in Anglo-American relations. Not only did Britain and the United States fail to launch a joint initiative to reflate the world economy and break the stranglehold of gold standard orthodoxy, the suspicion and hostility generated by events in London, notably between Roosevelt and Chamberlain, returned to trouble their relations throughout the 1930s. Interestingly, scholars who have studied the internal constraints on Roosevelt's freedom to make foreign policy as he would have wished, also now argue that the best opportunities to shape public opinion to a more internationalist outlook were squandered between 1933 and 1935[39].

The World Economic Conference and the Lessons of History

The utility of the World Economic Conference did not end in the summer of 1933. The materials and proposals collated in preparation for the conference provided the basis for war debt, trade and monetary negotiations in the years to come. Roosevelt, in particular, continued to be drawn to the idea of an international conference to settle the world's diplomatic and economic crises in the latter 1930s. FDR's call in 1938 for a "conference of all nations" to consider "correlated questions to be solved in a spirit of justice", the State Department's World Recovery Programme of 1939 and the Welles Mission of 1940 all had their genesis in the World Economic Conference of 1933[40]. After 1940, however, the history of the

[37] Discussed in: *P. J Cain, A. G. Hopkins*, British Imperialism. Crisis and Deconstruction, 1914–1990 (London 1993) 81–93.

[38] Communiqué from Roosevelt to Hull, 24 June 1933, SD 550.S1/Monetary Stab./47, Records of the State Department, National Archives II, Washington D.C.

[39] *T. Guinsburg*, The Triumph of Isolation, in: *G. Martel* (ed.), American Foreign Relations Reconsidered, 1890–1993 (London 1994) 101.

[40] Telegram from Roosevelt to Hitler, 27 September 1938, cited in: *R. D. Challener*, From Isolation to Containment, 1931–1950 (London 1970) 84–85. See also file series NA SD 600.0031/World Program, 1936–1939.

failure of the World Conference, and, in particular, the "bombshell message" came to serve a very different purpose as the American administration developed a much more critical view of its foreign policy efforts in the inter-war period.

The impulse to "learn the lessons of History" was never stronger than during the years which saw the widespread collapse of liberal democracy, the failure of the diplomatic and economic order created after 1919 and a bloody second world war waged within a generation of the first. History was now a "bruised witness" called to the stand to offer truthful testimony about what went wrong[41]. As Roosevelt made clear in 1943, he was determined to rectify the errors of the last peace: "the well-intentioned but ill-fated experiments of former years did not work ... It is my intention to do all that I humanly can as President and Commander-In-Chief to see that these tragic mistakes shall not be made again."[42] Errors in regard to the treatment of Germany were uppermost in the minds of the audience of this fireside chat, but for Roosevelt the lessons went further. Throughout the war American policy-makers were preoccupied as much with objectives and plans for the post-war order as with helping the "right side" win. (Indeed, in the first years of the Second World War, the American preoccupation with learning the lessons of the past and planning for the future frequently frustrated their British friends and later allies who were engrossed with more pressing concerns.)[43]

When it came to planning postwar international co-operation many of Roosevelt's advisors developed a particularly critical appreciation of American foreign policy in the interwar period. The myriad of individuals who had opinions on, though intermittent influence over, the evolution of American foreign policy under Roosevelt, has always made it difficult to trace precisely who influenced the development and articulation of American foreign policy and when. So, too, did the dramatic pace of events and the tremendous growth of the American economy at war that triggered structural change and a new constellation of interest groups which this economic change helped to stimulate, that were instrumental in recasting American foreign policy[44]. This is not the place to attempt to unpick the complex process by which the lessons of history were drawn, understood and implemented by the American administration, or to the potency of history as an

[41] The observations of the European-trained scholar of American foreign policy on this process in American policy remain interesting. See: *S. Hoffman*, Gulliver's Troubles or the Setting of American Foreign Policy (New York, London 1968) 33–110.

[42] Christmas Eve Fireside Chat on Tehran and Cairo Conferences, 24 December 1943, *S. I. Rosenman*, The Public Papers and Addresses of Franklin D. Roosevelt (New York 1950) 559; *E. R. May*, Lessons' of the Past. The Use and Misuse of History in American Foreign Policy (New York 1973) 4–5.

[43] For example, see memorandum by Horace Wilson, 9 November 1939, General Correspondence of the Foreign Office, Public Record Office, London (hereafter PRO FO371), FO371, 24247, 431/431/45.

[44] Institutions, like the Princeton Center for Advanced Study, the Yale Institute of International Studies and the Rockefeller Foundation, also forged significant international links between scholars and policy-makers.

analytical tool or the role of historians as policy advisors (perhaps something that can be taken up in discussion)[45]. However it is relevant to note that by 1942 American "irresponsibility" in the global system and the disaster that this wrought, was demonstrated by two key events: the failure of the United States to join the League of Nations and the impact of the "bombshell message" on the World Economic Conference in 1933.

Learning the lessons of history was not just about changing intellectual convictions and defining new policies at the highest level of the administration. American history also demonstrated the risk of ignoring congressional and public opinion, and it is here that the historical explanation for the failure of the World Economic Conference was revived and recast. For most, if not all, of the 1930s, the United States had viewed the history of the failure of the World Economic Conference as a multilateral failure, defending itself vehemently against, in particular, British accusations that the conference had failed because of American "irresponsibility". (Typical was Neville Chamberlain's assertion in July 1933 that "there has never been a case of a conference being so completely smashed by one of its participants"[46].) The United States saw its "responsibility" to the international economy as no greater than that of the other major powers and had sought to demonstrate a will for "partnership" not "leadership" in the build-up to the international economic negotiations in London. But after 1942 the administration expressed its "responsibilities" in hegemonic terms. The transformation is well illustrated by the writings of Herbert Feis, a prominent adviser to the State Department and War Department until 1946 who went on to become a Pulitzer prize-winning historian of the Cold War. Writing in 1934, he argued that the disintegration of the international economy could only be halted "when Great Britain, the United States and France ... [have] faced their responsibilities fully in both currency and political relations". By 1950 this multilateral account of international relations in the 1930s became one in which the United States failed to realise an economic potential that would "have made the difference between peace and war"[47].

The administration's public information program (read propaganda) after 1945 to sell America's new commitment to the new monetary and economic institu-

[45] The process is usually dated as taking place during the Second World War, but there are good reasons to suggest it was already underway in the 1930s.

[46] Private papers and diaries of Neville Chamberlain, University Library, Birmingham (hereafter NC), NC 18/1/836, Chamberlain to Ida Chamberlain, 15 July 1933. Such assertions were also made publicly and were in marked contrast to his complaint of May 1933 "I have a horrible time ahead of me with this awful World Economic Conference ... And it is difficult to see how anything valuable can come out of it." NC 18/1/827, Chamberlain to Hilda Chamberlain, 14 May 1933.

[47] LC Feis:16, Feis to Frankfurter, 29 March 1934; LC Feis:83, essay for Issues in American Life, 1953, 12–13. For further details see *P. Clavin*, *C. Wilhelm*, History as Propaganda: The role of German and British historians in "educating" the United States, 1933–1955, European Union Human Capital and Mobility Programme project "History and Historians in European and American Societies and Cultures" 1996.

tions of Bretton Woods, and in particular, the planned International Trade Organisation, made extensive use of the lessons of history[48]. When it came to presenting America's plans for the postwar order "History", in Harry Dexter White's words, offered "sex appeal" to counter the dryness of economics[49]. Accounts of the economic imperatives for US participation in the world economy were shunned in preference to an historical narrative which began with a brief history of British "responsibility" towards the highly successful world economy in the nineteenth century, climaxed with a vivid account of America's "selfish" imposition of the Smoot-Hawley tariff in 1930 and its "irresponsible" behaviour at the World Economic Conference, and concluded with an exploration of the new, enlightened self-interest which distinguished American leadership in the creation of a new economic order for the world. In this process, the *Pax Britannica* of the nineteenth century became the role model for the new *Pax Americana* designed to make the world "safe for democracy" in the twentieth century[50].

Arthur Sweetser of the Office of War Information and Cordell Hull agreed in 1942 that it was essential to educate the American public "gradually and cautiously". "People nowadays were afraid of 'great plans' and they might react against them."[51] Instead, in government propaganda initiatives, the devastating impact of the "bombshell message" served as explanation and lurid proof for the subsequent disintegration of economic and diplomatic co-operation, while the RTA served as a vital counterpoint to this sorry tale – the silver lining in the dismal history of American economic diplomacy in the 1930s[52]. In its presentations of the postwar order to the American public, the Anglo-American RTA, in particular, was presented as "a practical demonstration of positive international co-operation ... that produced results and the way people have got accustomed to the

[48] See for example the widely-circulated publicity document prepared by the Division on Commercial Policy entitled, "Fifty Facts on the Proposed British Loan", June 1945 in NA RG43, Lot 57D-284, Box 3. The document's verbatim repetition of the British position on war debt payments after 1931, and so vehemently denied by the USA throughout the 1930s, is particularly striking: Britain defaulted because "in 1931 the Hoover moratorium suspended debts .... we raised our already high tariffs in 1930" and "when Britain borrowed money it was loaned on to her allies...When Germany stopped paying reparations, the Allies stopped paying war debts and the whole World War 1 debt structure collapse like a pack of cards."

[49] NA RG 43, Lot 57D-284, box 3, comments on memorandum by A. Bloomfield, June 1945.

[50] Shaping the Lessons of History: Britain and the Rhetoric of American Trade Policy, 1930–1960, in: Freedom and Trade, vol. 1, History and Policy, *A. Marrison* (ed.), (London 1998) 287–307.

[51] Memorandum of conversation between Sweetser and Hull sent to Archibald MacLeish, 21 May 1942, Private Papers of Arthur Sweetser, Library of Congress, Washington DC (hereafter LC Sweetser), LC Sweetser: 32.

[52] FDR continued to argue that the escalation in world armaments and the severity of the global depression were linked. As he explained, "Between 1929 and 1932 almost all the nations went bankrupt – and their bankruptcy just about equalled their arms expenditure. That's an extraordinary fact – figure it out sometime.", LC Sweetser:38, Sweetser's notes of conversation with FDR, 29 May 1942.

gradual removal of trade barriers through his [Hull's] tariff policy"[53]. The State Department's "information program" launched in October 1945 to educate the American public, and therefore Congress too, as to the benefits of America's new commitment to multilateral tariff reductions made mention of the harm caused by American "irresponsibility" at the World Economic Conference. However, the central theme of the numerous speeches delivered, in particular, by Assistant Secretary of State William Clayton, was the importance of a strong Anglo-American partnership to support the American commitment to "Good Neighbourliness". Historical narratives continued to form the basis of the "educational" drive. "No other country", Clayton told the American public in October 1945, "has been as important to our international trade, or indeed, the international trade of the world as Great Britain"[54].

John Lewis Gaddis, echoed recently by John Young, has described the evolution of American foreign policy in the Second World War thus: "like the British from whom they *inherited* the tendency, Americans had traditionally associated their security with balancing the power of the world"[55]. But the transfer of a sense of global responsibility was not genetic. My contention is that as the United States sought to define the *Pax Americana* to govern international relations in the post-war period, it was not a question of "inheriting tendencies". American publicity campaigns reveal the conscious (and unconscious) adoption of the rhetoric and perceived history of British power in the nineteenth century. The history of the failure of the World Economic Conference was an important part of this process. The evolution of American foreign policy in the Second World War reflected Roosevelt's conviction that Woodrow Wilson had been right: economic stability and national security could be achieved only on a world-wide scale and America had to take the lead now that European leadership had failed[56].

But it would be wrong to suggest that all America's lessons of history were self-taught. It is striking how far the public presentation of the "ineffectiveness" and "irresponsibility" of American foreign economic foreign policy of the interwar

[53] LC Sweetser: 32,memorandum of conversation between Sweetser and Hull sent to Archibald MacLeish, 21 May 1942. The RTA has been criticised for its focus on eliminating discrimination in international trade than on liberalising domestic tariffs. See inter alia: *R. E. Baldwin, A. O. Krueger*, The Structure and Evolution of Recent US Trade Policy (Chicago 1984); *J. A. Conybeare*, Trade Wars. The Theory and Practice of International Commercial Rivalry (New York 1987), ch.3; *I. Drummond, N. Hillmer*, Negotiating Freer Trade: the United Kingdom, Canada and the Free Trade Agreements of 1938 (Waterloo 1989). At the same time, it remained the only sustained initiative to reduce protectionism in the 1930s and formed the basis for GATT, See: *D. Irwin*, The GATT's Contribution to economic recovery in post-war Western Europe, in: *B. Eichengreen* (ed.), Europe's Postwar Recovery 127–150.

[54] Memorandum on the information program of the United States, 4 Oct. 1945, RG43, box 3, Lot Files on International Trade, National Archives, Washington D.C.

[55] My italics. *J. L. Gaddis*, The End of the Cold War: Implications, Reconsiderations, Provocations (New York 1992) 9; *J. Young*, Britain and the World in the Twentieth Century (London 1997).

[56] *W. F. Kimball*, The Juggler: Franklin Roosevelt as Wartime Statesman (Princeton 1991) 186–87.

period echoed earlier stinging British criticism of American policy. After 1919 historical example informed and illustrated British criticism of American "selfish", "nationalistic" economic policies, despite the fact that in 1931 the British government, too, abandoned the internationalism which had characterised its overseas economic policy since the abolition of the Corn Laws. Throughout the interwar period the British government, in policy documents, diplomatic meetings and the British press, compared the development of American policy after 1930 to the historically "responsible" British economic policies in the nineteenth century: the Smoot-Hawley tariff of 1930, the cessation of American lending to Europe, the insistence on war debt repayment and the flotation of the dollar in 1933 were unfavourably contrasted with the promotion of free trade and the Bank of England's guardianship of the international gold standard.

Indeed, during the Second World War, the *Pax Britannica* critique of American foreign policy in the interwar years took on a more self-conscious and concerted character as the British Foreign Office employed historians, and consequently a host of historical motifs, first in their efforts to entice American into the war on Britain's side, and then as planning for the post-war world began, to shape American internationalism on an Anglo-American axis, a partnership based on common, historically-defined goals of security and stability for the "new" international system. The task of these historians was not to educate the American public as to the "facts" of history, but to use historical example to add validity and appeal to their propaganda message. Although Britain's strategies for disseminating information in the United States grew more sophisticated and extensive as the war went on, the story remained much the same. At the heart of Britain's propaganda message lay what the Foreign Office called the "doctrine of responsibility", in other words that the United States recognise and act on its "responsibilities to the world", with the aspiration that, in so doing, the United States would adopt policies favourable to Britain. The history of the World Economic Conference continued to be useful, but as a lesson of how not to approach the issue of international economic co-operation[57].

Emphasising that America should learn the lessons of history and recognise its responsibilities to the wider world was not without risks for the British government. Whenever possible, the Ministry of Information and its "agents of influence" sought to leave economics out of the picture, in part, because the recent

[57] In particular, the Ministry of Information (staffed by past or future historians like Denis Brogan, John Wheeler-Bennett and Harold Nicolson) sought to educate the American elite as to the international "responsibilities" of the United States in the international order to be created after the war's end. Refugee scholars, like the German Moritz Julius Bonn, were also used by the MOI in order to circumvent US suspicion of British propaganda. For a summary of American strategies to shape domestic public opinion see: *D. Frezza*, Psychological Warfare and the Building of National Morale during World War II, in: *D. K. Adams, C. A. Van Minnen* (eds.), Aspects of War in American History (Keele 1997) 173–196. For the continuation of Britain's information programme after war's end see: *C. Anstey*, Foreign Office Efforts to Influence American Opinion, 1944–1949 (Ph.D diss, London School of Economics 1984).

history of Anglo-American economic relations was a troubled one and only served to underline the diminishing base of British power. But Britain's commitment to the sterling area (which had grown only stronger in the war) and its opposition to American calls to set up an International Trade Organisation (ITO) were confused by its calls for American "responsibility" in the world economy. For all that British officials now chose to omit any reference to the role of free trade in the history of *Pax Britannica*, their American audience filled in the gap, in large part thanks to British criticisms of American foreign policy in the interwar period which had devoted a great deal of attention to the tension between America's status as creditor and its protectionism. (For Britain the lesson was to be careful what you wish for.)

History, as it unfolded after 1945, also made it clear that the rhetoric of a Pax Americana aside, there were limitations to US administrations' will and ability to "force the world to be free" and the benefits to be had from it[58]. In particular, the rhetoric of America's commitment to multilateral tariff cutting differed from the reality that saw the protectionist impulse of Congress destroy the ITO at birth and limit the effectiveness of GATT until the 1960s. The executive's failure to secure Congressional and public support for their lessons of history illustrated the limitations of analogical thinking. However, the narrative of a Pax Americana modelled on the interwar account of the Pax Britannica did not disappear with the end of the war. The historical motif had an important impact on the historiography of American economic foreign policy after 1945, particularly histories of American economic foreign policy written by former members of the State Department like William Adams Brown and Raymond Mikesell[59]. It is here that my paper comes full circle for the histories of Brown, Mikesell, alongside those of William L. Langer, S. Everett Gleason and Herbert Feis are the most critical accounts of United States economic foreign policy in the inter-war period. Writing in the 1950s and early 1960s, these former members of the State Department charted the development of American economic foreign policy as a linear history maturing progressively from the "blinkered, irresponsible and selfish" actions, exemplified by the Smoot-Hawley tariff and the World Economic Conference to its conversion into the new champion of the international economy during the Second World War. It was only later in the "Crucial Decade", that historians and political scientists began to question this historical model to ask how far America, or Britain for that matter, ever enjoyed truly hegemonic power.

[58] *K. W. Stiles*, The Ambivalent Hegemon: Explaining the "Lost Decade" in Multilateral Talks, in: Review of the International Political Economy 2 (1995) 19.

[59] *W. A. Brown*, The United States and the Restoration of World Trade (New York 1950); *R. Mikesell*, United States Economic Policy and International Relations (New York 1952).

Concluding Remarks

As the first part of this paper has sought to demonstrate, American foreign economic policy can only be held partly responsible for the ignominious collapse of the World Economic Conference in 1933. This was widely recognised at the time, but it served the varied national interests of Britain, France and Germany to denounce Roosevelt's actions more vehemently than the economic nationalism of their neighbours. (The language of the "bombshell message" certainly made their task easier!) By the outbreak of the Second World War, however, the United States had developed a much more critical perspective on the history of international economic cooperation in 1933. The historical narrative of the "bombshell message", in particular, formed a central plank of US administration efforts to educate the American public as to its new responsibilities in the international system and the dangers to world peace and prosperity if it failed to meet the responsibilities the progress of history had conferred on the United States. The "bombshell message" took on a new lease of life as a tool with which to educate the American public. The narrative of American irresponsibility in the 1930s, forged by the State Department and the Office of War Information, was influenced by a large variety of sources, not all of them American. These historical accounts, which placed almost sole responsibility for the failure of the World Economic Conference on the shoulders of the United States, helped to create something of a mismatch between the rhetoric and the reality of policy. The narrative of American "irresponsibility" also went on to shape the historiography of American interwar foreign relations in the period after 1945 summarised in the introduction of this paper.

Robert Skidelsky

The Great Depression: Keynes's Perspective

Introduction

Although Keynes's *General Theory* has often been called the theory of a very deep slump, the Great Depression is not in fact mentioned in Keynes's *magnum opus*. His theory is designed to establish the logical possibility of a low employment equilibrium – something denied by the classical economists. Its purity is not sullied by any reference to events.

Keynesian interpretations of the Great Depression are derived retrospectively from the *General Theory*. The best-known examples are by Peter Temin and Charles Kindleberger[1]. The main debate is between the Keynesians and the monetarists, the former emphasising the collapse in effective demand, the latter the collapse in the money supply. At issue is the direction of causation: from money to prices or from prices to money. There is also a Hayekian tradition which emphasises the role of credit-induced distortions in the structure of production. The contention here is that the pursuit of price stability when productivity is rapidly increasing may be inflationary, producing an asset boom followed by a bust. The reason for contemporary interest in this way of telling the story of the 1920s is obvious.

As one would expect, Keynes's own commentary on the Great Depression is more subtle and eclectic than the simplified Keynesian model would suggest. The bulk of his comments, including his suggested policy measures, occurred during the downward slide and before the *General Theory* model was developed. For America he advocated policies of monetary expansion identical to those Friedman later said should have been adopted; for England, tethered until September 1931 to the gold standard, he argued for a mixture of Protection and public works. He did not suggest currency devaluation in either country till it occurred; then he welcomed it. His espousal of expansionary fiscal policy ('unbalancing the budget') dates from 1933, when he believed that a liquidity trap might exist.

By 1936, the Great Depression was over, but the recovery – in the USA and Britain – had stopped short of full employment. The incomplete recovery from

[1] *Peter Temin*, Did Monetary Forces cause the Great Depression?, in: *W. W. Norton* (1976); *C. P. Kindleberger*, The World in Depression 1929–1939 (London 1973).

depression was the factual background to Keynes's logical demonstration of the possibility of equilibrium at less than full employment. By contrast, in his commentary on the Great Depression itself, Keynes is trying to analyse a process which is still in train, and whose outcome cannot be foreseen. Would there be a full recovery or only a partial recovery? And, if the latter, how long would it take? In the early 1930s, there were no clear answers to such questions. By the mid 1930s, more of the picture was available. Keynes's method switched accordingly from the theory of disequilibrium processes to the theory of equilibrium states short of full employment[2].

In the early 1930s, Keynes was trying to understand the Great Depression in terms of the model he had developed in the *Treatise on Money*. This was a theory of deep cycles, set in an 'open' economy, with a special focus on the British case of a 'jammed' economy in the 1920s. The analysis was in terms of disequilibrium prices. He applied this model to the American slump in 1931. By the end of 1932, Keynes had taken the analytic decision to 'close' the model, remove the price system and concentrate on the direct response of output to changes in effective demand. In face of the severity and world-wide character of the collapse, this seemed a sensible simplification. As Peter Clarke has emphasised, Keynes's models always had a direct reference to immediate events[3]. Keynes regarded this as a virtue; others have seen it as his greatest vice – his tendency to invest 'special cases' with a 'treacherous generality'[4].

Keynes's development as an economist has been described as 'a struggle to escape from the stranglehold of the Quantity Theory of Money'[5]. He never did 'escape' from it entirely. His first theoretical book, *Tract on Monetary Reform* (1923), scarcely goes beyond Irving Fisher, in its recognition that the price level is indeterminate in the short-run, because of the variability of the velocity of circulation. There is a chapter on 'Effects of Changes in the Value of Money', which shows how these changes have distributional effects which can affect the level of output and employment. This is because some prices (especially wages and rents) are stickier than others (business receipts). Like Fisher, Keynes argues for stability in the domestic price level, to be secured by banking policy. The innovatory argument is policy-oriented: there may be a conflict between domestic price stability and fixing the exchange rate. If so, the former ought to be given priority, because 'contracts and business expectations which presume a stable exchange rate, may be far fewer, even in a trading country such as England, than those which presume

[2] For a fuller discussion, see *Robert Skidelsky*, The Influence of the Great Depression on Keynes's 'General Theory', in: History of Economics Review 25 (Winter-Summer 1996) 78–87.

[3] *Peter Clarke*, The Keynesian Revolution in the Making, 1924–1936 (Oxford 1988) esp. ch. 4.

[4] As *Joseph Schumpeter* put it in his review of the GT in the Journal of the American Statistical Association vol. 31 (December 1936) 791–795; reproduced in *John Cunningham Wood* (ed), John Maynard Keynes: Critical Assessments, vol. 2 (London) 125.

[5] By *Richard Kahn*, in: The Making of the Keynesian Revolution (Cambridge 1984) 50–51.

a stable level of internal prices'[6]. Thus a managed currency is Keynes's precondition for domestic price stability. This was the basis of his rejection of the official policy of returning Britain to the gold standard at the pre-war sterling-gold parity.

From the point of view of the Quantity Theory, Keynes's *Treatise on Money* (1930) can be regarded as an analysis of the causes of short-run changes in the velocity of circulation, or 'demand for money to hold'. Behind velocity lies investment and consumption spending. Keynes identifies fluctuations in business confidence, leading to fluctuations in investment demand, as the motive force for changes in velocity. Thus monetary disturbances may, though they need not, originate in the 'real' economy – from the side of the 'demand for loans' rather than the 'supply of money'. This broke with the old 'classical dichotomy'. However, Keynes's faith in the efficacy of what Schumpeter calls 'monetary therapy' survived unchanged from the *Tract on Monetary Reform* to the *Treatise on Money.* The following passage from the *Treatise* is a representative statement:

> 'Those who attribute sovereign power to the monetary authority on the governance of prices do not, of course, claim that the terms on which money is supplied is the *only* influence affecting the price level. To maintain that the supplies in a reservoir can be maintained at any required level by pouring enough water into it is not inconsistent with admitting that the level of the reservoir depends on many other factors besides how much water is poured in.'[7]

Keynes never told a historical story about the Great Depression. But in the *Treatise on Money* he offered a general explanation. 'I am bold to predict, therefore, that to the economic historians of the future the slump of 1930 may present itself as the death struggle of the war-rates of interest and the re-emergence of the pre-war rates. Now, at long last, this will doubtless come by itself.'[8] The slump, that is, was rooted in post-war strains, themselves the result of wartime dislocations, which had kept interest rates too high relative to profit expectations. Chief among these were the large volume of government borrowing for consumption purposes and the deflationary tendencies associated with the botched return to the gold standard[9]. Keynes thought that the US collapse had dragged down the rest of the world.

We start then with Keynes's interpretation of the American collapse, move on to his analysis of the British problem and then say something about the role of the gold standard in his thinking about the slump. The paper concludes by asking whether another Great Depression could occur.

[6] TMR vol. 4 of The Collected Writings of John Maynard Keynes, published by Macmillan for the Royal Economic Society (1971–89) 126. All references to Keynes's own writings will be to this edition.

[7] TM, ii, CW vol. 6, 304.

[8] Ibid. 345.

[9] *Susan Howson, Donald Winch,* The Economic Advisory Council 1930–1939 (Cambridge 1977) 51.

The American Crisis

Despite some disclaimers, both Keynes and Hayek predicted the US slump, though for different reasons. Hayek thought that a credit inflation was proceeding in the USA in the later 1920s. This became the standard retrospective Austrian account. In 1934, Lionel Robbins argued that the slump originated in the expansionary policies of the Fed in 1927, partly to offset a mild inflation, mainly to help Britain stay on the gold standard. This unleashed an orgy of speculation which could not be checked by the dear money imposed subsequently[10]. The analytical basis of this story was that prices should have been falling, as goods were becoming cheaper to make. Keynes got involved in this debate in 1928, when his business partner Oswald 'Foxy' Falk concluded that business conditions in the USA were 'unsound'. Keynes denied that inflation was taking place at this time. The test of inflation, he repeatedly said, was the 'test of prices'. Judged by the commodity price index, there was no danger of inflation in 1927. Hence, by raising the discount rate gradually from 3.5% in January to 5% in June 1928, the Fed was imposing a progressive deflation on a thriving economy. This was the basis of Keynes's commentary in 1928. In July and September he argued that the danger facing the US was not inflation, but deflation. 'The difficulty will be', he wrote in September, 'to find an outlet for the vast investment funds coming forward – particularly if central banks resist the tendency of the rate of interest to fall'. On October 4 1928 he wrote: 'I cannot help feeling that the risk just now is all on the side of a business depression ... If too prolonged an attempt is made to check the speculative position by dear money, it may well be that the dear money, by checking new investments, will bring about a general business depression.'[11]

Keynes retracted one part of this analysis in the *Treatise on Money*. He conceded (in 1930) that the stability of the commodity price index between 1928 and 1929 had concealed a 'profit inflation'. However, he insisted that the speculation in real estate hid a more general tendency to under-investment relative to the volume of corporate saving. Both sides, that is, accused the other of looking in the wrong place. Orthodox banking opinion saw in the speculative boom a clear indication of unsound credit conditions crying out for 'correction'; Keynes believed that inflated prices on Wall Street were an inaccurate indicator of the state of the real economy. 'Thus I attribute the slump of 1930 primarily to the deterrent effects on investment of the long period of dear money which preceded the stock-market collapse, and only secondarily to the collapse itself.'[12] The implication of Keynes's view was that 'dear money' should be used only as 'shock therapy'. What was needed in 1928 was a short, sharp dose of dear money sufficient to break the market, thus avoiding the prolonged period of dear money which led up to the investment collapse of 1929.

10 *L. Robbins*, The Great Depression (London 1934).
11 *Skidelsky*, John Maynard Keynes, vol. 2 (London 1992) 341.
12 TM, CW, 6, 176.

But how should the US government or monetary authority respond to the business depression which developed after 1929? By 1934, Keynes was urging deficit spending on President Roosevelt. But this was not the advice he gave three years earlier. The *Treatise on Money* was published in January 1931. Keynes visited the USA in May 1931 to take part in a symposium on unemployment in Chicago. He also gave two lectures in New York. Soon after he arrived he reported to Falk that he had not realised how insolvent the banking system was. 'They have purchased great quantities of second-grade bonds which have depreciated in value and their advances to farmers and against real estate are inadequately secured'. To Hubert Henderson he wrote: 'At any moment bank runs are liable to break out almost anywhere in the country. All this tends towards a mania for liquidity by anyone who can achieve it.' 'Barmy' opposition from some New York banks was stopping the Fed from open-market operations to push up bond prices[13]. At this stage, Keynes still rated the possibilities of open-market operations by the Fed highly.

Keynes's lectures to the New School for Social Research, New York, were an attack on the 'orthodox' remedy of fighting the Depression by cutting costs. He said any such policy would 'shake the social order to its foundation'[14]. On the contrary, a massive monetary expansion – to increase the quantity and reduce the cost of bank credit – was needed to raise prices. This analysis was based on the orthodox (short-run) Quantity Theory of Money. Lowering interest rates would increase investment demand without immediately augmenting supply. 'And that is just what is needed to raise prices, to increase profits to normal and so to renew the motive to increase output and employment.'[15]

The three lectures he gave in Chicago in June/July 1931, before an audience of economists, were the last occasion he used an unmodified *Treatise on Money* framework to explain what was happening. The main characteristic of the 1925–28 boom he now saw as 'an extraordinary willingness to borrow money for purposes of new real investment at very high rates of interest'. There was also the growth of the hire-purchase system, which Keynes described as a 'sort of semi-investment' and the US's willingness to lend freely abroad. The resulting prosperity, based on 'building, the electrification of the world, and the associated enterprises of roads and motor-cars', spread from the US to the rest of the world, except Britain. In other words, the US expansion, with its associated foreign investment policy, kept the world in boom. 'A very few more quinquennia of equal activity might, indeed, have brought us near to the economic Eldorado, where all our reasonable economic needs would be satisfied.' The part played by inflation was 'surprisingly small'.

The slump which followed was caused by the collapse of investment. This was due to 'extraordinary imbecility', not to a 'natural' reaction against previous over-investment. Maintenance of the investment rate required falling interest rates, but

13 *Skidelsky*, Keynes, vol. 2, 390–391.
14 CW, vol. 20, 546.
15 Ibid. 549.

the Fed pushed them up to check Wall Street. Prolonged dear money had contractionary effects both in the USA and abroad. Also speculation was attracted to Wall Street away from foreign bonds. Once the decline started it gathered cumulative force. This was 'the whole explanation for the slump'[16].

His argument rested on the 'tacit assumption' that 'if the volume of investment falls off, then of necessity the level of business profits falls away also'. Here Keynes married the classical monetary disequilibrium analysis to his Treatise on Money definitions of saving and investment. Receipts from sales were more variable than costs of production – profits were more variable than wages. The first effect therefore of a credit deflation was a profit deflation. But profit (the difference between entrepreneurial costs and receipts) was equal (by definition) to the difference between saving and the value of investment. Thus 'the whole matter may be summed up by saying that a boom is generated when investment exceeds saving and a slump ... when saving exceeds investment'[17]. It was a characteristic of this type of analysis that saving varies less than investment over the cycle 'except ... towards the end of a slump [when the country] is very impoverished indeed'. The decline is eventually halted when 'negative saving' (or spending) by the government on the dole reduces the 'net volume of saving' to equality with investment. Keynes would describe this forced unbalancing of the state budget as 'Nature's way' of halting the economic rundown. But this process did not generate 'automatic' forces of recovery. There could be no permanent recovery till fixed investment had recovered to the level of full-employment savings[18].

Keynes rejected as impracticable, imprudent and unjust the attempt to restore profits by cutting business costs to below the depressed level of business receipts. The recovery required 'on the one hand, a fall in the long-term rate of interest ... and, on the other hand, a return of confidence to the business world ...' There was little which could be 'done deliberately to restore confidence'. Confidence was a by-product of a 'real improvement in fundamentals'. Keynes advocated loan-financed public works, chiefly because 'the government can borrow cheaply and need not be deterred by overnice calculations as to the prospective return'. But because he doubted whether they could be conceived and effected quickly enough, he also urged on the banking authorities (a) open-market operations to raise bond prices, and (b) lowering interest rates on deposits to 'drive depositors off deposits into bonds'[19]. What Keynes says about interest rate policy here is important, because I think it is a representative statement of his views:

'It may be that when confidence is at its lowest ebb the rate of interest plays a comparatively small part. It may also be true that, in so far as manufacturing plants are concerned, the rate of interest is never the dominating factor. But, after all the main volume of investment always takes the forms of housing, of public utilities and of transportation. Within these spheres the

[16] CW, vol. 13, 345–51.
[17] Ibid. 354.
[18] Ibid. 352–58.
[19] Ibid. vol. 20, 540.

rate of interest ... plays a predominant part. ... Every fall in the rate of interest will bring a new range of products within the practical sphere.'[20]

Interestingly, Keynes failed to distinguish between nominal and real interest rates, concentrating instead on blockages to the fall in nominal rates produced by risk premia over and above the 'pure' rate of interest and increased liquidity preference[21]. With US prices 10 per cent lower in 1931 than in 1929, the rise in the real cost of debt was swamping the 'fearfully slow' reductions in nominal rates.

Already by 1941, Keynes's American followers were convinced that monetary policy was useless as a macroeconomic tool, and Keynes, on a mission to Washington in 1941, had to remind them that 'a movement from a higher rate to a lower rate [allows] a greater scale of investment to proceed over a very much longer period than would otherwise be possible'[22].

The British Slump

Keynes regarded the US collapse as superimposed on a previous British depression, which it worsened. In the 1920s 'We were not participating in the enormous investment boom which the rest of the world was enjoying. Our savings were almost certainly in excess of our investment. In short, we were suffering a deflation.'[23] By 1930 'it is now fairly obvious that we are on the downward slope of an international credit cycle ... The intensity of our own problem today is due the fact that we now have the influence of this international depression superimposed on our own pre-existing troubles ...'[24] The American collapse, that is, increased the deflationary pressure already in evidence in the 1920s, making an adjustment back to full employment even more difficult.

The main significance of the British slump of the 1920s for the world slump was that it had left the USA as the only world growth engine. It had had to take over most of Britain's (and Western Europe's) pre-war role in this respect. Because Britain's slump (stagnation would be a better word, since, apart from 1920–22 the British economy did grow in the 1920s, though very slowly) was so well established and had been so exhaustively analysed by Keynes before 1929, he added little to the analysis of it after the world depression hit the British economy. The two grand inquests on the British slump to which he contributed in 1930 – the Macmillan Committee on Finance and Industry and the Economic Advisory Council's Committee of Economists – were backward looking, though Keynes was by then using the *Treatise on Money* framework.

20 Ibid. vol. 13, 358–66.
21 Ibid. vol. 20, 535–40.
22 q. *Moggridge*, op.cit, 658n.
23 CW, vol. 13, 347.
24 Ibid. vol. 20, 156.

As is well-known, Keynes's main explanation of the British 'slump' of the 1920s is that Churchill had overvalued the pound when he put it back on the gold standard in 1925. This had restricted export demand, while the high interest rates needed to defend the restored parity had curtailed domestic investment. Selling prices (profits) had fallen, real costs gone up, whence unemployment ...

It was the effects on output and employment of falling prices which first attracted Keynes's attention when the first post-war slump hit Britain in 1920. In a lecture to Cambridge students in the autumn of 1920 called 'Do We want Prices to Fall?' (one of his New York lectures in 1931 was 'Do We Want Prices to Rise?'), Keynes answered a resounding 'No'. He accepted the need to liquidate the post-war inflation, but rejected the official policy of reducing the price *level* in order to raise the exchange rate. Devaluation should be preferred to further deflation – 'we should accept a permanently diminished value for the standard coin measured in gold'[25]. Keynes explained the logic of this choice more clearly in a lecture in December 1922:

'The business of forcing down certain levels of wages, and so forth, into equilibrium is almost hopeless, or it will take a long time. The continuance of unemployment is to an important extent due to the fact that we have got the level of wages ... out of gear with everything else. The only way in which they will get into gear will be by an increase in the level of prices.'[26]

Keynes had posed the key issue of wage behaviour. British money wages had fallen by a third between 1920 and 1922 – the last example in British history of downward flexibility. But commodity prices had fallen even further, so recovery was incomplete. Keynes and the financial establishment drew different lessons from this experience. Keynes concluded that the deflation of 1920–22 had brought Britain to the 'verge of revolution' and that, as a working assumption, wage rates should be regarded as too rigid in the short period to adjust to 'the ebb and flow of international gold credit'. Hence his insistence that domestic price stability should be the main aim of monetary policy. The Treasury and the Bank of England concluded that wage costs had shown themselves sufficiently flexible to justify one further deflationary push to restore the pre-war gold standard.

That deflation causes unemployment because it causes costs to rise relative to selling prices remained central to Keynes's explanation of the British unemployment in the 1920s. It entered the *Treatise on Money* and it survives in the *General Theory* where the real wage is seen as a resultant not of nominal wage bargains but of the general price level. Thus the British unemployment problem was policy-induced.

The mechanism which connected monetary policy to the price level was the cost of credit. Keynes's contention in the second half of the 1920s was that the rate of interest required to defend the pound was too high to produce full employment at the given level of domestic costs. This was the same as saying that the pound was overvalued. Since an assault on costs was ruled out for political and social

[25] q. *Skidelsky*, Keynes, vol. 2, 45.
[26] Ibid. 133.

reasons (the experience of the General Strike of 1926 was not to be repeated), the British economy was caught in a low employment trap. Monetary policy was blocked by the gold standard and wages policy was blocked by the Trade Unions. It was at this time that Keynes began advocating controls on the export of capital, to improve the 'foreign balance' and thus enable interest rates to come down. The same kind of reasoning lay behind his advocacy of a tariff in 1930–31.

There was a muddle in all this which Keynes did not sort out till the early 1930s. At this point the transmission mechanism was from credit contraction to prices to unemployment. (Though in the *Economic Consequences of Mr. Churchill* (1925) and *Can Mr. Lloyd George Do It?* he had hinted at an alternative transmission mechanism from credit to output and employment, with price changes as the resultant of output changes.) Ralph Hawtrey confirmed this. He pointed out to Keynes in 1930 that 'If anything occurs to affect the demand for goods ... the first result is an increase or decrease of sales at *existing prices* ... There is always some interval of time before prices are adjusted ...'[27]

As a member of the Macmillan Committee in 1930 Keynes pressed the case for a loan-financed programme of public works. He used his familiar argument that business confidence was too low to allow full-employment investment at the prevailing interest rate. But he was trumped by Sir Richard Hopkins of the Treasury in a famous exchange. If business sentiment judged the programme unsound 'it is not itself a dynamic force towards a great renewal of activity and prosperity ... It might lead people to think ... it better to invest the next lot of money they had to invest [abroad].'[28] In other words, fiscal policies judged unsound could lead to psychological crowding-out. Keynes had no answer to this except to change businessmen's views of what was economically sound.

The same point came out in the Committee of Economists. This was appointed, with Keynes as chairman, by the Prime Minister, Ramsay MacDonald, on 24 July 1930, to enquire into 'the chief causes of our industrial position'. The inability of the economists to come up with an agreed diagnosis testifies to the disorder in contemporary theory. One of the Committee economists, Hubert Henderson, used the Ricardian equivalence theorem to attack the loan-financed public works which Keynes had been advocating. Keynes admitted that 'psychological factors and high taxation' had played a part in deterring investment, but said that much more important was the fact that interest rates were 50 per cent higher than prewar. 'Therefore I twist and turn about trying to find some reasonable means of permitting investment of a fairly sensible kind to take place in spite of its not yielding the current market rate of interest. The necessity for this is increased and not diminished by any deterrent effect on private effort which may result from high levels of taxation and of wages which are beyond remedy'. Henderson denied that 'wages were beyond remedy' and urged a curtailment of unemployment benefit. Robbins argued that Britain's unemployment problem was largely due to

[27] Ibid. 444–45.

[28] Macmillan Committee, Minutes of Evidence, 6500–24, 5650, 5654, 5684–6.

wage growth being in excess of productivity growth. Keynes riposted that most unemployment was due to the rise in sterling in 1924–25 having turned the terms of trade against Britain 'without this being compensated by a reduction of money wages...'

Keynes himself produced a terms of trade analysis of unemployment. Using the TM framework, he defined the 'equilibrium terms of trade' as those which prevail 'when the level of money wages at home relatively to money wages abroad is such that the amount of the foreign balance plus the amount of home investment at the rate of interest set by world conditions (ie. which just prevents gold movements) is ... equal to the amount of home savings ...' Keynes argued that the overvaluation of sterling in 1925 had worsened the equilibrium terms of trade. Britain could either *meet* the worsened equilibrium terms of trade by cutting money wages or *improve* them by reducing pressure to lend abroad (by a programme of loan-financed public works) or enlarging the foreign balance (through Protection). The first was ruled out on social grounds, the second would alarm business, so Keynes was left with the third as his most substantial proposal. The other economists added 'systematic reform of the whole system of unemployment insurance' and conceded that public works had a minor part to play 'if they are of a useful and productive character' (the revised Treasury view)[29].

Keynes was shaken enough by his colleagues' emphasis on supply-side rigidities to write in the *Nation* of 30 August 1930:

> 'The dominating factor in the whole business is, however, the failure of Britain's industrial system to adapt itself to the postwar world. This lack of adaptability, the outstanding characteristic of British economic life during the whole of the postwar decade, has manifested itself in a hundred ways ... the failure to carry out thoroughgoing rationalization ... rigid wage rates, immobility between trades and areas, severe Trade Union restrictions and regulations.'

But he basically believed that little could be done about these supply-side problems, hence his continued emphasis on monetary manipulation.

What would happen if the slump were allowed to run its course? Keynes argued before the Macmillan Committee that 'the continuation of the present state of affairs would in the end so impoverish the community that they would not have a sufficient margin of income to save, and when that had gone far enough we should find unemployment disappear'. The interesting point, in the light of Keynes's later theory of 'under-employment equilibrium' is that he thought that this low-income equilibrium would be a full-employment equilibrium. His idea was that as the machinery of production shrinks the unemployed find low-paid service jobs outside the industrial system – as 'gardeners and chauffeurs'[30]. However, this kind of rebalancing the economy, as well as being retrogressive, would clearly take a long time, so not unsurprisingly Keynes put it 'very low' on his list of remedies.

To the modern observer the absence of any proposal for the devaluation of sterling is the most striking omission in Keynes's proposed remedies for the British

[29] The debate is summarised in *Skidelsky*, vol. 2, 363–378.

[30] CW vol. 20, 127.

depression. Although he wrote to MacDonald on 2 August 1931 that 'it is now clearly *certain* that we shall go off the existing parity at no distant date', he back-tracked a few days later, telling the PM that 'it still probably lies within our power' to keep on the gold standard, and that he personally would support 'for the time being whichever policy was made, provided that the decision was accompanied by action sufficiently drastic to make it effective'. MacDonald took this to mean that Keynes was 'on side' for the defence of sterling[31]. There was nothing at this point in Keynes's theory to suggest that a defence of sterling based on a policy of wage reductions would not improve the economic situation. His objections to it were social. Perhaps an ingrained patriotism held him back for actually urging, or even positively wanting, devaluation. More important was Keynes's apprehension that a sterling devaluation would lead to currency wars.

Keynes's retrospective on the British problem was given in an article he wrote in April 1932:

> 'By the return to the gold standard in 1925, at an unsuitable parity, the Bank [of England] set itself a problem of adjustment so difficult as to be well-nigh impossible. On the one hand, it was obviously impracticable to enforce by high Bank rate or the contraction of credit a deflation sufficiently drastic to bring about a reduction in internal costs appropriate to the parity adopted. On the other hand, the maintenance of a low Bank rate, which would have rendered London unattractive to foreign short-term funds would, in the actual circumstances of our trade balance and readiness to lend abroad, have led to a rapid loss of gold by the Bank and a much earlier collapse of the gold standard ... The policy actually adopted was to preserve a middle course – with money dear enough to make London an attractive centre for short-term funds but not dear enough to force an adjustment of internal costs. In this way we tided over the immediate situation by exploiting London's immense reserves of credit and prestige. We were even able to continue lending abroad on a scale almost commensurate with our former strength, in spite of the increasingly adverse balance on account of current business. But the inevitable price of this temporary ease was the accumulation of a heavy burden of short-term liabilities ... Sooner or later, for good reasons or for bad, some loss of confidence might arise; and then ... the insecure structure had to tumble.'[32]

The Gold Standard

The impact of the American collapse on the financial positions of governments and banks and balance of payments positions of countries in Latin America and Europe was bound to bring about a collapse of the international gold standard, in the absence of US or concerted reflationary measures. But the way the gold standard worked in the 1920s was seen by Keynes as an independent source of deflationary pressure. Keynes's historical retrospect on this episode had to wait till 1941, when he was working out his plan for a post-war International Clearing Union, designed to re-establish a multilateral clearing system purged of the defects of the gold standard.

[31] *Skidelsky, Keynes,* vol. 2, 394; see also fn. 2, 672.
[32] CW, vol. 21, 68–69.

In a paper called 'Post-War Currency Policy', Keynes dismissed the classical theory of the gold standard. The flow of gold never did preserve equilibrium by adjusting relative price levels. Instead, Keynes claimed, there had been only two periods, each of about fifty years, when the use of commodity money in international trade had 'worked' – the silver inflation period of the 16th century and the gold standard of the late 19th century, when 'the system of international investment pivoting on London transferred the *onus* of adjustment from the debtor to the creditor nations'. But this experience showed that loans do not bring about a balanced position unless they create a new source of payments.

In theory the gold standard system provided for a symmetrical adjustment between surplus and deficit countries. In practice, adjustment was '*compulsory* for the debtor and *voluntary* for the creditor'. A creditor could always 'hoard' its surpluses. Keynes clearly had in mind the behaviour of the USA and France from 1928–29 onwards. But a debtor country could not readily adjust either. The theory of debtor adjustment ignored 'the lack of elasticity in the social structure of wages and prices' and the 'social strains' this imposed on a country trying to deflate its costs. Further, the debtor was generally a small country, least able to force its exports on the rest of the world by a one-sided change in the terms of trade. If the price of its exports had to be reduced to the same extent as their volume had to be increased the problem was insoluble. This may be taken to be a stylised account of the problems faced by Latin American countries in the late 1920s. 'Thus', Keynes wrote, 'it has been an inherent characteristic of the automatic metallic currency ... to force adjustments in the direction most disruptive to the social order, and to throw the burden on the countries least able to support it'.

The classical (or pre-first world war) system had mitigated these weaknesses by the system of foreign lending, but this had changed its character in the 1920s:

Up to 1914 the flow of capital funds had been directed from the creditor to the debtor countries, which broadly corresponded to the older and the newer countries, and served at the same time to keep the balance of international payments in equilibrium and to develop resources in undeveloped lands. In the first phase after the last war, the flow of fund continued to be directed from the creditor to the debtor countries, but a large part of the flow, namely from the United States (and also from Great Britain) into Europe ceased to correspond to the development of new resources. In the second phase ... complete degeneration set in and capital funds flowed from countries of which the balance of tade was adverse into countries where it was favourable.

This became, in the end, the major source of instability. If the favourable trade balance of the United States had been the only problem, the newly produced gold in the rest of the world would have been more than sufficient to discharge it. The flow of refugee and speculative funds superimposed on this brought the whole system to ruin ... Nothing is more certain than that the movement of capital funds must be regulated[33].

[33] CW, vol. 25, 27–31.

In short, the gold standard system lacked an adjustment mechanism. In the mid 1920s, the United States had stepped into Britain's position as the main supplier of foreign loans, though many of these had not created new resources for paying interest on, and repaying, debt. When the outward flow from the USA was reversed in 1928–29 and was followed by 'capital flight' from debtor countries in 1931, intolerable deflationary forces were unleashed which brought about a chain of defaults and caused the gold standard to collapse.

The main reason why Keynes resisted a unilateral British devaluation in 1931 was that he thought it would jeopardise the possibility of a reformed gold standard which might become the agent of worldwide reflation. The essential condition was to ensure that countries never had to deflate because of a shortage of gold. As a 'minimum' step towards a coordinated management of the gold standard, Keynes proposed that all central banks would be allowed to hold at least half of their legal reserve requirements in gold convertible currencies. But the 'ideal' arrangement would be to set up a supernational bank with which central banks would bank, which would have the power to create a fiduciary reserve asset (supernational bank money or SBM) which would count equally with gold as the legal reserves of the member banks. It would be able to lend SBM to the central banks of countries in balance of payments difficulties in proportion to their deposits of gold and securities. It would vary the quantity of SBM so as to stabilise its value in terms of a tabular standard of the major traded commodities and so to stabilise the world business cycle[34].

Schemes of this kind were rapidly overtaken by events. But the second world war gave them a new hearing and the Bretton Woods Agreement was the result.

Another Great Depression?

Is another Great Depression possible? This question was briefly asked after the East Asian financial crisis in 1997. It is now clear that there was no danger from this source. The economies concerned were too small for their collapses to have a major impact on the rest of the world, and (except for Indonesia) they are recovering.

But looking at the Great Depression of 1929–1932 through Keynes's eyes, one can see a number of disturbing similarities between then and now. As in the late 1920s, the United States is the only real locomotive of today's world economy, its insatiable consumption and investment demand sucking in imports of goods and capital from all round the world. The other major centres, the European Union and Japan, are stagnant. There is also the same attitude of hubris in the USA, built on the dynamic growth performance and stable prices of the 1990s.

[34] TM, CW vol. 6, 354–61.

A collapse of the United States economy could therefore trigger another major depression, via various transmission channels. There are two major weaknesses in the American position: Wall Street is overvalued and the US current account is heavily in the red. Certainly some of the same questions about the 'soundness' of American conditions can be asked today as Keynes and Hayek asked in the 1920s.

Keynes would be looking for an underlying weakness in effective demand; Hayek for the inflationary implications of a stable price level when inventions are making goods cheaper.

On the other hand, the major currencies are floating, not fixed. This provides an automatic adjustment mechanism lacking under the old gold standard, but also the possibility of heavy overshooting as capital funds are switched from falling to rising currencies.

Also, there are more governmental instruments available to deal with deflationary shocks. It is hardly conceivable that the US banking system would be allowed to collapse as it did in 1930–33. On the other hand expansionary Keynesian measures have not (so far) had much effect in Japan, and are officially abjured in the European Union.

The Great Depression of 1929–1933 was a result of a malign conjuncture of factors – a combination of events, ignorance, and lack of coordination, none of which, in isolation, would have brought the world economy crashing down. It is highly improbable that all would occur simultaneously today. Specifically, governments now know enough to break into the deflationary spiral at a much earlier point than happened in the 1930s. So while the newly globalised economy will be repeatedly 'shocked' by unexpected events, a second Great Depression would require a collective amnesia which is inconceivable.

Christoph Buchheim

The "Crisis Before the Crisis" – The Export Engine Out of Gear

It is common knowledge in economic history that there have been different phases of secular growth since the Industrial Revolution. The years from the outbreak of the First World War until the end of the Second on the one hand and those afterwards until the beginning of the seventies on the other provide a striking contrast. Whereas the first of these periods saw only very slow economic progress, the second comprised the so-called "Golden Age" of growth.

This paper mainly deals with a sub-period of the first, i.e. the twenties. Knut Borchardt once characterized the state of the German economy at that time as being "sick"[1]. However, it was not only Germany which then experienced a kind of continuous crisis. Britain was another case in point. In a way (Western) Europe as a whole already showed clear signs of sluggish development before the outbreak of the Great Depression. This being the case, it appears to be appropriate to look for a general cause. There might be a deeper reason for the economic problems for example in Germany and Britain than high labour costs or an obsolete capital stock. The proposition made here is that it was a weak dynamic of exports reflecting the lack of a liberal trading system which lay at the root of the problem.

Today the theory of catching-up is widely accepted as an explanation of the Golden Age. But it is clear that catch-up growth does not develop automatically if there is such a potential. Whether or not convergence will occur depends on the "social capability" of the follower countries. Moses Abramovitz identified the social capability of a country with its technical competence as well as its institutions[2]. Thus the social capability influences "the diffusion of knowledge, the rate of structural change, the accumulation of capital, and the expansion of demand", which among themselves determine the speed of catching-up[3]. Now, trade and export further each of the four factors listed. Trade in machinery is a most important means of the international diffusion of knowledge. Exports are, seen for each

[1] *K. Borchardt*, Constraints and Room for Manoeuvre in the Great Depression of the Early Thirties: Towards a Revision of the Received Historical Picture, in: *idem*, Perspectives on Modern German Economic History and Policy (Cambridge 1991) 157.
[2] *M. Abramovitz*, Catching Up, Forging Ahead, and Falling Behind, in: Journal of Economic History 46 (1986) 388.
[3] Ibid. 390.

country separately, an exogenous element of demand. An upswing of exports therefore normally induces new investment, which in turn leads to an increase of productivity. Exports and investment together greatly facilitate structural change. After 1945 world exports rose very quickly, and the share of exports in the gross national product of industrial countries multiplied. Therefore it is hardly surprising that post-war growth often is characterized as export-led. The growth potential offered by the possibility of catching-up was thus realized mainly through buoyant exports. Seen from this perspective it is astonishing that slow export growth in the interwar period often plays a much less conspicuous role in explanations for the poor performance of European economies.

The paper is organized in two parts. In the first the development of growth and exports after the First and after the Second World War is compared generally. In the second part the German case in the twenties will be analyzed in more detail. In conclusion some remarks will be made about the institutional setting of the world economy in both periods.

Growth and Exports

Catching-up growth occurs if more productive technologies used in a leading country are imitated by follower countries. Given the appropriate level of social capability this normally brings about convergence, because it seems to be more difficult and time-consuming to innovate and develop new technologies from scratch than to import and apply technologies which are already used successfully elsewhere. Therefore comparative productivity levels of leading and follower countries are a rough measure of the extent of potential catching-up growth.

Table 1: Average GDP per Manhour in Western Europe as percentage of U.S.

1913	1929	1938	1950	1973
64	61	60	50	73

Source: *A. Maddison,* Monitoring the World Economy 1820–1992 (Paris 1995) 249.

A big productivity gap between the United States and Western Europe[4] already existed before the First World War. However, in the next quarter of a century there was no catch-up growth. The contrary was the case, for in 1938 the gap was greater than in 1913. This clearly underlines the fact that convergence is not a necessary outcome even of quite large differences in productivity levels. After the Second World War a process of catching-up indeed developed. The gap was very much reduced in the quarter of a century after 1950. With regard to the interwar

[4] Throughout this paper "Western Europe" includes the following countries: Belgium, France, Germany, Italy, The Netherlands, Sweden, Switzerland, United Kingdom.

period, it is interesting that, according to the figures presented, the gap widened more before 1929 than after. The reason is that the U.S. economy grew much more vigorously than Western Europe before but not after the Great Depression[5]. Prima facie, this is plausible because the U.S. as a very large economy was much less dependent on exports than the smaller West European countries.

With regard to export performance, the First World War marks a turning point. Whereas real exports of West European countries rose by 3.4 per cent annually on average between 1899 and 1913, from then on to 1929 it was only 0.4 per cent. Manufactures had the biggest share in those exports. Manufactured exports grew with a rate of 4.0 per cent and 0.8 per cent respectively[6]. It is revealing to compare rates of growth of exports and social product per head before and after the War as is done in table 2.

Table 2: Growth of Total Exports and GDP per Capita (constant prices; % p. a.)

	1899–1913		1913–1929	
	Exports	GDP/capita	Exports	GDP/capita
France	2.7	1.3	0.8	1.9
Germany	5.6	1.6	−0.1	0.8
UK	1.8	0.5	0.0	0.3
Other Western Europe	3.9	2.0	1.2	1.5
U.S.	2.9	1.9	3.3	1.7

Sources: *A. Maizels*, Industrial Growth and World Trade (Cambridge 1965) 428–429; *A. Maddison*, Monitoring the World Economy 1820–1992 (Paris 1995) 104–107; 180–183, 194–197.

In all cases exports rose with a faster pace than living standards (GDP/capita) before the war[7]. After the war the reverse was true except for the U.S. Therefore, exports clearly were not an engine of growth in Europe after 1913. In the United States it was different especially with regard to manufactured exports which even increased by 5.8 per cent p.a. between 1913 and 1929 (1899–1913: 5.1 per cent), not least because overseas countries replaced European suppliers, which during the war could not deliver, by American, which could. West European countries themselves, however, were not such a good market for American manufactures, with export growth thereto being a third lower than in prewar years (1899–1913: 3.5 per cent p.a.). Together with the fact that manufactured exports of West European

[5] *A. Maddison*, Monitoring the World Economy 1820–1992 (Paris 1995) 196–197.

[6] *A. Maizels*, Industrial Growth and World Trade. An Empirical Study of Trends in Production, Consumption and Trade in Manufactures from 1899–1959 with a Discussion of Probable Future Trends (Cambridge 1965) 428–429; 432–433.

[7] This seems to have been true even before the turn of the century; compare for all countries included in table 2: *A. Maddison*, Dynamic Forces in Capitalist Development. A Long-Run Comparative View (Oxford 1991) 312–315 (volume of exports 1870–1899); *Maddison*, Monitoring the World Ecnomy, 194, 196 (GDP/capita 1870–1899).

countries to each other rose at only half the rate than those to other destinations this means that intra-industry trade in the twenties must have been especially weak[8]. And indeed the steeply rising tendency of manufactured imports in industrial countries from before the First World War was already interrupted or reversed in the twenties[9]. Only after the Second World War did it reemerge strongly, and then intra-industry trade between industrial countries proved to be the most dynamic element of world trade[10]. Three conclusions can be drawn from these observations:

1. As the growth of intra-industry trade heavily depends on a high degree of trade liberalization, the severe break in the upward development of this subdivision of world trade after 1913 clearly hints to much greater protectionism after the war than before[11].
2. The shrinking share of intra-industry trade in total trade meant lower competition from foreign suppliers in home markets of industrial countries. This must have been more damaging to the growth of productivity in the smaller countries of Western Europe than in the U.S. and therefore explains at least partly the lack of catching-up in the twenties.
3. Sharply rising intra-industry trade opened up worldwide markets to manufacturing enterprises of all industrial countries after the Second World War. It really was this kind of trade which made for export-led growth and thus reduced the pressure for the re-introduction of protectionist devices. On the other hand the lack of a similar dynamic of intra-industry trade could have been largely responsible for problems of overcapacity and low industrial investment in West European countries after the First World War.

In order to further substantiate these conclusions let us now compare the development of manufactured exports after the First and after the Second World War in some detail. To do this the years 1913, 1929, 1937, and 1955 are chosen, i. e. years for which Alfred Maizels has compiled comparable export figures from the trade statistics of industrial countries. The years mentioned generally were part of cyclical upswings, and in some cases they marked an upper turning point of the business cycle. 1913 and 1937 saw maxima of real world exports before the beginning of the respective wars. In 1929 the peak level of exports in the whole interwar period was reached[12]. The increase in exports between 1913 and 1929 therefore is a true measure of their dynamic in the twenties. The time span between 1913 and 1929 was about twelve years not counting the years of war. The same happens to be the case for the second pair of years (1937 and 1955). By comparing relative additions to manufactured exports between 1913 and 1929 and between 1937 and

[8] Intra-industry trade is very roughly defined here as exports and imports of manufactures between industrial countries themselves.
[9] *Maizels*, Industrial Growth and World Trade 156–157.
[10] GATT, International Trade 1954, 164–165; WTO, Annual Report 1998, 91, 158, 160.
[11] See the contribution of Forrest Capie in this volume.
[12] *Maddison*, Monitoring the World Economy 239.

1955 we therefore can make reliable statements about their different contributions to overall growth in the two postwar periods.

Table 3: Increase of Real Exports of Manufactures in Two Postwar Periods

	1913–1929	1937–1955
France	+ 32%	+ 167%
Germany	+ 7%	+ 62%
UK	– 7%	+ 66%
Other Western Europe	+ 59%	+ 75%
Total Western Europe	+ 14%	+ 77%
Among Western European Countries	+ 9%	+ 103%
Total Western Europe and North America	+ 36%	+ 83%
Among Western European and North American Countries	+ 28%	+ 116%

Source: *A. Maizels*, Industrial Growth and World Trade (Cambridge 1965) 432–433.

Table 3 fully confirms the above findings. Not only were manufactured exports, especially from West European countries, growing several times faster after the Second World War than in the twenties, but intra-industry trade among industrial countries which had risen still slower in the twenties quickened its pace even more than total manufactured exports after the War. That must have greatly contributed to full capacity utilization of West European economies in the fifties. Consequently investment ratios were much higher in those years than in the interwar period[13]. The rise in real national product in the second period was exactly double the increase in the first[14]. It appears plausible to suspect that this had a lot to do with the export surge.

The Case of Germany in the Twenties

The weakness of the economic development of the Weimar Republic led to low incomes from entrepreneurial activity[15]. Recently this observation has been persuasively confirmed by Mark Spoerer in his analysis of the profits of industrial joint stock companies. He showed that their equity yield was more than 8 per cent on average between 1886 and 1913, whereas from 1926 to 1929 it fell to 3.3 per cent[16]. Initially industrialists might have accepted low profits, "because they

[13] *Idem*, 76; see also *B. Eichengreen*, Mainsprings of Economic Recovery in Post-war Europe, in: *idem* (ed.), Europe's Post-war Recovery (Cambridge 1995) 11.
[14] *Maddison*, Monitoring the World Economy 180–183.
[15] *Borchardt*, Great Depression 156.
[16] *M. Spoerer*, Von Scheingewinnen zum Rüstungsboom. Die Eigenkapitalrentabilität der deutschen Industrieaktiengesellschaften 1925–1941 (Stuttgart 1996) 160.

judged this a temporary penalty which would disappear as export markets were regained and home demand returned to normal"[17]. Therefore they engaged in rationalization and expanded operations expecting a rise in profitability. In this context it is interesting that German industry managed to slightly reduce the productivity gap vis-a-vis the U.S. in the period 1925 to 1929[18]. And in fact, according to Spoerer, the equity yield also began climbing up from 0.2 per cent in 1925 to 4.2 per cent two years later. However, long before having attained the normal level of the pre-war years, it again fell to 3.3 per cent in 1928[19]. Now all hopes of industry for an imminent return to higher profitability were dashed and business pessimism surged. Fixed net investment of industry collapsed to 0.4 billion Reichsmark in 1929, i.e. 0.7 billion Reichsmark lower than one year earlier[20]. Entrepreneurs accused the state of greatly overburdening industry with costs. Industrial relations worsened appreciably, because fast growing wages were seen as the principal reason for the profit squeeze.

Whether or not the complaints of industry were borne out by reality has been a matter of debate in the so-called Borchardt-controversy. After a careful revision of the evidence Albrecht Ritschl concluded that real wages grew faster than productivity in the second half of the twenties compared to 1913, thus giving substance to the contemporary accusations of entrepreneurs and supporting Borchardt's opinion[21]. But if one also pays attention to the increase of the German terms of trade in the same years[22], the answer to the question of an undue wage pressure is less clear[23].

There is still more to be said about the case. This becomes obvious from an inspection of table 4:

[17] *T. Balderston*, The Origins and Course of the German Economic Crisis. November 1923 to May 1932 (Berlin 1993) 381.

[18] *S. N. Broadberry*, The Productivity Race. British Manufacturing in International Perspective, 1850–1990 (Cambridge 1997) 36.

[19] *Spoerer*, Scheingewinne 147.

[20] Statistisches Jahrbuch für das Deutsche Reich 1941/42, 610.

[21] *A. Ritschl*, Zu hohe Löhne in der Weimarer Republik? Eine Auseinandersetzung mit Holtferichs Berechnungen zur Lohnposition der Arbeiterschaft 1925–1932, in: Geschichte und Gesellschaft 16 (1990) 375–402; compare also *S. N. Broadberry, A. O. Ritschl*, The Iron Twenties: Real Wages, Productivity and the Lack of Prosperity in Britain and Germany Before the Great Depression, in: *C. Buchheim, M. Hutter, H. James* (eds.), Zerrissene Zwischenkriegszeit. Wirtschaftshistorische Beiträge. Knut Borchardt zum 65. Geburtstag (Baden-Baden 1994) 15–43. For Borchardt's original contention see *Borchardt*, Great Depression 154–157.

[22] *W. G. Hoffmann*, Das Wachstum der deutschen Wirtschaft seit der Mitte des 19. Jahrhunderts (Berlin 1965) 606–607; 612–615.

[23] See *R. Tilly, N. Huck*, Die deutsche Wirtschaft in der Krise, 1925 bis 1934, in: *Buchheim* et al. (eds.), Zerrissene Zwischenkriegszeit 50–53.

Table 4: Development of Costs in German Industry 1925 – 1929 (1913 = 100)

	1925	1926	1927	1928	1929
1. Productivity per man hour	89	98	106	105	110
2. Real hourly wages (deflated with cost of living index)	103	110	116	125	130
3. Real hourly wages (deflated with price index for manufactures)	101	110	113	123	132
4. Unit wage costs	113	112	107	117	120
5. Costs of material inputs relative to prices of manufactures	97	92	87	87	87
6. Unit variable costs relative to prices of manufactures	103	100	95	99	100

Sources: *A. Ritschl*, Zu hohe Löhne in der Weimarer Republik? In: Geschichte und Gesellschaft 16 (1990) 375–402; *T. Balderston*, The Origins and Course of the German Economic Crisis (Berlin 1993) 51; Statistisches Jahrbuch für das Deutsche Reich 1931, 262.

Lines 1 and 2 of the table reproduce Ritschl's figures. In line 3 a price index for manufactures instead of the index of living costs is taken for deflating nominal hourly wages, because from the perspective of industrial producers this seems more appropriate. If the price index for finished manufactures of the German Statistical Office[24] had been used for the calculation, the outcome would have been a lower level of real wages than shown in line 2. However, Theo Balderston's criticisms of the official index are accepted[25] and therefore the price index recalculated by him is taken in line 3. The not implausible result is that real wages in the later twenties behaved even more unfavourably from the viewpoint of entrepreneurs than is thought by Ritschl. Line 4 therefore is no surprise any more, signalling a continuous rise of wage costs from 1927 onwards, which obviously caused increasing business unrest. But what industrialists at the time ignored is that there was a balancing factor for the bigger wage costs. For input relative to output prices had apparently been declining since 1913, which can be seen in line 5 of the table. Here the official price index for raw materials and semi-finished products is used for the calculation. The fall in relative input prices was even greater for an index of raw material import unit values as employed by Balderston[26] – an indication of the high degree of cartelization in Germany which kept prices of homeproduced inputs higher. A rough index of unit variable costs combining wage costs and costs of input materials (without taxes and other contributions) is then constructed in line 6 assuming a ratio of its two elements of 2:3[27]. The result is clear: Variable

[24] Statistisches Jahrbuch für das Deutsche Reich 1931, 263.

[25] *Balderston*, Origins 50.

[26] Ibid. 55.

[27] The ratio of 2:1 used by *Balderston* in his calculation (Origins 55) seems far too high in the light of information supplied by the German Statistical Office. For example, the following ratios for single industries in 1928 can be calculated from information contained in "Stati-

costs of industry as defined had hardly changed in the second half of the twenties compared with the pre-war period. The inspection of wage costs alone therefore must lead to erroneous conclusions about the competitiveness of German industry before the Great Depression. In fact German manufactured exports were quite competitive on world markets, as Balderston has shown. Machinery exports of Germany for example quickly grew from their low after the stabilization, approaching their prewar share of world exports towards the end of the twenties[28].

If variable costs were not higher than in 1913 and the international competitiveness of the German industry not bad, why then were profits so much smaller in the twenties than before the war? The answer to this apparent paradox was low capacity utilization[29]. Thus the capacity utilization index of the "Institut für Konjunkturforschung" stood at 72 per cent in the second half of 1928[30]. Perhaps this figure derived from business reporting was overpessimistic, as Balderston is inclined to think[31]. Capacity utilization however continued to decline in 1929, whereas in 1925 it still was 76 per cent[32]. Rationalization after 1925 had obviously led to a further lowering of capacity utilization, possibly also aggravated by widespread cartelization. Anyway, it seems certain that capacity utilization towards the end of the twenties was poorer than in 1913. That can also be seen from machine-building, where capacity utilization apparently was more than 20 per cent below prewar levels in 1928[33]. Thus we arrive at the interesting fact that high competitiveness leading to a rising share of world exports in the later twenties was not sufficient for a satisfactory utilization of given capacity in the machinery industry. There, as well as in other branches of industry, lack of demand appears to have been the fundamental problem resulting in low profits. Not high variable costs because of wage pressure therefore were the primary reason for sharply reduced profitability, but much increased fixed costs per unit of production as a consequence of bad capacity utilization. Incidentally this might also explain why the productivity level attained by industry at the end of the twenties was only about

stisches Jahrbuch für das Deutsche Reich", various editions, and in "Vierteljahrshefte zur Statistik des Deutschen Reichs":

Table: Wages and Salaries as Percentage of Value of Material Inputs

Machinery industry	88	Cotton spinning	19
Iron and Steel	67	Tyre production	18
Knitting industry	46	Leather production	13
Production of cars	32	Soap industry	13
Clothing industry	24	Margarine industry	5

28 *Balderston*, Origins 83–128, esp. 111.

29 Svennilson mentions excess capacity, aggravated by collusion, as a serious problem in the industry of Europe as a whole; see *I. Svennilson*, Growth and Stagnation in the European Economy (Geneva 1954) 48–49.

30 Konjunkturstatistisches Handbuch 1936, 17.

31 *Balderston*, Origins 366.

32 *A. F. Mester*, Eine Zeitreihe der Ausnutzung des Sachkapitals (1925 bis 1938 und 1950 bis 1957), in: IFO-Studien 7 (1961) 81.

33 *Balderston*, Origins 370.

10 per cent higher than in 1913 which otherwise might call into question the effectiveness of the rationalization movement[34].

It is ironical that the literature refers to undue wage pressure as an important cause of the weak economic performance in the Weimar Republic on the one hand and to wage moderation having supported growth in the Federal Republic of the fifties[35] on the other, although the increase in wages was even slightly higher between 1950 and 1955 than between 1925 and 1930[36]. Strike activity in the first half of the fifties also was more widespread than later[37]. And, as has recently been confirmed, "the rhetoric of the unions and the counter-rhetoric of business and the liberal press were by no means moderate throughout."[38] The real difference of the two periods did not lie in the trend of wage growth but in the trends of capacity utilization and thus productivity growth and investment. These proved to be far higher after the Second World War, although in the twenties there already was ample scope for catch-up growth. However, lack of demand prevented its implementation after the First World War, which was, by the way, quite a popular explanation of low growth at the time. But the solution could obviously not have been even higher wages. Instead a much more dynamical growth of world trade would have led to the exogenous rise of demand for German manufactures, which was so urgently needed at the time. In this way it would have been possible to set into motion the virtuous circle of export-led growth already in the twenties, which finally did the job after the Second World War.

Concluding Remarks

It was protectionism of all sorts which brought the export engine out of gear after the First World War. For some time after the Second World War, however, protectionism was also flourishing – on a still higher level. In the interwar period the League of Nations tried to tackle the problem. Several world economic conferences passed sounding resolutions, but to hardly any avail. Why then was the situ-

[34] As is indeed done in *H. James*, The German Slump. Politics and Economics 1924–1936 (Oxford 1986) 146–155.

[35] See e.g. *B. Eichengreen*, Institutions and Economic Growth: Europe After World War II, in: *N. Crafts, G. Toniolo* (eds.), Economic Growth in Europe Since 1945 (Cambridge 1996) 45–46.

[36] Statistisches Jahrbuch für die Bundesrepublik Deutschland 1990, 502, 548.

[37] *J. Frerich, M. Frey*, Handbuch der Geschichte der Sozialpolitik in Deutschland, Bd. 3 (München [2]1996) 96.

[38] *H. Giersch, K.-H. Paqué, H. Schmieding*, The Fading Miracle. Four Decades of Market Economy in Germany (Cambridge 1992) 76; see also *K.-H. Paqué*, How Cooperative was the Spirit? A Note on the "Eichengreen-View" of Europe After World War II (Kiel Working Papers 701, Kiel 1995). The union rhetoric, however, might have been more frightful for entrepreneurs in the Weimar Republic in the context of state arbitration; compare *C. Zahn*, Arbeitskosten und Lebenslagen zwischen Inflation und Großer Krise. Zur Geschichte der Weimarer Lohnbewegung (St. Katharinen 1996).

ation after 1945 different? Why could protectionism then effectively be reduced and a liberal international trading system be established in the course of time?

A modern conceptualization of their possible role in the process of growth says that international organizations function as commitment mechanisms solving the problem of adherence to a code of good conduct by all involved[39]. The above questions can be reformulated to suit this theoretical framework: Why did the League of Nations or any of its sub-organizations fail to develop such a commitment mechanism in order to insure coordinated reductions of protectionism in the twenties, whereas after the Second World War exactly that could be done through OEEC and GATT? The fundamental problem therefore is how organizations fulfilling their role as efficient commitment mechanisms came into being, because obviously not every international organization does so.

A liberal and multilateral world trading system is clearly a kind of public good, which can only be attained by collective action. According to Mancur Olson, the incentive of each actor to commit himself to the achievement of such a good is very small. This is true even if he is a member of an organization with that purpose. But the situation is very different if there exists a dominant member with the same aim within the organization. In case of such a benevolent hegemony means will be made available by the strong member to bring about the coordinated action by the others necessary for the attainment of the public good.

This is the fundamental difference between the interwar and the post-war period. In the former, the United States as the dominant country was not very much interested in a liberal trading system. It abstained from the League of Nations and unleashed a spiral of protectionism. Then, however, the U.S. changed from being Saul to Paul. The first step in the new direction was the Reciprocal Trade Agreements Act of 1934. In the forties the U.S. repeatedly asked its allies for pledges to multilateralism – in the Atlantic Charter and in the Lend-Lease-Agreements. After the end of the second war it resolutely engaged in the erection of such a system. By the provision of special favours the U.S. finally secured the compliance of its partners with this course of action. In the first GATT negotiations, for instance, the Americans offered big tariff cuts against rather small and ineffective concessions by the others. The liberalization of intra-European trade and payments was achieved by the U.S. using Marshall Plan dollars as a carrot[40]. In this way the process of reducing protectionism was set into motion, the U.S. initially employing its hegemony to the advantage of its partners. In the end, however, all profited by the establishment of a free system of world trade thus achieved. The Europeans could exploit the potential for catch-up through export-led growth. But the American economy also grew with a higher rate than in the interwar period.

[39] *Eichengreen*, Mainsprings 5–7.

[40] Compare *C. Buchheim*, Die Wiedereingliederung Westdeutschlands in die Weltwirtschaft 1945–1958 (München 1990) 99–107.

Forrest Capie

The International Depression and Trade Protection in the 1930s

Trade protection seldom if ever disappears, but it reached one of its high points in the two decades between the two World Wars. It had been on the increase in the late nineteenth century when it was one manifestation of the spreading nationalism that characterised the period. The First World War did not resolve the problems of the world economy – indeed in some important respects it aggravated them. New nations were born, old differences remained, and international distrust intensified in the 1920s and 1930s. Rising protectionism accompanied the suspicion and distrust and resulted in the worsening of the intense nationalism that lay behind the First World War. The Americans set the pace with the Fordney-McCumber tariff of 1922 and other countries quickly followed suit. The Americans imposed further "skyscraper" tariffs with the Smoot-Hawley tariff legislation of 1930. When, in 1932, the British abandoned the free trade policies that they had held to for close to a century the curtain had finally come down. Fascism with its emphasis on self-sufficiency and its bilateral trading philosophy emerged in Europe, and as some see it the Second World War was not so much second, as the continuation of the First World War after an interlude full of tension. This unhappy experience of the interwar years with its associated depression made the allied countries determined to lay the foundations for a better, more secure and more prosperous world when the Second World War was over.

Our focus here, however, is on outlining in general what happened to trade protection between the wars. Facts do not tell their own story. "Letting the facts speak for themselves", is an empty cliché. Facts need to be evaluated in the light of theory. Werner Sombart expressed it neatly when he wrote, "Facts are like beads: they require a string to hold them together, to connect them. But if there is no string, no unifying idea, then even the most distinguished authorities cannot help producing unsatisfactory work." (1929, p. 5) Many economic historians accept this wholeheartedly and have become accustomed to employing explicit models in their work. Disagreements do arise over this approach but there is no escaping that theory is necessary at some level. In practice it may only be the basic theory that can ever be applied. Basic theory is what is needed to capture the essence of the issue. This paper, while largely descriptive, does nevertheless operate within an implicit theoretical framework and makes some use of explicit theory when it comes to considering the domestic impact of the tariff in Britain in the 1930s. It is of course vital to hold on to the basic facts; otherwise there is the danger of making remarks such as have appeared in a recent monograph that "The British simply would not accept the free trade doctrine" (Zeiler, p. 24) or "Free trade frightened the British" (p. 39).

In the first section we provide some indication of the types of protectionist measures employed in the period, and indicate how difficult it is to make quantitative estimates of impact. Section II outlines some of the appropriate international context including something of the mood of the time and the spread of protectionist sentiment and policies from the First World War onwards. Britain had been the prime advocate of free trade for close to a century but was not immune to the spreading protectionist forces. Section III indicates briefly how that change in policy came about. Section IV shows what the domestic impact in Britain was, and hints too at some international impact.

I.

On a similar theme on a previous occasion in Germany, when I argued that measuring protection was extremely difficult and, following Viner, that trying to quantify its impact was positively treacherous, Wolfram Fischer took me to task. He cited a number of studies on the impact of tariffs in a number of countries. At different times I have contributed to these calculations (on Europe in the nineteenth century and for Britain between the wars) but remain convinced that quantification is indeed treacherous – necessary perhaps but still treacherous.

Calculating the impact of protection is treacherous but calculating the impact of tariffs may well be the least treacherous part of any such exercise. There were many other protectionist devices that were much more difficult to assess. There were for instance quotas on an extensive range of goods, and while in theory they have a tariff equivalent, in practice many more data are required and a knowledge of parameters such as demand and supply elasticities; and any hope of estimation to any degree of accuracy begins to drift away.

There were also invisible barriers to trade on a huge scale. It is seldom easy to agree on what exactly constitutes an invisible barrier never mind measuring it (though again I was once involved in just such an exercise) given that they often take the form of safety or health regulations or some such. These barriers covered the whole spectrum too across industry, agriculture, and services. One example from Britain can suffice to illustrate. In the late 1920s there was an outbreak of a serious cattle disease in England. It was said to have originated in Argentina (the major foreign supplier of beef and competitor for empire suppliers). The strictest hygiene regulations were then imposed on the killing conditions in Argentina such that many producers were deterred from trying to comply and there was a great movement out of pastoral and into arable farming. (That of course can be achieved almost overnight but it takes some years to move back the other way.)

As a result of these measures Argentine's exports of meat to Britain dropped sharply in the late 1920s. But there were further and considerable knock-on effects of this. When British Empire countries met at Ottawa in the summer of 1932 to consider responses to the world wide depression one outcome was to produce policies which favoured Empire producers ahead of foreign producers. Quotas were then imposed on meat suppliers (meat was incidentally Britain's largest single import next to oil). These quotas were based on the three years immediately before the Ottawa year – the very years when Argentine's (the largest single supplier of meat) exports were at their lowest. Thus Argentina was damaged much further on top of the measures which most believe were based on a spurious reading of the evidence. This is just one illustration from a multitude. Trying to measure this protection is surely impossible and without measurement there can be little assessment of impact.

The principal legacy of the Ottawa meetings was, however, the extensive range of concessions extended to empire countries – imperial preference. The general principle at Ottawa was: Britain first, empire second, foreigners last. The main beneficiaries were of course primary producers which is what most of the empire was (though there were some exceptions such as cars from Canada – moved across the borders from Detroit), but the system angered many trading partners. Not least was the biggest trading partner of all, the U.S. Secretary of State Cordell Hull said the Ottawa Agreements represented, "the greatest injury, in a commercial way, that has been inflicted on this country since I have been in public life" (Quoted by Ikenberry, p. 170). Hull believed that the trading blocs centred on Britain, Germany, and Japan "were the root cause of the instability of the period and the onset of war" (ibid.). There is no doubt Ottawa poisoned relations between Britain and America, the two countries who might have been able to redirect commercial policy in the period.

An even more difficult device to measure and to assess the impact of, is that of exchange controls – something that most countries adopted in one form or another in the 1930s. This device was usually presented as a means of curbing excessive capital flows associated with financial crises at the beginning of the decade. Bilateral trading agreements also distorted and damaged trade. These took different forms ranging from barter (e.g. of German coal for Brazilian coffee), through clearing agreements, which some have argued Germany exploited effectively to borrow from poor neighbours, and on to payment agreements of which the Anglo-German agreement of 1934 was generally regarded as the model.

Between 1932 and 1937 Germany signed clearing agreements with every European country except Britain in the far north and Albania in the far south; and there were agreements with other countries farther afield. These agreements covered visible and invisible trade. More than half Germany's foreign trade was covered by such agreements. Germany was able to exploit its position as the major market for many of those countries – especially those of eastern and central Europe. For example if a country had a current account surplus with Germany then payments out of the clearing fund were greater than those flowing in. But with such a country's currency limited its exporters would have to await payment – in effect Germany borrowing from what were invariably much poorer countries.

It would surely be agreed that the proliferation of all these measures resulted in huge distortions to economies and serious misallocation of resources. In order to get some idea of just one element in all this – the tariff – we could simply look at the ratio of import duties collected to total imports. This is accepted by many in the field as a reasonable proxy for the changing degree of protection arising from this particular instrument. When this is done what unsurprisingly emerges is that for a whole host of countries there was a huge jump in protection in the late 1920s and early 1930s. And that is to judge from just one of the many measures used. In spite of all the difficulties mentioned there is surely still room to form judgements on both the scale and the direction of the impact even if no numbers can be attached.

II.

In the years between the two world wars the international economy was in considerable turmoil. A variety of problems dogged the immediate post-war recovery of many countries and severely hampered the progress of international economic relations. That in turn led to further problems or at minimum exacerbated problems within and between countries. A principal legacy of financing the great war was differential inflation rates and price levels in 1919/20 and hence exchange-rate problems. There had also been soaring domestic and international debt and diminished resources with which to service the debt. Domestic production and international trade patterns were badly disrupted. And added to all this was the burden of reparation payments for some and the difficulties of transfer for others.

Worse, there was no agreement internationally on what needed to be done to resolve many of the problems. The U.S. has sometimes been found culpable for failing to take up the role of international leader that Britain had held before 1914 but was in no position to continue to carry on with after 1920. The U.S. was regarded as becoming isolationist after WWI and regretting its involvement in what it regarded as a European problem. Whether or not that is fair or too simple, the U.S. did refuse to join the League of Nations which was one kind of signal. She certainly declined to take up the role of international leader. But worst of all from the point of view of international trade was the almost immediate adoption of new protectionist measures. Since in 1920 the U.S. was the biggest, richest, and least war-damaged economy in the world, these were the worst kind of signals to send to a world that urgently needed the opposite by way of example and encouragement.

When President Harding took office in 1921 he asked Congress for emergency tariff legislation. "I believe in the protection of American industry... and it is our purpose to prosper America first." (quoted in Eckes, 1998) In 1921 the U.S. introduced an Emergency Tariff Act, largely as a defensive measure against Europeans who showed signs of increasing protection. The Emergency Act was the forerunner to the Fordney-McCumber legislation that was passed in September 1922. That introduced tariffs that resulted in the average rate on dutiable imports being raised by almost 50 per cent from 26.8 per cent (already high by international standards) to 38.2 per cent or from 9 per cent to 14 per cent on total imports. Attempts at measuring the impact of this addition to the American tariff have proved notoriously difficult (see Falkus). These measures contributed to making it impossible for many debtor countries to earn the dollars they needed to make interest payments on their debt.

Protection quickly developed in another group of countries too – those that were deprived of European manufactures during the war years. They had developed their own substitute products. But when world manufacturing production began to get re-established these countries sought to protect their own new products. Further, the creation of new states in Europe increased the tariff frontiers by some 12.000 miles, as these new countries also sought to protect their own industry. Old countries were not immune. Many raised their tariffs on both industrial and agricultural goods. Primary producers were not to be left out and sought to protect their new industries on the one hand, and on the other their agriculture against the deteriorating terms of trade that it faced. An element in almost all of these cases was that tariffs would provide bargaining power in anticipated trade negotiations.

Such was the move to protection in the decade after the war that there were almost universal increases in tariff levels as the figures in the Table I show:

Table I: Tariff levels in 1913 and 1931

	1913	1931
Germany	16.7	40.7
France	23.6	38.0
Italy	24.8	48.3
Austria	22.8	36.0
Czechoslovakia	22.8	50.0
Hungary	22.8	45.0
Spain	37.0	68.5
United States	41.0	53.0

Source: Liepman, 1938, p. 415; Humphrey, 1955, p. 74.
Reproduced in fuller form in Conybeare, 1987, p. 236

The League of Nations was impotent in the face of such determined action by individual countries. World economic conferences were organised by the League in 1927, 1929, and 1930. These were all quite realistic in their ambitions, aiming to get rid of non-tariff barriers to trade and preventing any further increases in tariff levels. They all failed. Leaders invariably came away from the conferences making high-sounding statements and all in apparent agreement with one another on the need to bring about increased free trade. But they returned to their countries unable to resist the political pressures that awaited them. In 1933 at yet another world economic conference, held in London, an attempt at a tariff truce was made but failed.

The situation had worsened considerably between 1929 and 1933. In 1929 two Congressmen by the names of Smoot and Hawley channelled the growing pressure for protection in the U.S. and saw through the Bill that took their names, to the Smoot-Hawley Act of 1930. That Act contained the highest rates of duty in American history, though it was based on a relatively small range of goods. In terms of domestic impact this is another example of a case of protection where the assessments made are generally reckoned to have been small though it did contribute to the depression. The domestic impact was certainly of less significance than might have been expected from the attention it attracted at the time and from the amount that has been written about it since.

But there is surely no mistaking the international impact it had. When the leading economy in the world took such action it was seen as another indication of the breakdown in international trading relations. According to one of America's leading international economists, Richard Cooper, "the most dangerous single mistake any American president has made in international relations was Herbert Hoover's signing of the Hawley-Smoot Tariff Act into law in June 1930 ... The seeds of the Second World War both in the Far East and in Europe, were sown by Hoover's signing ...". (p. 291, 292) It certainly seems to have provoked a serious outbreak of retaliation even if the extent is still debated. The Japanese raised their tariffs in response. Italy boycotted U.S. goods and raised their tariffs in 1930 and 1931. The French did likewise. "... the French minister of commerce publicly declared that retaliation was the current basis of French trade policy." (Bailey, 1932, p. 96) In 1930 almost every trading country imposed quotas. Britain too was guilty. Apart from introducing the tariff in 1932 they implemented a number of quotas and other devices and turned increasingly to Empire. Other countries took exception in particular to these British measures and retaliated with similar measures. Germany was particularly aggrieved at the actions of both the Americans and the British and felt that she had been singled out and was being discriminated against in its trade. There were many claims at the time that the unemployment that this brought in Germany at minimum eased the way for Hitler coming to power.

But by 1933 it was too late for another conference to do anything about the deteriorating conditions. World trade had by that time collapsed and many countries were at the bottom of one of the worst economic depressions in their history. World trade fell from a base of 100 in 1929 to a level of 35 in 1933 and even further to 28 in 1935. It barely rose above that for the rest of the decade. Protectionism was responsible in good part for this collapse though of course it was inextricably bound up with the depression to which it had contributed.

By 1935 70 per cent of the world trading system was subject to bilateral balancing of some type of *non-tariff* barriers. When the extent of tariff barriers is added to this the huge scale of protection in the world can be readily appreciated.

III.

The return to protectionist trade policies in Britain after almost a century of commitment to free trade was a major source of concern in the world economy in the middle of the great depression. What led Britain to adopt such a policy, one that had had no place in British economic life for so long? This is a question that has long been debated, with a variety of answers given. These answers chiefly take the following forms. It was a desperate measure in the face of one of the worst economic depressions in history. Some find that too strong and suggest that the forces working for protection had been gaining strength in the 1920s, indeed from as early as the First World War. According to this latter account the return to protection was likely even without the depression of 1929–32. The third explanation emphasises the longer term. It draws on the fact that there are always groups who benefit from protection and where they can acquire power they are likely to encourage protectionism and adopt protectionist measures.

Britain's adoption of free trade, as was noted above, came in the first half of the nineteenth century when Britain was the dominant industrial power. British textile manufacturers were enthusiastic free traders so long as they had a virtual monopoly. That way they could delay the rise of foreign competition. Their views on free trade did not extend to machinery since the free movement of machinery would weaken their monopoly position. For roughly a quarter of a century from the repeal of the Corn Laws in 1846 free trade reigned supreme in Britain.

As the nineteenth century progressed and British dominance was more and more encroached upon, the sound of free traders began to wane and the jingle of protectionists could be heard more frequently. Just as theory predicts, there were increasingly cries from those who suffered competition and a number of organised attempts were made at reversing free trade policy.

It is difficult to prove that a build up of pressure was leading inexorably to the adoption of protection but there is considerable suggestive evidence. So at the outbreak of the First World War Britain remained firmly attached to the free trade doctrine, having come through years of increasing international competition and some industrial recession and growing protectionist pressure without really wavering on the policy.

According to some the implementation of protectionist legislation in 1931/32 should be seen as the culmination of a movement that was gaining strength from at least the 1923 election, an election that was fought on the issue of protection. It takes little effort to push that date back to the First World War. The Safeguarding of Industries Act passed in 1921, which allowed for a long list of items to be given protection even if the value of goods affected was quite low, was a victory for protection. British industries became increasingly protectionist in outlook. In 1923 the Conservatives were seeking re-election, and the election of that year can be said to have been contested very largely on the issue of protection. There was some backing from some of British industry.

This came immediately after one of the worst economic recessions in British history, 1920–21. But the electorate rejected protection and voted in the first ever Labour Government. The Conservatives regained power a year later and thereafter the iron and steel industry persistently sought protection throughout the rest of the 1920s. Most of the NFISM's executive committee and the director, Sir William Larke, were enthusiastic tariff reformers, and in early 1926 they gave their support to a sub-section of the industry, wire, when it made an independent application. But this application was rejected on the same grounds. The main application was renewed in 1927, but again it was turned down by reference to the original decision.

In 1928 the Iron and Steel Confederation tried a slightly different approach by asking the government to set up a committee to investigate competition in the home market. The industry argued that protection would allow them full capacity utilisation and economies of scale such as to allow lower prices. But much of British industry remained understandably sceptical of this argument, and feared that the price of their inputs would in fact rise.

There is no doubt Parliament had become increasingly influenced by businessmen (as opposed to landowners or the professions). According to one account, between 1919 and 1939 on average one-third of the Conservative Party in the Commons were employers or managers. It would be dangerous to draw conclusions too rapidly from a simple count of heads, bearing in mind the diversity of motives that take people into Parliament and conscious too that numbers alone do not accurately reflect the strength of respective groupings. But clearly the larger the numbers were, the greater was the chance that business interests were represented and the higher the probability that business demands would be heard, that numbers could be found for support and so on. Business groups had been accustomed to organising themselves for specific objectives for a long time and had a focus in the Chambers of Commerce.

Business organisations had been formed in the First World War with a view to defending business interests. Many of them were direct descendants of the pre-war tariff movements, but others were the product of new concerns raised by war. In January 1915, soon after the outbreak of war, a Unionist Business Committee was formed in the House of Commons to protect the interest of business in time of war. A high point of business pressure for protection came with the publication of a tariff scheme adopted by the London Chamber of Commerce on 25 May 1916. The Federation of British Industries (FBI) formed in 1916 was protectionist in outlook. In 1916 the British Commonwealth Union was established 'to form a solid business group in Parliament' and a fundamental element of this programme was tariff reform, and it was linked with Empire interests.

The foundations were laid in wartime and in the deep recession of 1921 the Conservatives exploited the collapse in trade for their protectionist ends. A powerful deputation from the National Union of Manufacturers (NUM) visited Baldwin, then President of the Board of Trade, urging prompt action. Baldwin agreed. The Safeguarding of Industries Bill soon followed, being introduced on

2 June 1921. It had no difficulty in its passage through Parliament and became law on 1 October. It was a clear case of the result of pressure.

A powerful pressure group evolved in Britain in the second half of the twenties. It was the Empire Industries Association, founded in 1924. It provided apparent concern for Empire with the need to protect against foreigners, and was thus ideally equipped for the particular problem of the time. It was to play an important part in advancing the protectionist case, and according to some view it gave the decisive thrust to that case.

Others see protection as a crisis measure brought about by the need to respond to the deep economic recession. The recession in Britain was not in fact deep. However, what was striking in 1930 and 1931 was the great rise in unemployment. Unemployment is sometimes, erroneously, used as a measure of economic activity. It is erroneous because while it may on occasions proxy output it certainly does not always do so and it can be affected by a number of other factors. Erroneous or not, as a measure of depression unemployment was still a fact to which politicians had to respond. A favourite response has always been that the blame must lie with foreigners, and demands for protection have arisen in these circumstances. This was the kind of mood that was being exploited by some in 1931.

A National Government, but one dominated by the protectionist Conservatives, came to power in the Autumn of 1931 and immediately found an excuse for introducing very high tariffs. They claimed that the scale of imports in October of that year were such as to constitute dumping and something must be done about them. In fact the evidence was slender to say the least. They compared manufactured imports coming into the ports of London and Harwich in October 1931 and the first few days of November with those of the corresponding period in 1930. There was not much difference for October but the early part of November did show an increase. On the strength of this the Abnormal Importation (Customs Duties) Bill was introduced in Parliament on 16th November and came into force on the 25th November. Duties of 100 per cent were permitted since the Act was designed not to tax but to prevent goods coming in.

There was no good evidence of dumping. There are difficulties in defining and observing dumping. Long-term dumping below the cost of production was unlikely given the risks. Short-term dumping, either of a sporadic or predatory type was always possible and it was this latter that was feared in late 1931. The second point is that while for some items there was a rise in imports at a time when world trade was collapsing, the likelihood is that the explanation lies in importers acting to beat the widely rumoured imposition of a tariff. Furthermore, there was a depreciation of sterling in the months following the severing of the link with gold. A third point is that the pattern of imports was often similar between products where one was expected to be protected and the other was not. In short the supposed abnormal imports did not exist. The operation was simply an excuse to dramatise the Government's concern and pave the way for the introduction of the General Tariff which was implemented in April 1932.

The return to protection in Britain after almost eighty years can therefore be seen as a triumph for the business pressure that had its origins in the years before 1914 and whose real foundations are found in the First World War. Thereafter the pressure built up steadily throughout the twenties. The performance of the economy between 1929 and 1932 was not the real cause. Unemployment was exploited, and spurious dumping concocted to pave the way for the protectionist measures the Conservatives had long favoured.

IV.

Following the war exchange rates were out of alignment after differential price experience in the years 1914–20. And there were problems of war debt and reparations. New nation states were born in the aftermath of the war and more protectionism and nationalism accompanied that. All of these factors meant that trading patterns were greatly changed. Further, since there were great technological advances in the war years it is not reasonable simply to look at pre-war patterns and make comparisons based on these, for the post-war world. Products had changed and comparative advantage had shifted. Many of these problems led directly or indirectly to the great depression that afflicted many countries in the years 1929–33. And all of this makes it that much more difficult to capture the effects of the tariff. For example the basic question: how much were imports reduced by as a result of a tariff, requires a knowledge of price elasticity's. But on what data could these reasonably be estimated given what has been said?

But we turn here to some indication of the impact of the tariff in Britain. The British economy grew faster in the 1930s than at any time in the previous half century. The correct way to measure growth is from one peak in the cycle to the next, in this case from 1929–37. Over that period the economy grew at more than 2 per cent per annum. That was faster than in the 1920s (1924–29) which in turn was better than anything since the 1870s. The depression of 1929–32 in Britain was not severe, not as deep as that of 1920–21, and mild compared with most other countries. That partly accounts for the good performance over the whole cycle. But more important was the very strong upswing of 1932–37, one of the strongest in British economic history. The economy grew by 24 per cent in that short period.

What lay behind this remarkable growth? The tariff and some other protectionist measures were introduced in 1932 and many have been content to argue *post hoc ergo propter hoc*, that it was protection that was responsible. The main objection to this is that a whole host of other factors might equally contend for that position. This was a time when a great deal was heard about managing the economy. A number of policies were introduced and as usual there were some exogenous factors that also operated. Where the whole explanation lies is not easy to determine, and this is not the place to pursue it. Our purpose here is to consider the part that the tariff might have played.

Some early assessments of the tariffs, which relied on rather casual investigations, found favourably. Some attributed the fall in imports directly to the tariff. Khan claimed that imports of manufacturers were reduced by 60 per cent inside eighteen months. Arthur Lewis felt that the tariff was too low to be of much use. Benham, one of the most distinguished contemporary investigators believed that the way in which the tariff assisted recovery was by stimulating investment in iron and steel. This is of particular interest in view of some specific results that we shall turn to in this section. Finally, in a lengthier study Richardson concluded that, "the effects of the general tariff were not very significant" (1967, p. 408).

One development in trade theory in the 1960s / 70s offered an explicit formulation of what had been implicitly appreciated by producers and economists alike, on the impact of tariffs and that was what was called effective protection. We use that here before referring to some different approaches to investigations of the impact of tariffs at this time.

Effective protection has become a useful way of looking at the impact of tariffs both within an economy and when making international comparisons. It is particularly useful for looking at the likely impact of protection on resource flows – those industries getting the greatest amount of effective protection should attract more resources than those beneath them in the list. It is important to be clear that there are many problems in the calculation of effective rates. There are problems relating to the assumptions and there are problems of data. However, if effective rates can be provided for a reasonable coverage of British industry and ranked in order of the effective protection given, it becomes possible to talk in general terms about the likely impact. Effective rates calculated for British industry for this period allow something to be said about the likely impact of the tariff and its contribution to economic growth.

The effective rates of protection range in the main between 40 and 60 per cent and that is not surprising since they are typically of the order of twice the size of the nominal tariff. But although that is the range there are some that lie well outside the range and those are of particular interest because of the nature of the industries involved.

One case that is of considerable interest is the construction sector. It was the biggest sector of all, and almost twice the size of the next largest sector, iron and steel manufacturing. Much of the credit for the beginning of recovery in the early 1930s has been given to construction, particularly residential building. (A huge proportion of interwar semi-detached houses date from 1932 as does a great deal of commercial property.) For example Benham writing some few years after the depression, and later Richardson in one of the most thorough historical studies, have credited the building industry with the crucial contribution to the recovery. Most historians of the period since then have not disputed this judgement.

The great expansion in building rested on a large number of factors on both the demand and supply side. There were demographic factors that meant a growing population of house buying age and this coupled with rising real incomes for the great bulk of the population. Real wages had in fact risen quite steeply through the depression years since money wages were relatively sticky but prices fell quite sharply. Supporting the demand side there was an important institutional factor and that was the availability of finance from the building societies at relatively modest interest rates. Mortgage finance was a growing area in the inter-war years and building societies prospered enormously. Thus there is no difficulty in accepting that the size of construction was such as to make whatever happened there important. There will always be questions raised about precise timing, but the evidence is persuasive that this sector did provide the initial boost to recovery, and thereafter it contributed greatly to the strong upswing in the rest of the decade.

Having said all that what is of interest is that the effective rate of protection for this sector is negative. This is not a controversial result. It comes about because the final product is not tradable but many of the inputs into building were tradable. So the final product, housing, had no tariff on it but importable inputs which made up 42 per cent of the final product had tariffs on them – slates, glass, woodwork, metal door and window frames and even bricks – at rates that ranged from 15 per cent to 33.3 per cent.

The building industry was therefore taxed in a greater way than others, put at a disadvantage in relation to the rest of industry. Even if refinements are made to the effective protection result there is little prospect of the construction sector coming off the bottom of the list. In other words resources would have been pulled away from this sector and attracted to others. The point to stress is that while acknowledging that this industry contributed greatly to economic recovery it has to be accepted that the tariff diminished its contribution.

A similar point has to be made about the iron and steel industry. It comes out second to bottom in the rankings of effective protection. This industry again partly by virtue of its size is one that reputedly gave great stimulus to recovery. The nature of the industry makes the calculation of the effective rate more difficult than many others. The industry was made up of two main parts. There was what was called the "heavy" part that produced pig-iron, semi-finished products and the simpler rolled products. And there was the "light" part where re-rolling and finishing was carried out along with the production of more specialised goods. It is the fact that the raw material passes through so many stages before it reaches its final form that means it is difficult to define the industry. Some firms covered most processes.

It was mostly those firms engaged in the "heavy" part who actively sought the tariff and those in the "light" who were opposed to it. The heavy part was dominant in every way and these were successful in obtaining high tariffs. The light part resisted the tariff of 33.3 per cent on their raw materials and semi-finished products even though they were given a 20 percent tariff on their finished product. This was one of these rare occasions in tariff history when the tariff placed on the input was greater than that on the final product. The end result is an effective rate of protection that is very low.

Here then is an industry which was given little protection – least of all by far in the manufacturing sector – and yet this industry is credited with having made the greatest contribution of all manufacturing industries to the recovery. Accepting that it did make such a contribution we are nevertheless forced to conclude that it was handicapped by the tariff. We would have to look elsewhere for the reasons – possibly to the rationalisation of the industry. The tariff would have resulted in resources being drawn away from iron and steel.

These two sectors – construction and iron and steel – which come at the bottom of the rankings of effective protection made up almost 40 per cent of total industrial output. These are the two sectors that are said to have contributed most to the very strong surge in economic activity from 1932–37. They were both considerably handicapped by the tariff and on this basis we would have to conclude that the contribution of the tariff to economic revival was minimal.

Britain had returned to a gold standard in 1925 and remained on that standard until September 1931. The debate on protection had taken place in the context of a fixed exchange rate regime. International trade theory deals with the differential impacts that can be expected from tariffs under fixed and floating exchange rates regimes. The basic position is that the tariff can be effective under fixed rates, though the extent will be affected by the impact on money supply and the general price level changes. But tariffs will be ineffective and possibly perverse under floating rates.

Britain left the Gold Standard in September 1931 and shortly thereafter implemented protectionist policies. It was at this stage that Keynes gave up his advocacy of the tariff. On leaving the gold standard Britain did not however permit completely free floating. It was at this time that the Exchange Equalisation Account was established and the exchange rate entered a period of dirty floating. Under fixed exchange rates a tariff diverts demand to home goods and domestic output can thus be encouraged, and incomes raised. But under a floating rate there is ultimately no change. Within a simple macroeconomic framework with floating rates, the tariff would bring about a rightward shift in the IS curve and a rise in interest rates. That would induce a capital inflow and so lead to an appreciation in the exchange rate. This then diverts demand from home goods back to imports and that process continues until interest rates are back at their initial point. Therefore there should be no expectation of protection contributing to economic growth. In fact Mundell went further than this in showing that under floating rates a new tariff was likely to be contractionary – it would actually reduce national output and income.

An aspect that must be taken account of is the impact British protectionism had on the rest of the world. The impact on the world economy has already been alluded to above. Britain was still the major trading country in the world economy and when it took the measures there were all manner of responses around the world. To isolate the domestic impact of tariffs in Britain is to ignore this and the ramifications that it had for world trade. The reverberations that undoubtedly swept around the world and back to Britain can only have damaged British external trade and hence economic growth.

This paper has suggested that a large move towards protectionist policies was underway from at least the First World War onwards and that that process accelerated rapidly in the 1920s such that by the time of the great depression the world had the highest levels of protection. It may be difficult to assess accurately the extent of the increase that took place or to be precise about the actual scale of protection in any one year but when all the measures employed are considered it can hardly be disputed that the world was in one of its most severe protectionist phases. As ever, there were many factors at work but the protectionist devices must take a large part of the blame for the poor economic performance in the world economy in the 1930s. The damage to the world economy is reflected in the collapse in world trade between 1929 and 1937. Of course falling incomes had a major part to play in that but incomes were generally rising after 1932 while trade continued to fall for several years. There will continue to be debate over the contribution, if any, of protection to the domestic economic recovery in the different countries but there is a lot of evidence to suggest that in some that contribution was tiny and in some cases perverse. There is no doubt that protection reduced imports – that is what it is good at – but that can be the problem for the world at large. Richard Cooper may have overstated the significance of the Smoot-Hawley tariff but when that is put in the wider context of the protectionist movement there is a clear case for saying that protection was amongst the most damaging aspects of international relations in the interwar period.

References

Bhagwati, Jagdish N., Protectionism (Cambridge, Mass. 1988)

Capie, Forrest, Depression and Protectionism: Britain between the Wars (London 1983)

Capie, Forrest, Effective Protection and Economic Recovery in Britain, 1932–1937, in: Economic History Review 44,2 (1991) 339–342

Conybeare, John, Trade Wars: The Theory and Practice of International Commercial Rivalry (New York 1987)

Cooper, Richard N., Trade Policy as Foreign Policy, in: *Robert M. Stern* (ed.), US Trade Policies in a Changing World Economy (Cambridge, Mass. 1987) 291–322

Eckes, Alfred E., Opening America's Market (Chapel Hill u.a 1995)

Eichengreen, Barry, Sterling and the Tariff (Princeton 1981)

Estevadeordal, Antoni, Measuring protection of the early twentieth century, in: European Review of Economic History 1,1 (1997) 89–125

Falkus, Malcolm Edward, The Industrialisation of Russia, 1700–1914 (London 1972)

Federico, Giovanni / Tena, Antonio, Was Italy a Protectionist Country?, in: European Review of Economic History 2,1(1998) 73–97

Gerschenkron, Alexander, Bread and Democracy in Germany (Berkeley, Los Angelos 1943, New York 1966, Cornell 1989)

Gordon, Margaret S., Barriers to World Trade: A Study of Recent Commercial Policy (New York 1941)

Humphrey, Don D., American Imports (Twentieth Century Fund 1955)

Kitson, Michael / Solomou, Solomos / Weale, Martin, Effective Protection and Economic Recovery in the United Kingdom during the 1930s, in: Economic History Review 44,1 (1991) 328–338

Kitson, Michael / Solomou, Solomos, Protectionism and Economic Revival: The British Interwar Economy (Cambridge 1990)
Liepman, Harry, Tariff Levels and the Economic Unity of Europe (New York 1938)
Neal, Larry, The Economics and Finance of Bilateral Clearing Agreements: Germany, 1934–8, in: Economic History Review 32,3 (1979) 391–404
Ritschl, Albert, Nazi economic imperialism and the exploitation of the small, in: Economic History Review 54,2 (2001)
Sombart, Werner, Economic Theory and Economic History, in: The Economic History Review 2,1 (1929) 1–19
Zieler, Thomas, W., Free Trade the Advent of GATT (Chapel Hill 1999)

Solomos Solomou

Trade Protection in the 1930s

Post-war policy makers created the foundations of a new international economic order around a number of beliefs about inter-war trade policy: protection and depression were seen to be inextricably related in a causal manner, as was protection and the disintegration of world trade and the collapse of multilateralism. This view continues to find support today (Capie, 1992; Capie, 1994). However, the picture of inter-war protection that is emerging in recent research is far more complex: some countries gained, others lost. Some trading blocs were able to expand trade in the adverse circumstances of the 1930s, others were not successful at doing so (Eichengreen and Irwin, 1993; Kitson and Solomou, 1990; J. Foreman-Peck et al., 1992).

In order to understand why countries chose protectionism in the early 1930s it is not sufficient simply to argue that protection policies were an outcome of interest group policies that did not serve countries well. We need to understand the historical context of this policy response. Two key features need to be emphasised: first, the 1930s was a period when existing institutions were failing to generate high employment and output levels; secondly, the policy framework was still very much based on *national* decision making, with very limited international policy co-ordination. In such circumstances it is possible that trade protection offered an appropriate national response to external shocks. It is misleading simply to point to the lost opportunities that accompanied the abandonment of free trade. Countries had the choice of raising interest rates and deflating further to control their worsening balance of payments problems or to protect. Protection offered a viable national-specific policy option.

This picture differs from that drawn by policy makers in the early post-war period. To reconcile these differing views it is important to realise that post-war policy makers were attempting to build the foundations for a New Economic Order by creating institutions that were going to re-stabilise the world economy in the long run (such as GATT). A qualified evaluation of the protectionist measures adopted during the inter-war era would not have been a politically viable way of generating institutional change. However, one important function of historical analysis is to identify the complexities of actual policy choices.

Business cycle shocks during the inter-war period had persistent effects on aggregate macroeconomic performance partly because the inter-war epoch did not have an equivalent set of international adjustment mechanisms to the pre-1913 era. The pre-1913 gold standard survived for so long partly because there existed viable international adjustment mechanisms to national-specific shocks, including international migration flows, trade protection and overseas investment (which stimulated the tradable sector). These adjustments manifested themselves in long swing fluctuations in a number of international economic variables, such as exports, overseas investment and international migration (Solomou, 1998). The inter-war era saw an abrupt end of many of these adjustment outlets. Legislation in the New World prevented mass emigration as a solution to mass unemployment. The disintegration of world trade, partly due to protection policies and a collapse of overseas investment during 1928–38, prevented export growth from stabilising the effect of domestic demand shocks. Instead, severe business cycle shocks left economies with high unemployment and low output levels. The 'passing of the Kuznets cycle' (Abramovitz, 1968) in the inter-war era is of central importance to business cycle experiences, just as the presence of Kuznets swings before 1914 represented the workings of various stabilising cyclical adjustment mechanisms in the international economy. The occurrence of large shocks and the failure to co-ordinate policy at the international level meant that national policy responses had to be pursued and trade policy offered a direct response to serious balance of payments problems.

The type of insights we gain from analysing the inter-war period can help us think about the type of pressures we might expect in future periods. It would be ahistorical to argue that particular regions should learn from the experience of the 1930s and avoid protection at all costs. The optimal policy response of the regions of the world economy must be a function of the nature of shocks and the nature of the adjustments that are possible (including the degree of international policy co-ordination). Judged in this context the protectionism of the 1930s was a rational response to specific historical circumstances that determined policy options. Pointing out that a different mix of institutions can result in improved economic performance may be sobering but anachronistic.

During the 1930s Government policies disrupted the flow of international trade with higher levels of tariffs. Quotas were also used on an extensive basis for the first time, particularly in France and Switzerland. International trade also became increasingly discriminatory, leading to the development of trading blocs between Britain and its Empire, Germany and Eastern Europe, Japan and the 'Yen Bloc', France and its Empire.

The discriminatory protection policies in the inter-war years are also assumed to have led to a collapse of multilateral trade (Pomfret, 1988; League of Nations, 1939). Both Britain and Germany practiced discriminatory trade policies in the 1930s and saw a proportion of their trade being managed with bilateral trading agreements. To evaluate the effects of these developments I consider two aspects of tariff policy in the 1930s. First, section I sets up a framework for analysing the national effects of tariffs. This is then used to evaluate the impact of tariffs on Britain. Section II considers the question of whether the world economy witnessed a collapse of multilateralism using long run quantitative evidence from the trade patterns of the major industrial economies.

I. National Effects of Tariffs

In considering the national effects of tariff policies during the 1930s the following aspects need to be considered:

'Initial conditions'
The initial state of an economy may affect its response to protection in the circumstances of the 1930s. Thus, economies that failed to reconstruct successfully in the 1920s, burdened with slow economic growth and overvalued exchange rates may behave differently to the more competitive economies. Thus, if the sectors protected in the 1930s were facing adverse competitive conditions in the 1920s (as in the case of Britain), protecting these sectors may have given them the necessary time to adjust, stimulating cyclical growth.

'Beggar-thy-Neighbour' effects
The initial benefits of a change in trade policy may be negated by the impact of retaliation and the decline in world trade. What proportion of the decline in world trade can be attributed to protectionism? The existence of 'trading blocs' complicates the analysis significantly. The alternatives are not simply rapid growth of world trade or slow growth of world trade; the growth of 'trading blocs' provided a means for some economies to expand trade.

Qualitative Policy Shifts
One needs to distinguish between quantitative increases in existing tariff rates and a policy regime shift towards protection. For example, most of British industry operated under free trade rules until the inter-war period. Thus, the policy initiated by the General Tariff of 1932 can be viewed as a qualitative shift and its effects would be expected to be different from the policy adjustment of many other economies, which simply involved raising tariffs from already existing high levels.

Balance of Trade Effects
Lewis (1949, pp. 59–61) suggests that the spread of protectionism may have had beneficial effects in reducing the amplitude of the downswing but negative effects during the upswing. Lewis argues that if one country cuts its imports then trading partners whose exports have fallen must cut their imports to maintain trade balance. To achieve external balance without recourse to policy their overall level of imports will have to fall by some multiple of their deficit, resulting in deflation. The introduction of a tariff allows trade flows to be adjusted in a targeted way, arresting the need for internal deflation.

The Overall Policy Regime

The effects of tariffs will be influenced by the nature of the exchange rate regime. In a simple macroeconomic model, to the extent that a tariff improves the trade balance it may act to appreciate the nominal exchange rate; to the extent that a tariff is a price raising measure it will act to appreciate the real exchange rate. However, such simple models rarely provide an accurate description of the way economies respond in historical time. In the circumstance of managed exchange rates in the 1930s the effects on the nominal exchange rate may be filtered via policy feedback. Empirical evidence also teaches us that "history matters". Even if a tariff has effects on the real exchange rate there may be enough time for significant adjustments to have been made. Thus we need to be aware of the possibility of hysteresis effects that may arise from trade policy, whereby a transitory event may result in longer-term effects. During the 1930s the links between protection and exchange rates are even more perverse. Countries that used protection as a means of sustaining the gold parity were more likely to face adverse effects than countries combining protection with devaluation. Thus, although all countries were raising tariff rates in the 1930s, in analysing the effects of these policies we need to allow for interactions between protection and exchange rate regime.

The structure of Protection

To better understand the expected impact of a tariff structure we need information on both the nominal and effective rates (Capie, 1983). Effective rates are important to determining the relative magnitudes of protection afforded to different industries. The nature of tariff changes varied significantly across countries. For example, in the case of the UK, protection was offered to the industrial sector but not to food and raw materials; in contrast, in France the rise of tariff rates was mainly on food and agricultural products. Inter-sectoral effective rates need to be considered in conjunction with intra-sectoral rates: thus, a non-tradable sector, such as building, that uses tradable inputs will be adversely affected by the price effects of a tariff structure. Within a particular sector different industries will receive different levels of effective protection.

Such effects are likely to lead to a diversity of impacts at the national level. Setting out the aggregate effect on the world economy then becomes extremely difficult. This framework will be used to evaluate the effects of the General Tariff of 1932 on Britain during the 1930s. In a more speculative way the section also uses this framework to consider the effects of French protection during the 1930s.

In February 1932 the UK imposed a General Tariff of 10 per cent *ad valorem* on imports from foreign countries: this was a protectionist device designed to shield the domestic industrial sector from foreign competition. To appreciate the nature of the change in Britain's trade policy we need to place it in the wider context of protectionism in the world economy. The UK was the only major industrial country to pursue a *unilateral* free trade policy in the period 1870–1913. Even by 1925 the limited extent of protection in the UK meant that the average tariff level on manufactured goods was only 5 per cent *ad valorem*: the McKenna Duties

(1915) and the Safeguarding of Industries Act (1921) had already protected some of the new industries such as motor cars, chemicals and scientific instruments. In contrast, the average tariff for Continental Europe was 25 per cent (Liepmann, 1938) and the United States 37 per cent (Bairoch, 1986; Eichengreen, 1989).

The early 1930s saw a sharp rise in tariff levels and quotas throughout the world economy, initially induced by falling food and raw material prices in 1928–29 which forced many European countries to raise the level of agricultural protection in order to alleviate distress in the sector. Such trends suggest that to analyse the effects of the General Tariff the relevant question that needs to be addressed is whether the UK pursued an appropriate *second best* trade policy in the 1930s in the context that the world trading system was already highly distorted. A policy of continuing with *unilateral* free trade, which assumes no existing distortions, was simply not viable.

Given that a tariff creates a wedge between domestic and foreign prices a starting point for analysing the effects of the General tariff is to consider effects on prices. The pricing response of domestic and foreign producers to changes in tariff rates is critical to determining the magnitude of change in competitiveness. If domestic producers simply use the protection afforded by tariffs to raise prices and foreign producers respond to the loss of competitiveness by cutting prices, competitiveness may, in fact, be little changed. Such information on the 'pass-through' properties of the tariff requires a disaggregated analysis of the pricing behaviour of domestic and foreign firms. This issue was partially addressed in a contemporary Board of Trade analysis of the General Tariff by Leak (1937). Leak considered the impact of the tariff on import prices relative to domestic prices for manufactured goods. A summary of Leak's results is presented in Table 1. Imports were split up into two categories: the first category, sample A, relates to classes of commodities of which domestic production exceeded £1 million in 1934. Two major features stand out: first, import prices were lower than those for similar domestic products. Secondly, there was a fall of approximately 19 percentage points in the relative price of imports from 1930 to 1933; this corresponds closely to the average duty imposed in 1933. This indicates that the domestic price of imports (average value plus duty) relative to the average value of domestically produced goods was not substantially altered by the tariff (see final column of Table 1). This would imply that for sample A, domestic manufacturers took advantage of the tariff to increase prices *or* that importers decreased their prices by a similar amount, or a combination of both processes.

Sample B was chosen on different criteria, being those goods for which imports in 1930 accounted for at least a third of the domestic market. In 1930 the relation of average values of imports to average values of domestic products was consistently lower for sample B than for sample A[1]. The impact of the tariff was to make

[1] *Leak* suggests that this may be because a price advantage was required to enter the UK market. However, this may also reflect the pricing strategies of foreign firms in order to take a rising share of the UK market.

Table 1: Imports Liable to Duty (Millions of Pounds)

Sample A

	As Declared	As Declared plus duty	At Average values of goods produced Domestically	a/c (%)	b/c (%)
	(a)	(b)	(c)		
1930	87.2	87.2	91.8	95.0	95.0
1933	31.4	37.1	41.0	76.6	90.5
1934	34.4	40.7	44.2	77.7	92.1

Sample B

	As Declared	As Declared plus duty	At Average values of goods produced Domestically	a/c (%)	b/c (%)
	(a)	(b)	(c)		
1930	39.6	39.6	49.0	80.8	80.8
1933	19.0	22.5	25.2	75.4	89.1
1934	21.4	25.3	28.6	74.8	88.4

Source: Leak (1937, p. 583)

the internal price of sample B imports (inclusive of the tariff) some 10 per cent below the price of similar home produced goods compared with 20 per cent below in 1930. Thus in 1933/34, these imports were approximately 10 per cent less competitive in the domestic market compared with 1930. Leak suggested that this relationship prevailed because domestic manufacturers were able to reduce prices due to expanding production.

Leak's evidence on pricing behaviour shows that the inflationary effects of tariffs were not always strong in the depressed conditions of the early 1930s. This result has some intuitive appeal. In a depression period, with a high level of excess capacity, the inflationary effect of tariffs will be expected to be small (Foreman-Peck, 1979; 1981). Moreover, under conditions of oligopolistic competition tariffs will lead to falling mark-ups for imported goods, increasing the degree of competition for domestic producers; the existence of economies of scale may encourage domestic producers to keep their new competitive edge against imported goods by *not* raising prices. Finally, the protectionist response of the early 1930s is general to the world economy; what will matter in determining changes in international competitiveness is the *relative* impact of tariffs on prices. The average tariff *changes* of France, Germany and America were comparable to those of the UK during 1927–31. Thus, although there is clear evidence that the real effective exchange rate appreciated between 1932–37 (Broadberry, 1986; Redmond, 1980) this cannot simply be attributed to the effects of the tariff. Moreover, as noted above, the policies of devaluation and tariffs complemented each other in the impact period by giving domestic producers a higher share of the domestic market in 1932–34.

The most direct effect of tariffs is expected to be on imports. Despite a significant growth of national income between 1929–37 imports of manufactures fell by 17.6 per cent, a sharp contrast to the rise of 65.7 per cent between 1920–29. The result was a very large fall in the share of imports of manufactures relative to net manufacturing output (Maizels, 1963; Kitson and Solomou, 1990). The downward shift of imports was also observed for aggregate imports as a proportion of GDP (Matthews et al., 1982; Beenstock and Warburton, 1983). In the face of major changes in world commodity prices in the early 1930s and the devaluation of sterling in 1931 we clearly cannot attribute the fall in imports only to the effects of the General Tariff. However, there exists a *prima facie* case that the new policy *contributed* to these trends. Since the General Tariff had its greatest impact on manufacturing imports we need to consider whether tariffs had a significant effect on this component of demand. Kitson and Solomou (1990) test this by estimating an import function for UK manufacturing imports during the period 1924–38.

Specifying the import function for manufactures as:

$$\log M = a + b_1 \log Y + b_2 \log P + b_3 \tau + \varepsilon \qquad \ldots(1)$$

M = *Manufacturing imports at constant prices*
Y = *Real GDP*
P = *Relative price of foreign to home manufactures*
τ = *ad-valorem tariff rate*

Specifying the import function in this general form explicitly considers the impact of the tariff, controlling for the effect of other important variables. The results are presented in Table 2. The fit gives an R^2 value of 0.89. All the variables have the expected sign and the income and tariff coefficients are statistically significant at the 99 per cent confidence level. The relative price variable is significant at the 95 per cent level (one-tailed test). The results suggest that UK manufacturing imports were income elastic with an elasticity above 2. The tariff had a large depressing effect on import demand – a one percentage point increase in tariff rates resulted in a 3.4 percentage change in manufacturing imports. The relative price effect is significantly smaller (a one per cent change in relative prices gave rise to a 1.06 per cent change in manufactured imports)[2].

[2] Imposing the restriction that the coefficient on logP and t are equal is rejected (*Kitson, Solomou*, 1990).

Table 2: Regression Results for UK Manufacturing Import Function 1924–38 (t values in parenthesis)

Results of Regressing:

$\log M = \alpha + \beta_1 \log Y + \beta_2 \log P + \beta_3 \tau + \varepsilon$

α	−6.772	−(1.83)
β_1	2.114	−(7.41)
β_2	−1.064	−(1.86)
β_3	−0.034	−(10.30)

$R^2 = 0.89$ DW = 2.07 F = 37.02

Note: P relates to the lag of the relative price variable; the tariff rate used aims to capture the effect of the policy change in 1932 and takes the value of zero between 1924–31 and the manufacturing average tariff rate reported in Kitson and Solomou (1990), Table A4.1 between 1932–38.

These results suggest that the impact of tariffs on import demand did not work through a simple price effect; the tariff effect was significantly higher than the non-tariff relative price effect. One interpretation may be that the tariff (because of its permanence) is capturing a long-run price elasticity of demand for imports which is significantly higher than the short run elasticity. The results are also consistent with the view that tariffs had significant *indirect* effects on the demand for imports; to the extent that tariffs stimulated scale-intensive industries, the behaviour of pricing and production of such industries had a significant indirect effect on import demand.

Given the degree of excess capacity in 1932, and the success of tariffs in reducing the demand for imports, protection is expected to generate a process of import substitution in production. The 'newly-protected' industries of 1932 received a favourable stimulus, improving their standing relative to the non-protected and already protected industries (for example, under the 1921 Safeguarding of Industries Act). In an empirical evaluation of this hypothesis Richardson (1967, p. 249) concludes:

'The tariff had little effect on the growth of newly protected industries between 1930 and 1935'.

This conclusion was based on Richardson's evaluation of the effects of protection on output, employment and trade in the newly protected industries of 1932 relative to those protected earlier. Richardson's argument is developed in two steps. The first simply compares the newly protected industries with other industries during the benchmark years 1930 and 1935 (the choice of these two years is determined by the available data: the censuses of production provide extensive disaggregated data). Given that between 1930 and 1935 the fall in imports in newly protected industries was less than the fall in imports of other industries, Richardson favours a non-tariff explanation for the healthy performance of the newly protected industries: recovery in the newly protected sector was thus seen as simply reflecting general economic recovery in the 1930s. The second step of Richardson's evidence is based on calculating import replacement ratios for the newly protected and other industries between 1930 and 1935. The Import Replacement Ratio of an industry is defined as:

$$IRR = \frac{\text{Rise in Gross Output} - \text{Change in Exports}}{\text{Fall in Imports}}$$

If a process of import substitution is observed in the 1930s then the fall in imports should lead to a proportional expansion of production for the home market (rise in gross output *minus* change in exports), assuming a constant level of demand. Thus, *ceteris paribus*, the ratio should tend to unity if import substitution is successful (a one per cent fall in imports should result in a one per cent increase in production for the home market). Given that the level of demand was not constant Richardson tests for the impact of the tariff by comparing the *relative* performance of the newly protected and other industries between 1930–35; if the tariff succeeded in generating a process of import substitution then the IRR is expected to be closer to unity for the newly protected industries than for other industries. In fact the IRR takes the value of 3.0 for the newly protected industries and 2.0 for other industries. From this evidence, Richardson concludes that import substitution was not observed in the 1930s recovery and thus industry output movements were independent of tariffs.

Kitson and Solomou (1990) question the methodology behind this result. A major weakness in Richardson's analysis is the implicit assumption that the newly protected and other industries begin from similar initial conditions in 1930. There is no attempt to compare the economic performance of the newly protected and other industries over a longer period that would allow us to test this assumption. The initial conditions in the 1920s will be unimportant only if industries were comparable in economic performance. We know this was not the case. The newly protected industries of 1932 consisted of many of the under-performing industries of the 1920s. The relevant question that Richardson's study does not address is the extent to which protection in 1932 reversed this path of relative decline. In order to evaluate this we need more information on the behaviour of the two groups of industries in the pre-protection period. Only by making such inter-period comparisons can we hope to test for the effects of policy changes.

The data contained in the Censuses of Production of 1924, 1930 and 1935 are at a sufficient level of disaggregation to allow us to distinguish the performance of the newly protected industries of 1932 relative to other industries. However, instead of comparing the relative position of the newly protected industries only for the years 1930 and 1935, we can use the benchmark comparisons of 1924, 1930 and 1935 as a way of capturing changes in relative performance in the light of the initial conditions faced by different industries before the policy shift in 1932. Thus, the *inter-period* difference in performance between 1924–30 and 1930–35 is the relevant measure to consider. The import duties of 1932 covered the majority of manufacturing industry, accounting for some 85 per cent of manufacturing output. The remaining industries had been protected under earlier legislation, including motor cars, scientific instruments and synthetic chemicals.

In order to evaluate whether sectoral growth was stimulated by tariffs let us consider the relative performance of the newly protected industries with respect to output and productivity growth. Output growth in the newly protected group of 1932 was stagnant between 1924–30, whilst other industries saw a growth of 2.7 per cent per annum (see Table 3). However, during 1930–35 there occurred a substantial turnaround as the newly protected group grew at 3.8 per cent per annum whilst the other industries grew at 2.3 per cent per annum. The impact of the policy shift on rates of productivity growth was also favourable (see Table 4).

Table 3: Output Indices for the Newly Protected and Non-Newly Protected Manufacturing Sectors (1935 = 100)

	Newly Protected	Non-Newly Protected
1924	83.22	76.13
1930	82.83	89.18
1935	100.00	100.00
	Growth Per Annum (%)	
1924–30	– 0.1	+ 2.7
1930–35	+ 3.8	+ 2.3

Source: Kitson and Solomou (1990, p.77).

Table 4: Labour Productivity Indices for the Newly Protected and Non-Newly Protected Sectors

	Newly Protected	Non-Newly Protected
1924	85.1	85.4
1930	87.4	93.0
1935	100.0	100.0
	Growth Per Annum (%)	
1924–30	+ 0.45	+ 1.43
1930–35	+ 2.73	+ 1.46

Source: Kitson and Solomou (1990, p.77).

The General Tariff of 1932 is correlated with a turnaround in the performance of UK manufacturing industries. Studies that have not managed to distinguish this effect have confused a number of very different economic processes. Comparing the newly protected industries of 1932 with the performance of other industries only in the 1930s (as Richardson has done) is equivalent to describing the life cycle and business cycle behaviour of these industries. By taking a longer run comparison over 1924, 1930 and 1935 we can document the magnitude of *change* in the

1930s relative to the 1920s which is more likely to capture the impact of the protectionist policy regime.

As has been argued above, the structure of protection, as measured by effective protection rates, offers further insights into the expected effects of tariffs. The concept of effective protection was first used by Capie (1978) to analyse the effects of the tariff structure on the British recovery of the 1930s. However, one should not regard effective protection rates as being assumption free. The calculated effective rates of protection depend very much on the way in which protected industries are assumed to behave. The assumption often made in studies of effective protection is that the law of one price holds in the domestic market, and that the country concerned is a small participant in the world market, so that any tariff has no effect on the world price of the goods concerned. The implication of this is that a tariff raises the prices of both imports and home sales to the domestic market by the full amount of the tariff. This assumption is unlikely to hold in a major depression (Foreman-Peck, 1979).

Another feature of the approach is that non-tradable industries (such as building) will almost certainly face some increase in costs[3], but they are assumed not to raise their prices. As a result such industries will have a negative rate of effective protection. In this respect the approach suggests that protection hindered economic recovery during the 1930s, because the housing sector played an important role in recovery. However, we need to be aware that effective protection represents only one framework for analysing the resource flow effect of tariffs on the industrial structure. Nominal tariff rates will also be important to the extent that they influence consumption decisions and the macroeconomic process of import substitution. Moreover, effective protection rates are calculated using macroeconomic assumptions that are clearly restrictive, such as full employment. Thus, paradoxically, if the income effect of the tariff is large enough, non-tradable industries may not be adversely affected.

Another feature that has not been fully emphasised in the literature is that effective protection rates can be calculated across a number of domains. The literature on Britain has focused on intra-industry rates (Capie, 1978; Kitson, Solomou and Weale, 1991). However another feature of British tariffs is that food and raw materials could still be imported tariff free. Thus, the manufacturing sector was relatively favoured by the tariff structure relative to the primary sector. If we take an inter-sectoral perspective to economic recovery in the 1930s, the evidence suggests that explaining the rapid revival of the manufacturing sector is central to the story. In terms of sectoral growth accounting, it is clear that to understand the strength of UK economic revival in the 1930s, the building sector is of second order importance to the role of the manufacturing sector (Kitson and Solomou, 1991).

[3] During the 1930s imports accounted for approximately 40 per cent of inputs into the industry.

The overall policy regime also needs careful consideration when thinking about the effects of tariffs. The use of protection as an instrument of national economic revival in a flexible exchange rate regime has been a controversial policy issue. The historical literature has drawn on Mundell's (1961) seminal paper to argue that tariffs were unlikely to have been expansive in the circumstances of the 1930s (Broadberry, 1986). Mundell recognised that under fixed exchange rates, and in the absence of extensive retaliation, a tariff may generate higher output and employment via import substitution effects. However, under flexible exchange rates, the appreciation of the real exchange rate, resulting directly from the imposition of tariffs, will render commercial policy ineffective. Applying such a framework to the 1930s experience is not straightforward. First, in the circumstances of the 1930s the sterling exchange rate was clearly operating in a framework of managed exchange rates, not floating rates. Hence, although the real effective exchange rate appreciated during 1932–37 (Redmond, 1980) this cannot simply be attributed to the General tariff. Secondly, the British trade data shows that trade policy generated persistent changes during the early 1930s. The import ratio for manufactured goods saw a sharp fall in 1932 (by about one third), a fall that was sustained from 1932 through 1938. Such behaviour cannot be explained within Mundell's floating exchange rate model, which implies a long-run equilibrium that is not affected by trade policy. Clearly, the evidence is consistent with a concept of path-dependence. The trade policy changes of 1931–2 generated large competitiveness changes that were complementary on impact. Moreover, the induced changes were large enough to generate a permanent change in the import penetration of the economy. Even if the Mundell model is seen as offering an explanation of the behaviour of the real exchange rate in the 1930s it does not follow that tariffs were neutral. Clearly, trade policy had large and persistent effects during 1932–4.

The evidence presented suggests that the impact of tariffs was important to the recovery of the UK economy after 1932. Between 1932–37 the U.K. economy witnessed a marked fall in import ratios that can be partly attributed to the impact of the General Tariff. The newly protected sector of 1932 saw an improvement in economic performance relative to the poor performance of the 1920s; these industries significantly increased their annual growth rate in the period 1930–35 compared with 1924–30. In contrast the group of industries protected throughout the inter-war saw a fairly constant growth performance between the two periods. These conclusions need to be kept in perspective. Tariffs were successful in stimulating economic revival, partly because they were acting as a catalyst in the context of very favourable conditions. For example, devaluation contributed to the recovery by improving competitiveness and facilitating the introduction of cheap money in 1932. Similarly the process of wage bargaining did not prevent the new trade policies from generating improved competitiveness and initiating import substitution.

The framework that has been set out above suggests that the national effects of trade policy need to be evaluated country by country. Briefly comparing Britain and France illustrates the dangers of generalising. In France the average tariff rate rose from 23% in 1927 to 38% by 1931 (Liepman, 1938). As noted above France also used quotas as a form of new protection during the 1930s. Clearly French trade policy represented a quantitative incremental policy change, to be distinguished from the General Tariff in Britain, which represented the end of unilateral free trade. Moreover, the main aspect of tariff changes in France was the rise in the tariff on foodstuffs, which rose from 19% in 1927 to 53% in 1931. The tariff on manufactures rose only marginally from 26% to 29% over the same period (Woytinksy and Woytinksy, 1955). Hence, the major aspect of French policy was to protect the agricultural sector from the collapse of international food prices. In terms of the structure of protection, the tariff changes of the 1930s meant that effective protection rates were clearly rising in agriculture relative to manufacturing. The effect on industrial sector cyclical revival was likely to be limited and indirect. In addition the overall policy regime that France sustained as a member of the Gold Bloc was unfavourable to recovery during the 1930s. The fate of the Gold Bloc during the 1930s was one of low cyclical growth rates, relative to the countries that exited from the gold standard (Eichengreen and Sachs, 1985; Solomou, 1996). To the extent that tariffs impacted to reduce imports and import ratios in the 1930s their effect on national economic recovery was positive, to the extent that tariffs helped to sustain the gold parity of France, their effect was adverse.

II. Bilateralism and Regionalism

Developments in the international trading system during the inter-war period are considered as the prime example of a collapsing multilateral trading system (Arndt, 1944; Lewis, 1949; Nurkse, 1944). For many contemporary observers the increase in discriminatory protectionist policies, partly resulting from the world depression of 1929–33, was assumed to have led to a collapse of multilateral trading patterns (League of Nations, 1936, 1942; PEP, 1937; Pomfret, 1988). This view has now become accepted in surveys of the period (Kindleberger, 1973; 1989; Capie, 1994).

A quantitative evaluation of this proposition is undertaken by considering an index of bilateralism for the four core industrial countries (Britain, France, German and America) during the period c.1870–1938. Bilateral trade entails the direct balancing of trade between pairs of countries. This contrasts with multilateral or triangular trade where a country will purchase goods (imports) from one trading partner but will sell (exports) to another country. There was a significant increase in the number of bilateral agreements during the 1930s. A number of these agreements sought to achieve bilateral trade balances while others provided preferential trading arrangements which represented a departure from the multilateral Most Favoured Nation policy (Irwin, 1993).

A simple measure for bilateralism is Pomfret's adaptation of the Grubel-Lloyd intra-industry trade index (Pomfret, 1988, p. 51):

X_i = value of exports from country i
M_i = value of imports to country i

$$B = \left[1 - \left\{ \frac{\sum_{i=1}^{n} |X_i - M_i|}{\sum_{i=1}^{n} (X_i + M_i)} \right\} \right] \times 100$$

This index is constructed in such a way that if all trade is settled on a bilateral basis, i.e.

$$\sum_{i=1}^{n} |X_i - M_i| = 0$$

then B will take the value of 100 but if all trade is settled on a multilateral basis, then

$$\sum_{i=1}^{n} |X_i - M_i| = \sum_{i=1}^{n} (X_i + M_i)$$

and the index will take the value of zero. Thus, if the bilateral agreements of the 1930s led to increase bilateralism this would lead, ceteris paribus, to an increase in the value of B. The value of this index is affected by business cycle shocks that affect trading relations differently across countries. Thus, a major shock that affects countries to different degrees, in terms of amplitude, timing and duration, will displace existing trading patterns giving rise to cyclical fluctuations in this measure of bilateralism. Despite this the long run movements offer us quantitative information on the effects of more persistent policy changes such as regionalism and discriminatory protectionist measures.

Figures 1–4 plot the long run data for the UK, France, Germany and America over the late 19th Century and the inter-war period. Although all countries display long run shifts it is not clear that the 1930s have an observable effect on the structure of trade settlements. With the exception of Germany no other country sees a discernible increase in bilateralism in the 1930s relative to the 1920s and pre-1913 trends. In the case of France and Britain the level of inter-war bilateralism is comparable to that observed in the immediate pre-1913 period. In the case of America the average level of the index is higher than that observed over the period 1875–1913; however this is valid for the inter-war period as a whole, not the 1930s. A number of studies have suggested that the period 1870–1914 witnessed a trend towards multilateralism (Saul, 1960). The trends for France, Germany are consistent with this hypothesis but the trends for the USA and the UK do not show a stable trend towards multilateralism in the pre-1913 period.

Figure 1: Bilateralism Index, UK

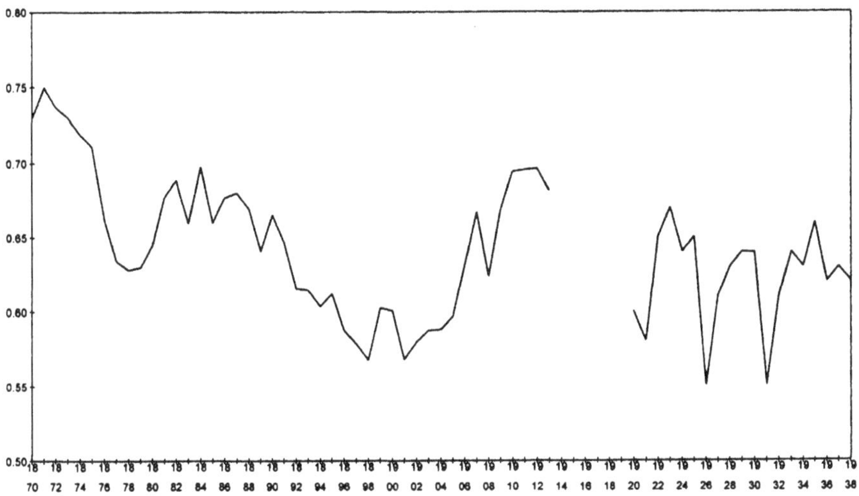

Figure 2: Bilateralism Index, France

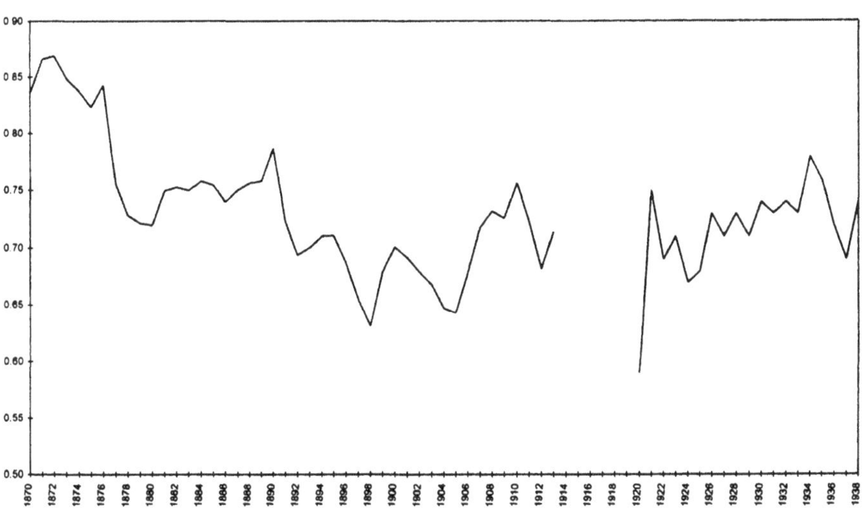

Why did the proliferation of bilateral trading agreements during the 1930s not lead to a rise in the overall level of bilateralism? It seems clear that, with the exception of Germany, the impact of discriminatory trade agreements in the 1930s was not to increase bilateralism but to foster regionalism. For countries such as the UK, France, Netherlands and Italy a growing proportion of trade was conducted with their respective Empires (Tovias, 1988). Furthermore, currency blocs also

Figure 3: Bilateralism Index, Germany

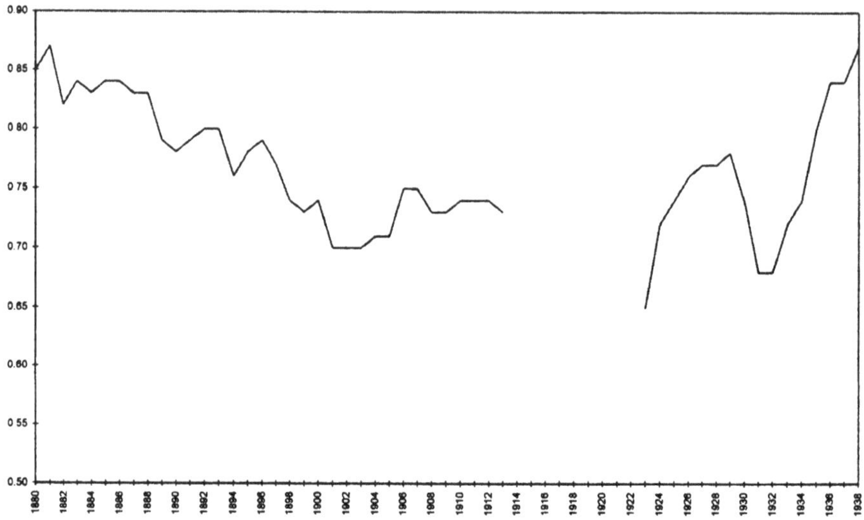

Figure 4: Bilateralism Index, USA

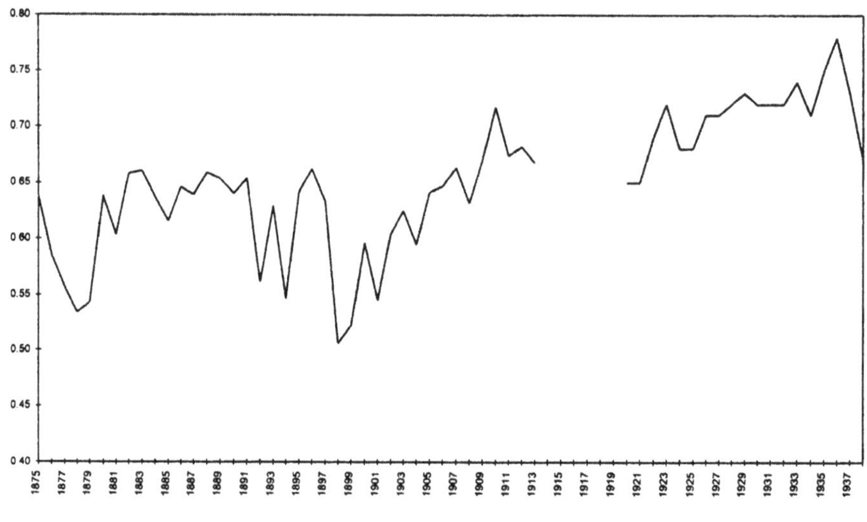

grew in importance as countries sought exchange rate stability within different policy zones. As the scale of trade expanded within these regional blocs a form of 'regional multilateralism' evolved in importance during the 1930s. The German experience is a unique outcome of the military objective of autarky and should not be seen as representative of the impact of trade policies in the 1930s (Kitson, 1992; Kitson and Solomou, 1995).

The evidence suggests that the discriminatory trade policies of the 1930s did not result in the widespread increase in bilateralism. The contrasting experience of Germany and the rest of the world illustrate this point clearly. The long-run evidence presented here does not support Pomfret (1988, p. 50) who notes that in the 1930s "increased discrimination was reflected in a growing resort to bilateralism". The experience of Germany cannot be separated from the Nazi policy of striving for autarky for political and military reasons. Other countries, however, sought pragmatic solutions to the shocks of the 1930s around regional blocs. Bilateralism was not an inevitable outcome, despite the signing of bilateral trading agreements. The evidence suggests that discriminatory trade policies during the 1930s resulted in new trade blocs, but within the trading bloc trade continued to be conducted on a 'multilateral' basis. A clear distinction between the development of trading blocs and the collapse of multilateralism is essential to understand the experience of the inter-war years.

Conclusion

The study of trade policy remains a politicised topic. The economic history of inter-war trade policy has been constrained by a post-war vision on the problem. The evidence considered above suggests that we have a long way to go before we can claim to understand the effects of trade policy on the world depression and recovery during the 1930s. Only by carefully building evidence at the national level can we hope to move towards an aggregate picture. Those who claim to know the answer need to articulate their case. Finally, to understand why nations pursued trade policies we need to bear in mind the overall problems facing economies during the inter-war period. In a world with few policy instruments and severe economic shocks, national protection provided a viable and in some cases an effective policy tool.

References

Abramovitz, M., The Passing of the Kuznets Cycle, in: Economica 35 (1968) 349–367

Arndt, H. W., The Economic Lessons of the 1930s (Oxford 1944)

Beenstock, M. / Warburton, P., Long Term Trends in Economic Openness in the United Kingdom and the United States, in: Oxford Economic Papers 35 (1983) 130–140

Bairoch, P., Commercial Policies and Economic Development in History: Myth and Reality of Protectionism, in: Journal of Regional Policy 4 (1986) 512–534

Bhagwati, J., Multilateralism at Risk: The GATT is Dead, Long Live GATT, in: The World Economy 13 (1990) 149–169

Bhagwati, J. / Irwin, D., The Return of the Reciprocitarians: US Trade Policy Today, in: The World Economy 10 (1987) 109–130

Broadberry, S. N., The British Economy Between the Wars: A Macroeconomic Survey (Oxford 1986)

Capie, F., The British Tariff and Industrial Protection in the 1930s, in: Economic History Review 31 (1978) 399–409
Capie, F., Depression and Protectionism: Britain between the Wars (London 1983)
Capie, F., Effective Protection and Economic Recovery in Britain, 1932–1937, in: Economic History Review (1991)
Capie, F., Trade Wars; A Repetition of the Inter-War Years, Current Controversies No. 2, (Institute of Economic Affairs, London 1992)
Capie, F., Tariffs and Growth (Manchester 1994)
Customs and Excise Department, Annual Statement of Trade of the United Kingdom 1921, 1925, 1929, 1933, 1935 and 1939, HMSO, London
Eichengreen, B. J., The Political Economy of the Smoot Hawley Tariff, in: Research in Economic History 11 (1989) 1–44
Eichengreen, B. / Irwin, D., Trade Blocs, Currency Blocs and the Disintegration of World Trade in the 1930s (1993) mimeo
Eichengreen, B. / Sachs, J., Exchange Rates and Economic Policy in the 1930s, in: Journal of Economic History 45 (1985) 925–946
Foreman-Peck, J. S., Tariff Protection and Economies of Scale: The British Motor Car Industry before 1939, in: Oxford Economic Papers 31 (1979) 237–257
Foreman-Peck, J. S., The British Tariff and Industrial Protection in the 1930s: An Alternative Model, in: Economic History Review 34 (1981) 132–139
Foreman-Peck, J. S. / Hughes-Hallet, A. / Ma, Y., The Transmission of the Great Depression in the United States, Britain, France and Germany, in: European Economic Review 36 (1992) 685–694
Irwin, D. A., Multilateral and Bilateral Trade Policies in the World trading System: An Historical Perspective, in: *J. De Melo, a Panagariya* (eds.), New Dimensions in Regional Integration (Cambridge 1993)
Kindleberger, C. P., The World in Depression 1929–39 (Berkeley 1973)
Kindleberger, C. P., Commercial Policy Between the Wars, in: *P. Mathias, S. Pollard* (eds.), The Cambridge Economic History of Europe, Vol. VIII (Cambridge 1989)
Kitson, M. / Michie, J., Depression and Recovery: Lessons from the Inter-war Period, in: *J. Michie, J. Grieve Smith* (eds.), Unemployment in Europe (London 1994)
Kitson, M. / Solomou, S., Protectionism and Economic Revival: The British Inter-war Economy (Cambridge 1990)
Kitson, M. / Solomou, S. / Weale, M., Effective Protection and Economic Recovery in the UK in the 1930s, in: Economic History Review 44,2 (1991) 328–338
Kitson, M. / Solomou, S., Bilateralism in the Interwar World Economy, in: Bulletin of Economic Research 47, 3 (1995) 197–219
Krugman, P., Is Bilateralism Bad?, in: *E. Helpman, A. Razin* (eds.), International Trade and Trade Policy (London 1991)
League of Nations, Balance of Payments and Foreign Trade Balances, Vol. II, League of Nations, Geneva
League of Nations, International Trade and Balance of Payments, 1913–1927, Vol. II, 1926–1928, Vol. III, League of Nations, Geneva
League of Nations, International Trade Statistics, 1930, 1931, and 1932, 1934, 1935, 1937 and 1938, League of Nations, Geneva
League of Nations (1936): World Economic Survey 1935/36, League of Nations, Geneva
League of Nations (1939a): Review of World Trade 1938, League of Nations, Geneva
League of Nations (1939b): World Economic Survey 1938/9, League of Nations, Geneva
League of Nations (1942): Network of World Trade, League of Nations, Geneva
Leak, H., Some Results of the Import Duties Act, in: Journal of the Royal Statistical Society, C. Part IV (1937) 558–595
Lewis, W. A., Economic Survey 1919–1939 (London 1949)
Liepmann, H., Tariff Levels and the Economic Unity of Europe (London 1938)

Maizels, A., Industrial Growth and World Trade (Cambridge 1963)
Matthews, R. C. O. / Feinstein, C. H. / Odling-Smee, J. C., British Economic Growth, 1856–1973 (Oxford 1982)
Nurkse, R., International Currency Experience, League of Nations (Geneva 1944)
PEP (Political and Economic Planning) (1937): Report on International Trade, PEP, London
Pomfret, R., Unequal Trade: The Economics of Discriminatory International Trade Policies (Oxford 1988)
Redmond, J., An Indicator of the Effective Exchange Rate of the Pound in the Nineteen-Thirties, in: Economic History Review 33 (1980) 83–91
Rooth, T. J. T., Tariffs and Trade Bargaining: Anglo-Scandinavian Economic Relations in the 1930s, in: Scandinavian Economic History Review 34 (1986) 54–71
Saul, S. B., Studies in British Overseas Trade 1870–1914 (Liverpool 1960)
Solomou, S. N., Themes In Macroeconomic History: The UK Economy 1919–1939 (Cambridge 1996)
Solomou, S. N., Economic Cycles (Manchester 1998)
Statistisches Reichsamt (1933 and 1938): Monatliche Nachweise über den Auswärtigen Handel Deutschlands, Ergänzungsheft, Berlin
Svennilson, I., Growth and Stagnation in the European Economy (Economic Commission for Europe, Geneva 1954)
Temin, P., Lessons From the Great Depression (Cambridge, Mass. 1989)
Tovias, A., Trade Discrimination in the Thirties and Eighties, in: World Economy 11 (1988) 501–514
United States Tariff Commission (1942): Foreign Trade and Exchange Controls in Germany, Report 150, Washington
Woytinksy, W. S. / Woytinksy, E. S., World Commerce and Governments-Trends and Outlook (1955)

Harold James

The Creation of a World Central Bank? The Early Years of the Bank for International Settlements

The Bank for International Settlements had two purposes, which its founders may have intended to be complementary, but which proved instead to be quite contradictory. On the one hand, the Bank was supposed to end the politicization of the reparations issue, which had plagued the international financial system of the 1920s, and provide a neutral, "market" solution. On the other hand, the Bank would act as an instrument of central bank cooperation, making the international capital markets less volatile. It would institutionalize the informal central bank cooperation that had developed under the tutelage of Montagu Norman (Governor of the Bank of England) and Benjamin Strong (Governor of the Federal Reserve Bank of New York) in the mid-1920s, and make it less dependent on individual personalities. Norman was deeply aware of the financial destabilization that followed from the death of Strong in October 1928. In effect, as a central bankers' central bank, the BIS was intended as a sort of world central bank.

The fact that this was a "Reparations Bank" in practice ensured that France and Britain would be locked in conflict as to the role and function of the Bank. Norman, more than the British Foreign Office, regarded reparations as pernicious and saw the Bank as being a valuable instrument in demonstrating the absurdity of the entire concept. France, and the Banque de France shared this sentiment, saw the Bank as a means to guarantee the continuation of German payments for French reconstruction until the date, 1988, established in the Young Plan adopted by the international conferences in The Hague. A consequence of this conflict was to poison Franco-British discussions of monetary policy, and more generally – and with very long-lasting effects – bring about an intellectual bankruptcy in discussions of monetary policy. For a long time, central banks and central bank cooperation were associated with the terrible failures of the depression era. This "lesson" of the depression influenced the design of the Bretton Woods order; and it was only in the 1980s and especially in the 1990s that an assertion of the value of independent central banks reappeared generally (Germany and the Bundesbank played a role of a model in this discussion).

The Goals of the Bank

The Young Plan replaced the previous mechanism for the transfer of reparation payments through an Agent-General, whose responsibility it was to convert the Marks paid by the German Government into foreign exchange, and to make a judgment as to whether the foreign exchange market would allow such a large transaction. Instead, Germany was to pay her reparations Marks to a new institution, the Bank for International Settlements (BIS). The BIS replaced the transfer protection mechanism of the Dawes Plan through its discretionary power to reinvest reparation payments in German securities, and thus to remove pressure from the exchange rate. The Bank also acted as the Fiscal Agent for the Dawes and Young Loans, as well as other international loans (the 1930 International Loan of Austria).

The BIS, however, was intended as rather more than merely a reparations bank. Its founders saw it as a way of mending the international order: stabilizing money, and providing depoliticized solutions to economic problems. Sir Charles Addis, a member of the Organization Committee established at The Hague conference to design the new bank, wrote: "It was hoped by this plan to fulfill the dream of Genoa by the gradual development of the BIS into a cooperative society of Central Banks, the governors of which would regularly meet together in concert in order to exchange information, and to devise means for promoting economy in the use of gold and for preventing by a common policy undue fluctuations in its value."[1] Later the objects of the Bank were described as collaboration to "evolve a common body of monetary doctrine" and to "smooth out the business cycle, and to contribute toward a greater equilibrium in the general level of economic activity"[2].

Montagu Norman formulated a very ambitious program as a way of implementing these objectives. He saw the prime task of the bank as lying in the "centralization of international monetary relations". It would prevent excessive credit leading to "overproduction when prices are artificially maintained (rubber etc.)". There was thus, initially, a restrictive or negative approach to credit creation. (Norman was thinking of the abortive Stevenson scheme, which had made rubber exports dependent on the price, had briefly raised rubber prices, and then led to over-planting and a catastrophic price collapse during the depression years.) The Bank could thus act to improve the international circulation of capital, and provide an answer to the excessive amount of short-term capital moving internationally. One common diagnosis of the ills of the 1920s contrasted the long-term nature of pre-war international capital movements with the volatile short-term flows of the 1920s (a debate reminiscent of some analyses of the ills of the 1990s). "To attract short-term capital to long-term markets is another task which can only be

[1] Bank of England Archive (BoE) G1/1, 28 July 1929 Addis to Leith-Ross (British Treasury).
[2] Fifth Annual Report, also quoted in *Barry Eichengreen*, Golden Fetters: The Gold Standard and the Great Depression (New York 1992) 263.

accomplished by identifying the policies of the Central banks, by coordinating the movements of their discount rates, by increasing the control of each in its own market."[3]

France agreed about some of these goals. The French expert Pierre Quesnay saw a desirability of centralizing the statistical work of the various central banks in order to know more about the problems raised by international capital flows. But French thinking went much further and proposed that the BIS should adopt a new gold currency (*grammor*) as a unit of account. The idea, characteristically French, goes back intellectually to the proposals of Napoleon III for a world monetary standard at the 1867 International Monetary Conference. Stripped of the gold element, however, it also looks forward to Keynes's discussion of an artificial international currency, *bancor*, in the negotiations preceding Bretton Woods. The result would be that the defense of a currency in the case of a speculative attack would not require the sale of another currency (and hence the likelihood of transmitting the attack elsewhere)[4]. There were enormous hopes. The BIS, in fact, was the last great attempt to establish international economic cooperation before the Second World War.

Its statutes laid down the Bank's responsibility as "to promote the cooperation of Central Banks and to provide additional facilities for international financial operations". It began operations on 17 May 1930 with an initial capital of 500 m. gold francs suisses, subscribed by Central Banks or (in the case of Japan and USA) banking groups[5]. (To give some idea of the contrast in size with other institutions: the capitalization of the BIS amounted to 0.107% of 1930 U.S. GNP; the capital of the IMF was 4.019% of U.S. GNP in 1945.)

Its constitution, however, represented a rather political sort of compromise. The Paris experts, the Hague conferences, and the Organization Committee left the BIS in the words of one of its Directors "vague, obscure, badly arranged and sometimes inconsistent"[6]. In the first place, its membership betrayed clearly its origins as a reparations bank: it excluded all of South and Central America, Africa, the British overseas dominions, and Asia, with the exception of Japan, which owed its inclusion to its status as a (very small) reparations creditor. In Europe, Spain was left out. The USA, however, was brought in, though the representation was inevitably unofficial in that the Federal Reserve System was forbidden to participate (because of the risk of involving the United States officially in the reparations quagmire). As a consequence, the BIS held its dollar deposits at two leading private New York banks.

The Bank was not located in any major financial center: the choice of site initially lay between the small countries of Europe, Belgium, the Netherlands and Switzerland, with France strongly advocating a Belgian location and Britain and

[3] BoE OV5/1, 24 April 1930 Conversation between Quesnay and Norman.
[4] BoE G1/1, 16 October 1929 Addis to Norman. See also Neue Zürcher Zeitung, 185, 30 January 1930, "Bank für internationalen Zahlungsausgleich".
[5] *R. Auboin*, The Bank for International Settlements 1930–1955 (Princeton 1955).
[6] BoE G1/1, (no date) Otto Niemeyer memorandum.

Germany equally militantly opposed. In Switzerland, the eventual choice, Zürich was rejected because although a major financial center, it was too German; Geneva involved too much of an entanglement with the League; and thus the choice fell on Basle. Norman had actually urged an even more peculiar Swiss choice, Bern, which had "the advantage of being a diplomatic, university and scientific center and less of a money-making atmosphere"[7]: the intention of maintaining the club-like atmosphere of 1920s in a rarified air was clear. Basle also had the advantage in the railway age of being at the intersection of the major European routes, London-Hoek van Holland-Rome, Paris-Vienna, Berlin-Madrid.

The staffing took place in accordance with the principle of national representation. The first President of the Bank, Gates McGarrah, was an American; but the General Manager in charge of the actual operation of policy was an extremely talented young Banque de France official, Pierre Quesnay, entirely dedicated to French national interests. German protests (especially from the Reichsbank President, Hjalmar Schacht) that he had been the figure responsible for organizing a speculative attack on the Mark in the spring of 1929 were ignored. Quesnay in fact had a powerful claim to his new position. Owen Young, the architect of the new reparations plan, hailed the 36 year old economist as the principal author of both the Young Plan and the Bank[8]. In order to conciliate Germany, Quesnay's Deputy was a German, Ernst Hülse from the Berlin Reichsbank. He proved a blinkered and unimaginative bureaucrat, more intent on warding off invasions of his administrative turf than on rescuing the international financial system[9]. The result would have been a complete deadlock or a descent into routine and trivial business had Quesnay not possessed rather more imagination and initiative than Hülse.

It was difficult after the deliberations of the Organization Committee to avoid the conclusion drawn by a later British Director of the Bank, Sir Otto Niemeyer: "No one who started out to construct a Super Bank for world cooperative purposes could conceivably have hit on the constitution proposed for the BIS."[10] The capital of the Bank came from the participating banks of issue. When the BIS began operations, its resources were so limited that the banking policy soon ran into a dead end: within months, by August 1930, the BIS approached complete illiquidity at the same time as the signs of world deflation and depression had become quite obvious[11]. In the first year of its activity, the BIS had 1800 m. Swiss francs in deposits, of which 300 m. were reinvested in Germany, 650 m. were short-term deposits by the reparations creditors who had not yet transferred their annuities, and 800 m. represented other central bank deposits. Its only business that fitted in with Norman's vision was a stabilization credit for the Spanish Peseta

[7] BoE G1/1, 19 October 1929 Norman to Addis.
[8] Neue Zürcher Zeitung 185, 30 January 1930, "Bank für internationalen Zahlungsausgleich".
[9] e.g. BoE G1/4, 2 September 1931 Rodd to Siepmann.
[10] BoE G1/1, Otto Niemeyer memorandum.
[11] BoE G1/2, 12 August 1930 Siepmann memorandum on phone conversation with Rodd (BIS).

of £3 m. in April 1931, which was designed to allow Spain to return to the gold standard (in fact the world financial crisis intervened).

The Bank was not permitted to make medium or long term investments (outside Germany) of the kind that might have been needed in drawing up stabilization packages. One of its staff now came to the conclusion that: "If things continue to take their present course, the Bank will be in a completely frozen position within a month and unable to meet its liabilities without borrowing."[12]

The Kindersley-Norman Proposals

The urgent need for medium term credits arose out of the world depression which immobilized many bank loans: this was where a lender of last resort might have played a powerful role in freeing the world from the incubus of frozen debt and illiquid banks. A Sub-Committee of the BIS in autumn 1930 started an inquiry into how the Bank might make up the shortfall caused by the growing bank problems of Central Europe:

> The [commercial] banks ... are no longer prepared to continue this custom [the Central European tradition of making long term credits to commercial and above all industrial borrowers], which, from the point of view of rigid banking principles might be called an abuse, as, owing to the post-war economic depression these credits have become frozen almost everywhere, with the result that the banks are no longer prepared to invest money in companies with which they have already invested large sums not to mention the further fact that this freezing of credits has transformed a considerable portion of the liquid funds of the banks into fixed investments[13].

The sub-committee recommended that a sum equivalent to the BIS's capital, in addition to some permanent deposits, should be placed in medium term bills bought from banks in order to thaw Central European credit. A more ambitious variant of the scheme appeared in February 1931 from the Bank of England and became known as the Kindersley scheme (Sir Robert Kindersley was a Director of the Bank of England and of the BIS). It aimed to overcome the failure of international bond markets, where – because of the collapse in security prices – new issues had become practically impossible. Kindersley and Norman recommended the creation of an international corporation with a capital of £25–50 m., which might issue bonds up to three times its capital to "foreign governments, municipalities, mortgage banks, harbour boards, railways and public utility companies". "At a period like the present, when the capitalist system is largely under the microscope and is being attacked from many sides, it is of the greatest importance

[12] BoE G1/2, 10 August 1930 HAS(Siepmann) Note on telephone conversation with Mr. Rodd.

[13] BoE OV4/84, 29 October 1930 Quesnay to Siepmann, attaching memorandum by Dr. Simon.

that capitalists as a whole should thus make an effort to find a remedy for at least one important difficulty which faces the money markets of the world today."[14]

In fact the scheme, which attracted German support – since there the danger of financial collapse became ever more acute – found the French hostile and suspicious of an attempt to chip at the French power political advantage arising out of the strength of the French capital market. The Governor of the Banque de France, Clément Moret, argued that a BIS participation in the Kindersley scheme would be contrary to the Bank's statutes. Moreover, it was French banks which were supposed to subscribe most of the bonds under the scheme, "without being given the means of controlling the use of the funds furnished"[15]. The debtor countries had only themselves to blame for the current weakness of international capital markets: "If a number of borrowers at the present time do not possess all the desirable facilities for procuring the capital of which they are reasonably in need, this is mainly because in the course of previous years too large a number of them have not strictly kept the engagements which they had undertaken with respect to their creditors." There could be no point in relying on guarantees given by a borrowing state, since, "in practice the creditor is powerless before a defaulting State; he comes into conflict with the 'sovereignty' of his debtor, and the political evolution of the last few years seems to have strengthened the force of this conception. The security given has only a very relative value and generally no value at all (for example Mexico, Turkey ...)." The perils of sovereign lending became obvious to all during the depression.

Moret's view in retrospect seems plausible. The first defaults came in Latin America. Bolivia had let its currency slip against gold in October 1930, and in January 1931 defaulted on its debt. Peru followed in March, Chile in July and Brazil and Colombia in October. There then came the Central European defaults: exchange control in Austria, Hungary and Germany in 1931, and defaults by Hungary, Yugoslavia and Greece in 1932 and Austria and Germany in 1933[16]. There was growing skepticism about sovereign loans. By the mid-1930s, the liberal Swedish economist Per Jacobsson, chief economist at the BIS, was writing: "Political influence in lending is, as a rule, very costly; when a government has to put its influence behind a loan, the likelihood is that there is something wrong with the security of the loan."[17] But Moret's pessimistic analysis does not take into account the possibility that early action might have limited the extent of financial contagion.

It was not, however, merely French opposition that brought down the Norman-Kindersley scheme. The American financiers were not sympathetic to a

[14] BoE OV4/84, 2 February 1931 memorandum "Kindersley scheme".

[15] BoE OV4/84, 27 February 1931 Moret to McGarrah.

[16] See *B. Eichengreen*, *R. Portes*, Debt and Default in the 1930s, Causes and Consequences (London 1985) also in: *R. Portes*, *A. K. Swoboda* (eds.), Threats to International Financial Stability (Cambridge 1987). Also *J. T. Madden*, America's Experience as a Creditor Nation (New York 1936) 111–13.

[17] BoE OV50/6, May 1936 Jacobsson, "Problems of International Financing".

large-scale rescue operation. BIS President McGarrah cabled to Morgan partners Lamont and Gilbert that the proposal was impractical and that it would have been much better to organize an investment trust through private banking channels. The Morgan bankers agreed with this assessment[18]. Thus the proposal disintegrated, and Governor Norman noted sadly: "The fact is that the BIS is already slipping to the bottom of a ditch and in that position seems likely to do no more than helpfully perform a number of routine and Central Banking operations."[19]

A more modest, but in some ways more interesting, proposal made by the middle term credit sub-committee under the chairmanship of the influential Belgian commercial (not Central) banker Emile Francqui, for the rediscounting by the BIS of commercial paper up to £10 m. in order to prepare the way for a semi-private corporation to be built up by the speculative Swedish financier Ivar Kreuger, fared little better. The idea was that rescue efforts involving central banks and official institutions alone would be doomed to failure. It was essential to "bail in" (to use more modern terminology) the private sector. But Francqui's initiative was not at all well received by the two hostile camps in BIS policy-making. On the one hand, the British and Germans at the BIS regarded the idea as inadequate and limited; on the other, Moret described it as "utopian", since "an issue of bonds at the present moment would, to say the least of it, be difficult"[20].

Governor Moret's pessimism was not unjustified, since the BIS Board meeting at which he delivered the death blow to the Francqui as well as Kindersley plans took place one week after the collapse of the Vienna Creditanstalt. The Central European credit crisis now set in: the Viennese panic brought down banks in Amsterdam and Warsaw. In June and July the scare spread to Germany, and from there immediately to Latvia, Turkey, and Egypt; but within a few months to England and USA. Less than one year after he was supposed to devise a scheme that might rescue the Central Bankers and the Central European banks, Ivar Kreuger had killed himself in a Paris hotel room.

The Central European Credit Crisis

The major failure of the BIS was the mishandling of the Austrian crisis. Austria had been remarkably and surprisingly calm until the spring of 1931. There had been a few small failures in 1929, but the general consensus was that these had not been enough to purge Austrian banking. "In spite of recent failures", *The Banker* noted, "there are still too many banks in Vienna, expectations of whose develop-

[18] FRBNY(Federal Reserve Bank of New York Archive) 797.3 BIS, 18 March 1931 McGarrah cable for Lamont and Gilbert.

[19] BoE OV4/84, 3 March 1931 Norman to Harrison.

[20] BoE OV4/84, 7 May 1931 report of Francqui sub-committee; 22 April 1931 Mcgarrah to Norman; 18 May 1931 BIS Board meeting.

ment as an international financial centre have failed to materialize."[21] The announcement of a customs union between Germany and Austria, and then the French protest against this demarche, increased nervousness; but there do not appear to have been any significant withdrawals of foreign short term credits. The shock came suddenly: the Creditanstalt announced a delay in the publication of its accounts, and then, in the night of 11–12 May, revealed losses of 140 m.sch., which it attributed to the costly aftermath of the absorption of the Bodenkreditanstalt. Before 11 May, most foreign creditors had not realized what was occurring: but after this the affair became highly political. Depositors lost confidence in the Creditanstalt. By the end of May, the bank had lost 200 m. sch. in deposits. But only a quarter of this sum was deposited with other banks: the rest moved out over the exchange[22]. As a run on the schilling started, the Austrian exchange was threatened, and Austria appealed for help. An important part of the intrigue about who was to rescue Austria took place at the BIS in Basle.

Governor Norman staged a rescue operation that was specifically intended to stop the French using the Austrian position for foreign policy advantages. But Norman was also aware from the first of the dangerous international financial repercussions of the Creditanstalt case. "Nor must we forget", he cabled to the New York Federal Reserve, "that a monetary breakdown in Austria might quickly produce a similar result in several other countries"[23]. It took two weeks of tense negotiations to provide what was in the end a token amount, and which did nothing to restore confidence in Austria or in any other country.

The problem lay in the French response to Norman. The Governor of the Banque de France, Clément Moret, knew, on the basis of information supplied from Basle by Pierre Quesnay, in this matter quite assiduous in the pursuit of France's national interest, that the London market was too weak to help Austria. The London Rothschilds could not afford to support the Creditanstalt: "It can thus be foreseen that the Austrian Government will sooner or later be obliged to sell its shares to a private group. In this respect it appears that the London Rothschild house will not be capable of acting. M. Quesnay announces the possibility that this offers to interested French banks."[24]

Norman's initiative resulted in two central bank loans organized by the BIS, though in July Moret tried to block the second Austrian loan because he could now argue that the international capital market had been so destroyed that it would be impossible to float a bond issue to pay off the loan[25]. But these loans were a classic case of "too little, too late": the initial 100 m. sch ($14 m.) loan did not even correspond to the first, grotesquely minimal, estimate of the Creditan-

[21] The Banker 1929 82.
[22] BoE OV 5/3, 9 July 1931 G.W.F. Bruins report.
[23] BoE OV32, 20 May 1931 Norman to Harrison.
[24] BdF (Banque de France Archive), Country File Austria, 15 May 1931 note.
[25] BdF, Conseil Général Procès-Verbaux, 13 July 1931

stalt's losses. Charles Kindleberger's verdict is on the mark: "The niggardliness and the delay proved disastrous."[26]

In mid-June, the bank's losses were calculated at around 500 m. sch., and the National Bank had 690 m. sch. worth of Creditanstalt paper. But even these figures under-estimated the extent of the losses, which only became apparent in the course of an audit: at the end of 1931 the losses were reckoned to be 923 m. sch. or 725 m. sch. more than the nominal capital and reserves *after* the government inspired May 1931 reorganization of the bank. The assets included frozen loans to Austrian and Central European industry. As the Dutchman van Hengel appointed by the creditors to supervise the affairs of the Creditanstalt wrote in his report to the creditors: "It must be understood that the Creditanstalt is not a bank. It still carries on a larger banking business than any other bank in Austria, but this, compared to its total business is relatively small and has contracted with the decrease in banking activity all the world over. The Creditanstalt is largely a holding company, most of whose holdings are industrial and in a very weak state."

The BIS intervention in the next stage of the Central European crisis, the German bank collapse, was not any more successful. On 20 June 1931, the Reichsbank received a $100 m. credit organized by the BIS (to which the BIS contributed one quarter), but the new reserves were rapidly lost in the following run, and an appeal by the Reichsbank on 9 July for further BIS assistance produced no help. There were other bank consortia, similar to that in support of the Reichsbank, for assistance to Hungary, Yugoslavia and the Bank of Danzig.

The Intellectual Bankruptcy of the Concept of International Central Banking

The credit crisis of the summer of 1931 meant the end of discussions about how the role of the BIS might be extended, and also in practice the collapse of attempts at central bank cooperation. The central bankers themselves acknowledged their failure. "The BIS feel that the Central Banks and the politicians each having had their chance and missed it, the next thing to do is to have a really good Committee of private bankers on which only those countries would be represented which have either given large credits to Germany or would be in a position to give credits."[27] But when such a committee met, to negotiate the Standstill Agreement, it was essentially conducting a work-out. The hope that any new credits would be forthcoming proved quite vain. By 1932, the Bank of England concluded that the BIS could only be rescued by complete reorganization: most immediately the dismissal of Pierre Quesnay, the abandonment of the idea of national representation

[26] *Charles P. Kindleberger*, The World in Depression (Berkeley 1986) 147.

[27] BoE G1/459, 24 July 1931 telephone conversation with Mr. Fraser; OV 4/25, 8 July 1931 HAS Note of telephone conversation with Mr. Rodd.

in management, and a move to Brussels where the energetic Emile Francqui might be able to perform a dramatic resuscitation[28].

In practice, none of this happened, and the BIS transformed itself into an institution for economic analysis, in brilliantly conceived *Annual Reports* from the pen of Per Jacobsson, and for the collection of statistics about the world economy. None of this impressed Norman, who had a quite different concept of what was involved in central bank cooperation. He told the central bank governors that: "He was against statistics: he thought the figures were misleading and he believed that if central banks or currency Authorities worked on statistics, even the best statistics, they were more likely to be misled than anything else."[29]

This collapse of the BIS into a center for merely routine operations was only part of a broader breakdown of the theory of Central Bank action. As the depression deepened, and as criticism mounted on all sides, central bankers more and more believed that their only mission lay in announcing loudly that they could do nothing: that monetary policy could not influence the development of the real economy. This was a complete break with the Central Bank activism of the mid-1920s. It was also of course theoretical nonsense, which arose out of the (forgivable) feeling that politicians' rather than central bankers' blunders had made the financial mess. If this was what was meant by a "common body of monetary doctrine", it was one that led away from giving central banks a great room in international financial matters.

In dealing with the League of Nations' Inquiry into the gold problem, the central bankers adopted the position that monetary policy was ineffective, and their view informed the majority report of June 1932 (a more far-ranging minority report signed by Sir Henry Strakosch as well as Sir Reginald Mant and Albert Janssen recommended concerted international action to raise commodity prices).

The modest recommendations centered around the restoration of freedom of exchange. Central banks should allow the automatism of the gold standard to operate: "gold movements must not be prevented from making their influence felt both in the country losing gold and in the country receiving gold."

Governments were to take the burden of adjustment: accumulating budget surpluses and repaying debt in the deficit countries. "In each individual country the necessary steps should be taken to restore and to maintain equilibrium in the national economy. This means that the budgets of the State and other public bodies must be balanced on sound principles, and also that the national economic system as a whole, and especially costs of production and costs of living, should be adjusted to the international economic and financial position, so as to enable the country to restore or to maintain the equilibrium of its balance of international payments."[30]

28 BoE G1/417, 1 December 1932 memorandum.
29 BoE OV5/6, 11 December 1932 BIS Governors' Meeting.
30 Report of the League of Nations Gold Delegation, 24.

In private, the Central Bank view was stated even more explicitly:

We are quite unwilling to lend our authority to those who would exonerate politicians and businessmen from responsibility by explaining the terrible tragedy of the present world crisis as being due solely to a scarcity of gold ... But it was evident to the Delegation, as is clearly expressed in the Second Report, that the causes responsible for this maldistribution were mainly of a general economic, financial and political nature. As these causes were not primarily monetary, monetary policies could not be expected to cure the world of the resulting ills.

The Italian Finance Minister Guido Jung explained that "it would be disastrous to the reconstruction of the world if in a report of ours we were to give to people the impression that there exists a monetary witchcraft, which can, by its own force, work miracle and avoid the necessity of facing manly and solving the political and economic problems"[31].

Part of the task of the 1933 London World Economic Conference lay in the discussion of the contribution of central banking policy to crisis, but the central bankers themselves resented the interference. The preliminary meeting of American economic experts held at the Federal Reserve Bank of New York was quite characteristic. In the presence of Hoover's Secretary of State (Henry Stimson) and the Secretary of the Treasury (Ogden Mills), Governor Harrison and the Chairman of the Board Eugene Meyer "emphasized the necessity of keeping off the agenda of a governmental conference purely central bank questions such as for example central bank credit and gold policies. They also pointed out that most of the monetary questions which could be placed on the agenda were of interest to central banks and that they thought it was of the utmost importance for the World Conference to avoid invading the central bank field or making any suggestions or giving any instructions to central banks which might prove embarrassing."[32]

At an unofficial meeting of the BIS Governors in February 1933, the Belgian National Bank president urged against any Central Bank agreement before London because this "would give a catastrophic reinforcement to the erroneous idea that the monetary factor is a primary factor which plays a preponderant role in the world crisis". Norman agreed wholeheartedly. Eventually, the BIS Governors did produce a document to preempt London, entitled "Rules of the Gold Standard": it contained, perhaps it is needless to say, nothing but platitudes.

It began with a statement that "the restoration of the proper functioning of the gold standard depends to a large extent upon forces and influences which lie outside the field of monetary policy as entrusted to central banks", and argued that the most important measures would be the settlement of inter-governmental debts, a restoration of freedom in the general movement of goods and services, and of capital, the balancing of budgets and the "restoration and maintenance of

[31] League of Nations Archive (LoN) R296.2, 12 January 1932 Bonn, Mlynarski and Chalendar to President of Gold Delegation; 8 January 1932 Jung to Trip.
[32] FRBNY 797.41, 12 November 1931 Crane memorandum.

that sufficient degree of flexibility in the national economy without which an international standard cannot function properly"[33].

The Banque de France and the Federal Reserve Bank of New York wanted to reach a separate agreement, outside the framework of the conference, on currency stabilization: but they were unable to do this. The British and US governments were unwilling to stabilize, since they by now rejected the Central Bank message and held that "much of the improvement which we have had ... had been initiated by the hope of inflation"[34]. The governments by now realized that money was too important to be left to the central bankers.

When attempts at international stabilization were made in the 1930s, they did not occur through the central banks, but through Finance Ministries or their Stabilization Funds (that is the significance of the otherwise rather modest 1936 Tripartite Pact). This anti-central bank sentiment influenced the design of the postwar order. The International Monetary Fund was to be owned by governments (in practice by Finance Ministries), rather than central banks. Central banks were thus deliberately left out of the beginnings of international monetary cooperation in the postwar world. The Bretton Woods resolutions also called for the winding up of the BIS: on the grounds that the Basle Bank had collaborated with Germany and compromised its neutrality. But this accusation was a pretext for a more general feeling that international central bank cooperation had proved itself decisively to be a failure.

[33] FRBNY BIS, 12 February 1933 BIS Unofficial meeting. Stenographic notes of Dr. Michaelis.
[34] FRBNY 3010.2, 11 June 1933 Harrison diary, quoting Sprague.

Barry Eichengreen

Averting a Global Crisis

In the autumn of 1998, for a brief period at least, the specter of "global depression" was in the air. Already in the first half of the year, economic activity had gone into free fall in Asia, while the Japanese economy remained becalmed in the doldrums. Russia's default and devaluation then dealt a heavy blow to an already fragile international financial system. The impact showed up most dramatically in the distress and last-minute rescue of the now-notorious hedge fund Long-Term Capital Management, but few segments of the financial community were unscathed. Institutional investors scrambled for liquidity, setting off a flight to quality and exciting fears of a global credit crunch. Investment plans were put on hold. International investors withdrew from the market, tightening the screws on Brazil and other countries that depended on international capital markets for financing their external deficits. This was the context in which Alan Greenspan warned that the United States could not long remain an oasis of stability in a crisis-ridden world.

The outlook two quarters later is noticeably less gloomy. Despite the battering absorbed by the world economy, the International Monetary Fund projects growth at the rate of 2.2 per cent in 1999[1]. This is slow growth, to be sure, but it is growth nonetheless. Latin America may not share in that growth this year: as of March the consensus forecast for 1999 was for a contraction of 1.2 per cent in the region, with Brazil, Ecuador and Venezuela underperforming the other countries. But at the risk of sounding Panglossian, this hardly qualifies as a depression. The fears of a catastrophic economic and financial meltdown that were so pervasive in the final months of 1998 have receded almost as quickly as they appeared.

What does this tell us about the resiliency and risks to the world economy? Did policy makers avert a serious economic and financial crisis by dint of good luck, or are there powerful stabilizing forces that work to right the world economy when it veers off course? Is the global financial system about to "come apart at the seams", as George Soros would have it, or is it surprisingly robust?[2] Is there a pressing need for institutional reform, or are existing arrangements good enough?

[1] According to the Interim World Economic Outlook released at the end of December.
[2] The quote is from *Soros* (1998).

My answer falls in the middle. If the comparison is with the 1930s, then there exist powerful stabilizing mechanisms that should help us to avoid a repeat of that history. At the national level they include automatic fiscal stabilizers, deposit insurance, and a social safety net. At the international level they include multilateral organizations like the International Monetary Fund, the Basle Committee of Banking Supervisors, and the World Trade Organization. None of this is to deny that individual countries can still run off the tracks, as Indonesia's tribulations make clear. But Indonesia's depression is not a global depression. Russia's default may have similarly done serious damage to that country's economic prospects, but it did not precipitate a complete and total collapse of global financial transactions as occurred in the 1930s. And for the time being at least, the firebreak in South America has held.

That prevailing arrangements were strong enough in 1998 does not mean that they will suffice to cope with all the shocks that may affect the world economy in the future. A larger shock or a different shock may strike where the system is most vulnerable. There remains a need to strengthen policies and institutions to enhance disaster preparedness. Reforming the international financial "architecture" may imply excessive ambition, but there is a pressing need for reform to strengthen financial systems, rationalize exchange rate arrangements, and create an alternative to ever-bigger bailouts.

I lay out this argument in three stages. The first two are designed to suggest that the risk of a global crisis should not be dismissed – that fears to this effect in the fall of 1998 were more than journalistic sensationalism designed to sell magazines. I make this case by emphasizing structural weaknesses in the world economy (in Section 1) and also by revisiting the Great Depression of the 1930s (in Section 2), emphasizing the parallels with recent events. Section 3 then attempts to explain why 1998 did not turn into another depression, attributing the difference to a more agile policy response and more robust institutions. Section 4, in concluding, identifies remaining vulnerabilities and sketches the agenda for reform.

1. Why 1998 Was Ripe for a Crisis

The events of 1998 are widely seen as threatening a global crisis unlike anything witnessed since the 1930s. The intervening decades had seen recessions but none that threatened to engulf the entire world. Recessions in the advanced-industrial economies typically did not coincide with recessions in the developing countries. When the debt crisis hit Latin America and Eastern Europe in 1982, the United States and the United Kingdom were already beginning to recover from the Reagan-Thatcher recession. And when the U.S. and Europe entered recession in 1991–2, growth was accelerating in much of the developing world. Perhaps most importantly, no previous recession had created such serious financial difficulties, actual or potential. While the list of postwar banking panics is long, those banking problems occurred in different countries at different times[3]. On no prior occasion did financial instability rise simultaneously in so many different places.

Why the difference? Four factors created the scope for a global crisis in 1998: leverage, financial deregulation, capital-account liberalization, and commodity-market integration.

Leverage

The problems that leverage can create are well known: commercial banks engaging in fractional-reserve banking may not have the liquidity to meet a depositor run, creating scope for self-fulfilling banking panics, while investors in securities taking positions on credit may be forced to sell into a falling market to meet margin and collateral calls, amplifying asset-price volatility. These linkages appear to have operated powerfully in 1997–8 during the run on the Indonesian banking system, when Korean banks that suffered losses from the Asian crisis were forced to sell off their holdings of Brazilian Brady bonds, and when Russia's default forced highly-levered institutions like Long-Term Capital to liquidate assets in other markets. One can see how these mechanisms created positive-feedback dynamics in financial markets and worked to transmit financial distress across borders.

While it is difficult to quantify, there are good reasons to believe that leverage has been rising. Advances in financial engineering have made it easier for market participants to take on leverage. The growth of markets in derivative securities has allowed them to unbundle leverage from positions in specific instruments that are subject to different margin and capital requirements. Modern risk-management practices (value-at-risk models, for example) create the belief, real or illusory, that high levels of leverage can be safely managed. The growth of hedge funds, managed-futures funds, and a population of high-income investors prepared to assume the risk of doing business with them has swollen the ranks of leverage-hungry collective investment vehicles operating outside the regulatory net. Inside the net, meanwhile, public bailouts have encouraged the belief that large financial institutions will not be allowed to fail. The fall over time in the capital ratios held by banks in the United States and other countries (the mirror image of rising leverage) is, at least in part, a consequence of this moral hazard[4].

Financial Deregulation

A key lesson drawn from the Great Depression was the need to tightly regulate financial institutions and markets. Governments in industrial and developing coun-

[3] See *Caprio / Klingebiel* (1996) for the list.
[4] See *Kaufman* (1996). The author estimates that the ratio of capital to total assets in the banking system has fallen from 0.23 in 1870–1913 to 0.07 in 1970–1992, while that held by nonfinancial firms has changed little (though the data in this case is less complete).

tries alike laid on a heavy regulatory hand for several decades after World War II. That these policies of "financial repression" had costs in terms of efficiency and growth is now widely accepted. Studies by authors like King and Levine (1993), Levine (1997), and Jayarante and Strahan (1996) have established beyond a shadow of a doubt that countries with more developed financial markets grow faster, and that removing repressive regulation was a precondition for developing the deep and liquid financial markets that are the elixir of growth.

But keeping a tight lid on financial markets, notwithstanding these costs, also limited the scope for financial instability. In the industrial countries, banking crises were few and far between; only with widespread deregulation in the 1980s did they again become a pervasive problem. The record of the "less developed countries" was more checkered, since (by definition) their capacity to effectively regulate their financial institutions and markets was less developed. But there as well, banking crises rose in frequency and severity in the 1980s and 1990s, as deregulation gathered momentum. Even if the countries in question purchased faster growth and economic efficiency by buying into financial deregulation, those same policy reforms lifted the lid on the box in which financial crises had been confined for several decades after World War II.

Capital Account Liberalization

Precipitous financial deregulation and rising levels of leverage would have heightened financial fragility even in isolated economies closed to transactions with the rest of the world. Of course, the economies threatened by crisis in 1998 were anything but closed. International financial liberalization had gathered steam in the 1980s. By the end of the decade, the advanced-industrial countries had all but removed the last of their capital controls. Developing countries followed suit: the IMF's index of exchange restrictions (a cross-country average of restrictions on capital account transactions, multiple exchange rates and requirements to surrender export proceeds) fell sharply after 1990. In the lead-up to the 1996 meetings of the World Bank and the International Monetary Fund, the Fund and the U.S. Treasury pushed the laggards to follow suit.

How this shift toward capital-account liberalization heightened financial fragility will be apparent even to the casual reader. By facilitating international financial transactions, it created new channels (including but not limited to those described above) for financial distress to spill across borders. It allowed financial institutions under water and gambling for redemption to borrow abroad as a way of levering up their bets. And – especially in countries committed to the maintenance of a currency peg – it constrained the ability of the monetary authorities to act as a lender of last resort.

Commodity Market Integration

The decline of tariff barriers, the growth of trade, and the international integration of commodity markets are not usually cited as increasing the scope for instability. But in fact, countries' macroeconomic fortunes are linked not just by the financial linkages but by trade and production linkages as well. In Asia, shifts in competitive advantage due to currency depreciation (the "competitive-devaluations" channel) was one factor contributing to the contagious spread of the crisis. More generally, as commodity markets have become more integrated, business cycles have become more synchronized. Frankel and Rose (1998) show that countries that trade more heavily with one another tend to have more tightly synchronized business cycles. When one country experiences a crisis and its economy turns down, it drags down its trading partners with it. Trade liberalization, like financial liberalization, has manifest benefits in terms of efficiency and growth, but it also increases countries' vulnerability to disturbances from abroad, creating additional channels through which national problems can turn into international problems.

Thus, there are important structural reasons for thinking that the risk of a global financial crisis was greater in the late 1990s than for several generations. If this was not sufficient grounds for concern, there were in addition striking parallels with the Great Depression, to which I now turn.

2. Disturbing Parallels

The distinctive feature of the 1998 crisis was its global scope. It is thus striking that the depression of the 1930s was also a global phenomenon. Not only did it infect the whole of the world economy, but weaknesses in the operation of the international system themselves contributed to the severity of the downturn.

Excessive Reliance on Short-Term Capital Flows

Unsustainable international capital flows, short-term capital flows in particular, were probably the most important factor priming the world economy for its fall. The nature of those capital flows will sound familiar to observers of the recent episode. Whereas in the 1990s capital flowed toward the newly stabilized and liberalized economies of Latin America and the rapidly industrializing economies of East Asia, in the 1920s the analogous flows were directed toward both the emerging markets of Latin America and Eastern Europe and the "reemerging" markets of Europe's west, which had been devastated by World War I and had an insatiable appetite for capital to finance their reconstruction. The war had weakened Europe's balance of payments, not just by disrupting her capacity to export but in addition by prompting new competition[5]. And the postwar network of war debts

[5] Thus, with the disruption of wheat exports from the Crimea, Canadian, Argentine and

and reparations required the ongoing transfer of financial resources from Europe to the United States.

The stability of the pattern of international settlements thus hinged on the U.S. lending the money back. This it did through the summer of 1928. High interest rates in capital-scarce Europe, in conjunction with low funding costs for banks in the United States (reflecting the low discount rates maintained by the Federal Reserve System), were the mechanism for bringing this about. Although much of this lending initially took the form of 20 and 30 year bonds issued by European borrowers and marketed in the United States, a growing amount was short-term lending, bank-to-bank lending in particular. Contemporaries did not refer to this as the "carry trade", the term we use today, but it is easily recognizable as such. Banks funded themselves in the U.S. and other markets where costs were low and on-lent to Germany and Austria, where deposit rates were high.

And in the 1920s, as in the 1990s, the exchange rate was key to this story. The borrowing countries had gone back onto to the gold standard in the first half of the 1920s, pegging their currencies in order to receive the gold-standard "good housekeeping seal of approval"[6]. A pegged exchange rate was regarded as an important signal of policy credibility, the assumption being that countries committed to its defense would follow sound and stable policies. The gold standard having prevailed for decades before World War I, investors were confident that exchange rates, once stabilized, would remain credibly pegged, relieving them of the risk of exchange rate changes. Eventually, of course, that image of stability proved to be an illusion, as in the 1990s.

The capital-market parallels go on. There was the fact that much of this foreign lending was underwritten by U.S. banks new to international business, many of which set up foreign offices for the first time in the 1920s. (Shades of rapidly growing investment bank presence in Asia in the 1990s.) There was the fact of new investment vehicles – investment trusts as opposed to emerging market mutual funds – which provided small savers ignorant of the risks a convenient way to buy into this high-yield market. There was the low level of commodity prices, which, as in the late 1990s, weakened the condition of financial institutions doing business in agricultural regions. And, of course, there was the fact of low interest rates in the major money center, which poured fuel on the fire of the carry trade, much in the manner of low Japanese rates in the mid-1990s.

Australian producers leapt in to fill the void, expanding their acreage under cultivation. With the disruption of British textile exports to the Indian Subcontinent, Japanese producers penetrated the Indian market for the first time. American exporters established beachheads in South American markets that had been the traditional preserve of European producers. All these were factors intensifying the competitive pressure on European producers following the war.

[6] As documented by *Bordo / Edelstein / Rockoff* (1998), countries which pegged their exchange rates under the provisions of a gold standard statute enjoyed favorable borrowing rates on international markets.

Frothy Asset Markets

Above all, there was the stock market. There is no greater consensus among economic historians about the causes of the stock market boom and crash of the 1920s than there is among financial market pundits today about the factors supporting the high level of the market and whether it is destined to come down with a crash[7]. But I would emphasize two parallels. First, the market was supported in the 1920s by so-called "new era" theories that the business cycle had been banished and the economy had entered a golden age of rapid growth and cyclical stability. The founding of the Fed, which was to supply an elastic currency, had abolished the business cycle, it was asserted, while the advent of modern mass production methods, as epitomized by Henry Ford's assembly lines, had inaugurated a new era of high productivity growth. Since there would be no more recessions, there would be no more occasions on which earnings would collapse, and the high level of stock prices was justified. (Expectations of rapid productivity growth of course worked in the same direction.) One cannot help but be reminded of the so-called "new economy" and "new paradigm" theories invoked in the 1990s to justify the run-up of the U.S. stock market.

In addition, the rise of share prices was fueled by investors' appetite for the shares of high-tech companies. The high-tech wonders of the 1920s were companies like RCA, or "Radio" as it was known, whose technologies were thought to have unbounded growth potential. In the event, RCA would pay no dividends for years to come. The analogy with today's Internet companies could not be more direct.

The high level of the stock market created the same dilemma for the Fed as in 1998–9. The phrase then was "excessive speculation" rather than "irrational exuberance" but the worry was fundamentally the same. Reducing interest rates to stimulate economic growth threatened to inflate an already over-full stock market bubble, but raising rates and pricking the bubble threatened to provoke a major correction that would plunge the economy into recession. In the event, the Fed opted to burst the bubble by tightening credit conditions; we now know that it was all too successful[8].

[7] See *White* (1990) for a review of the literature. Interest-rate increases are a possibility, although the timing is not obviously right. While the Massachusetts Department of Public Utilities refused on December 11th to allow Boston Edison to split its stock four to one on the grounds that the stock's price was already higher than could be justified by future earnings, there was no immediate reaction of utility stocks to that decision. The failure of Clarence Hatry's commercial empire and its impact on the London market have been blamed for undermining confidence in New York, but there was in fact little generalized fall in share prices in London (declines being largely limited to Hatry's companies and American railway securities traded there). While the well-known financial pundit Roger Babson made a speech to the National Business Conference warning that "sooner or later a crash is coming..." for every Babson there was an Irving Fisher who believed that the top had not yet been reached.

[8] The same pattern is evident in virtually every emerging market crisis of the 1980s and 1990s – a sharp rise in interest rates in the major creditor countries, which interrupted the flow of funds to developing countries and burst asset market bubbles abroad – with the notable

Deleveraging

In 1928–9, the 150 basis point rise in U.S. interest rates helped to plunge the world into recession by precipitating an even more dramatic monetary contraction in other countries. Those other countries relied on the United States for capital imports. They had pyramided a large volume of liabilities on a narrow base of international reserves, typically foreign exchange reserves instead of gold reserves. Higher interest rates made foreign investment less attractive, and as a result New York stopped lending. And when New York stopped lending, the capital importing countries developed serious balance of payments problems. Given the fragility of their payments position, they had to tighten their monetary policies even more dramatically than the U.S. to defend their gold standard parities. Thus, between 1927 and 1928, the growth rate of M1 declined by 2 percentage points in North America but by fully 5 percentage points in Latin America and 4 percentage points in Europe. Between 1928 and 1929 M1 growth in North America declined by 4 percentage points in North America but by fully 5 percentage points in Latin America and 5 percentage points in Europe[9].

When exchange rates then began to be devalued, the shock to confidence led central banks to scramble out of foreign exchange reserves in favor of gold. The share of foreign exchange in global reserves fell from 37 per cent at the end of 1929 to 11 per cent at the end of 1931. There was a flight to quality, in other words. With fewer reserves to back their liabilities, central banks curtailed the supply of the latter. And with less central bank credit available, commercial banks curtailed their lending. The Bank for International Settlements, lacking the resources and precedents on which the IMF could draw in the 1990s, failed to arrange support for the crisis countries. Deleveraging was dramatic.

In 1997–8, deleveraging and credit stringency again spread infectiously across countries. This time the mechanism was different, however. Korean commercial and investment banks were forced to liquidate their positions in Brazilian Brady bonds to raise funds late in 1997 in reaction to the losses suffered on their Korean holdings, transmitting the crisis to Latin America. In 1998, losses in Russia forced international banks and hedge funds to liquidate positions in other emerging markets in order to meet margin calls and raise liquidity. The transmission mechanism may have been different, but the underlying factor, leverage, was the same[10].

exception of the Asian crisis in 1997. This is a point emphasized by *Eichengreen / Fishlow* (1998). Although there was no equally dramatic monetary tightening in the U.S. and Europe in 1997, there were increases in interest rates in the United Kingdom and Germany in the spring. Japanese long rates ticked up in March as the outlook for the Japanese economy temporarily brightened.

[9] Regional averages are from *Eichengreen* (1992). The Far East stands out as not conforming to the pattern, precisely because Japan did not return to the gold standard until 1931.

[10] It is interesting to compare the analyses of *Galbraith* (1954) and International Monetary Fund (1998) in this regard.

Crony Capitalism and Implicit Guarantees

To this point, the story of the capital flows of the 1920s has been told in terms of problems on the lending side. It takes two to tango, of course. Too many countries used their borrowed funds indiscriminately, building municipal swimming pools in Germany and railways from no place to nowhere in Bolivia and Peru, leaving behind the same legacy of unfinished infrastructure projects that today define the skyline of Bangkok. Fishlow (1985) emphasizes that capital transfer was smooth in the 19th century because borrowed funds were put to uses that enhanced the debtor country's capacity to export. This was less obviously true in the 1920s and, we now know with benefit of hindsight, in the 1990s[11].

In addition, there was the familiar problem of implicit guarantees for banks in the borrowing countries, to which so much attention has been paid in the recent literature[12]. In Central Europe, banks had long been the instrumentality of governments' industrial and financial policies. In Austria, for example, the government leaned on the largest Viennese bank, the Creditanstalt, to absorb a smaller bank, the Bodencreditanstalt, which ran into trouble in 1928–9. Having done the government's bidding, the Creditanstalt received in return an implicit guarantee. What better bank to lend to than one effectively backed by the government? Thus, even after other capital flows dried up in the summer of 1928, foreign banks continued to pour short-term deposits into the big Berlin and Vienna banks in 1929 and 1930. The parallel with Asia in the 1990s is striking.

Policy Mistakes

The remaining element of the story was devastating policy mistakes. Monetary policy was left on a contractionary setting, as the Fed hesitated to cut interest rates. Some central bankers feared that interest-rate cuts in response to the collapse of the Wall Street bubble would only encourage the formation of an even bigger bubble, setting the economy up for an even bigger fall[13]. Central bankers

[11] And where capital was plowed into export-oriented sectors like semiconductors and steel, as in South Korea, the relevant export markets were already saturated.

[12] For examples, see *Dooley* (1997) and *Krugman* (1998).

[13] The literature on this subject is immense. It suggests that some Federal Reserve officials seemingly lacked the intellectual acuity to distinguish between real and nominal interest rates. Noting the decline in nominal rates, they argued that money was cheap, plentiful, and "sloppy". Others inferred from the low level of member bank borrowing that the banks must have been flush with cash. *Friedman* and *Schwartz* emphasize the death of Benjamin Strong, the influential head of the Federal Reserve Bank of New York. Only Strong, in their view, had the insight, intelligence and influence to lead the Federal Reserve Board to a sensible decision. In his absence, the liquidationist interpretation of the Crash and the recession was allowed to carry the day. This was the view that the speculative excesses of the 1920s had set the stage for the stock market boom, the crash, and the slump, and that to reflate the economy would only set the stage for a bigger bubble and a bigger slump subsequently. It was better to allow the excesses to be leeched out of the system. As the point was famously put to President Hoover by his Treasury Secretary Andrew Mellon, "Liquidate stocks, liquidate the

stood by as banking systems collapsed around them. Fiscal policy was not used to a significant extent in the U.S. or other countries in the doctrinaire fear that uneconomical public works spending would undermine confidence and crowd out private investment[14].

Here too the parallels with the 'nineties are disturbing. Japanese policy makers have been reluctant to use monetary policy to jump-start their economy for fear of creating another bubble economy. Their use of fiscal policy has been erratic, reflecting fears that inefficient public investment will damage market confidence. As late as the middle of 1998, the government had taken only tentative steps to deal with the country's banking crisis. In Asia and Latin America, central banks have hiked interest rates and taxes and cut government spending despite the spreading economic slowdown, again to stem the depreciation of the exchange rate. In much of Asia and Latin America, macroeconomic policy has thus done little to stem the deepening crisis and in some cases has only compounded it.

In sum, many of the same vulnerabilities that set the stage for the depression of the 1930s were evident in Asia and other emerging markets in the 1990s. There was good reason to worry last year, in other words, about the risk of a serious economic and financial meltdown.

3. Reassuring Differences

And yet the turbulence of 1997–98 did not precipitate a global slump. This brings us to the contrasts between the two periods.

farmers, liquidate real estate...purge the rottenness out of the system." A stronger economy would emerge, in this view, only from this process of financial consolidation, which justified inaction in the face of the deepening slump. The Fed may also have been rendered reluctant to act by the exchange-rate constraint under which it operated until Roosevelt succeeded Hoover in 1933. It was required to hold 40 per cent gold cover against its monetary liabilities. As the gold-exchange standard began to disintegrate, confidence in the convertibility of the dollar began to dissipate, and other countries began liquidating their dollar reserves and demanding gold in return. The Fed lost gold and began to fear that this constraint would bind. In addition, there was the requirement that the Fed had to hold the other 60 per cent of the backing in either eligible (commercial) paper or gold, and the supply of eligible paper began to fall off significantly as the level of economic activity declined. Whereas *Epstein / Ferguson* (1984) and the early *Wicker* (1966) emphasize the importance of free gold, *Friedman / Schwartz* dispute it, observing that the Fed would have circumvented the free-gold constraint by initiating expansionary open market or foreign exchange market operations. This, however, would have required US central bankers to step out of their established mind set, which was dominated by the Real Bills Doctrine, according to which the provision of additional liquidity was justifiable only when it was done for legitimate business purposes – in other words, only when it could be done by discounting commercial paper, not something which in 1931 was in abundant supply.

[14] The exception to this generalization was government spending on rearmament, most notably in Germany and Japan (and elsewhere toward the end of the 1930s).

Continued Strong Growth in the United States

This may be the most significant difference. In 1929 the U.S. economy had descended into recession even before serious financial difficulties developed at home or abroad. The business-cycle peak (in August) preceded the stock market crash by several months. It preceded the spread of bank failures and currency devaluation by even longer intervals. Thus, the U.S. was unprepared to act as an importer of last resort as the crisis spread beyond its borders. By imposing the Smoot-Hawley Tariff, it pulled the plug on the international trading system. In 1998, in contrast, the U.S. economy continued to grow robustly, even accelerating in the final quarters of the year. The country's trade gap widened as it absorbed exports from Latin America and East Asia.

The difference may be partly explicable by the different institutional arrangements governing trade in the two periods (as I suggest below). But the very fact that the U.S. economy was expanding vigorously in 1998 and unemployment had fallen to historically low levels minimized the pressure for trade protection. A global crisis is easier to avert for political as well as economic reasons when the world economy has a locomotive.

G-7 Interest Rate Cuts

In 1998 the G-7 countries, led by the United States, quickly cut interest rates in order to re-liquify international financial markets. The Fed lowered the discount rate three times in succession in the final months of the year. Canada and the United Kingdom quickly followed, and the 11 European central banks about to become founding members of that continent's monetary union fell into line in December. In Japan, where interest rates were already low, the central bank reduced them to zero. Interest rates having been cut, financial-market participants who had taken losses in Russian GDOs and other high-risk, high-yielding assets found it easier to finance their positions, obviating the need to sell into a falling market. Investors who wished to take advantage of the distress sales of others similarly found it easier to finance their positions. Overly-excited financial markets thus began to settle down.

Why this difference from 1929? The simple answer is that central banks had learned a powerful lesson from history and were concerned to avoid repeating the mistakes of 70 years before. A subtler answer is that the major economies, not being on a gold standard, enjoyed more freedom of action. In the 1930s, financial uncertainty caused flight from national currencies and a scramble for the limited global stock of gold. Even the largest central banks, committed to defending their gold parities, had little scope for cutting interest rates. In 1998, with the dollar, the yen and the major European currencies floating against one another, this constraint no longer bound. However unfashionable the argument, there is little question that floating exchange rates had a stabilizing influence on the world economy.

Intervention on Behalf of Distressed Financial Institutions

The New York Fed-led rescue of Long-Term Capital worked in the same direction. By bringing together 14 of the firm's principal creditors, it signaled that major financial institutions would not be allowed to fail. The concern of officials was for the stability of the financial system, not for LTCM itself. They worried that placing the firm into receivership and forcing it to liquidate its positions might add to the volatility of already volatile financial markets and create additional difficulties for other market participants. Had LTCM been forced to file for bankruptcy protection, the provisions of repurchase and reverse repurchase agreements would have permitted its creditors to sell the collateral securing those repos and swaps. It is important to recall that Russia's default and the subsequent flight to quality had already reduced liquidity and created fears of a credit crunch. Historians will debate whether intervention was justified by the public interest in market stability. But the New York Fed certainly felt that the case was strong.

Again, social learning explains the contrast with the 1930s, when officials stood by as the banking system collapsed around their ears. The banking panics of that year left an indelible mark on policy[15]. That this problem showed up in a nonbank firm like Long-Term Capital rather than a major U.S., European or Japanese bank points up the other important difference with the 1930s: bank regulation has been strengthened, and deposit insurance has been extended, heading off the banking-panic problem (in the advanced-industrial countries at least).

[15] If anything, policy makers learned this lesson of history too well, leaving them loath to allow a major financial institution to fail. Thus, the New York Fed's provision of its good offices has been criticized for creating moral hazard. By saving LTCM from outright failure, it lost the opportunity to teach investors a painful lesson, which only served to encourage risk taking by other hedge funds. While the moral-hazard argument cannot be dismissed, it is hard to attach too much stock in it, given that shareholders in LTCM still lost 90 per cent of their stake. There is, in addition, the allegation that the knowledge that the New York Fed was prepared to arrange a meeting of the firm's creditors encouraged LTCM's partners to reject a competing proposal (by the renowned investor Warren Buffet) that would have essentially wiped out 100 per cent of their stake. Be that as it may, moral hazard risk must in any case be balanced against meltdown risk, especially in circumstances where Federal Reserve officials apparently felt that there existed a serious threat to systemic stability. LTCM may not have been a bank, but it was still too big to fail. In addition, there is the fact that the Fed put up no money of its own. Rather, its effort to facilitate a lifeboat operation in which other financial institutions took over the portfolio and operations of a fundamentally-sound financial institution is the classic, textbook responsibility of a lender of last resort, with precedents stretching back as far as the Baring Crisis of 1890 (*Bordo / Schwartz* 1998). It is not clear that this lifeboat operation could have been arranged without the help of the Fed; not only were there formidable large-numbers and free-rider problems to be surmounted, but commercial and investment banks that might have otherwise been prepared to collaborate in LTCM's rescue first required assurances that they would not be subject to legal action for having colluded.

Japanese Bank Restructuring

While the Japanese economy continued to contract in the final quarter of 1998, some progress was finally made in bank restructuring. A massive bank rescue package was announced in the autumn. More than $100 billion of public funds was pledged to underwrite capital injections and help the banks write off bad loans (and also to finance the takeover of weak banks and buttress the deposit insurance fund). The authorities closed Hokkaido Takushoku, nationalized Long Term Credit Bank and Nippon Credit Bank, and engineered a number of bank mergers. They forced banks to cut costs and close loss-making foreign operations in return for access to public funds. The newly-established Financial Supervisory Agency demanded fuller disclosure of the bad loan situation, reassuring investors that there would not be more bad news to come. As a result, a number of banks were able to raise new capital by issuing preferential shares.

This approach may be second best to a U.S.-Savings-and-Loan-style workout, in which bad loans are removed from the books of the financial institutions and auctioned off to the highest bidder. But for those who believe that its banking system has been holding back Japan's recovery and that Japan has been holding back Asia's recovery, it is better than nothing.

The Brazilian Firewall

In 1998 the IMF leapt into the breach with a multi-billion dollar package of financial assistance for Brazil. This is in contrast to the failure of the Bank for International Settlements to marshal support for the Central European countries engulfed by crisis in 1931. Observers blessed with 20–20 hindsight criticize the Fund for supporting yet another unsustainable currency peg and invoke Brazil's eventual abandonment of that peg in support of their argument. It would have been better, in their view, for the IMF to have pushed Brazil to devalue three or four months earlier. But it is worth recalling that, from the vantage point of 1998, the situation was not so clear. Financial markets were still in the intensive-care ward. The flight to quality was still underway, and investors were ill prepared to take another hit. Although Brazil devalued anyway, there is an argument that its devaluation would have had much more devastating effects had it been allowed to occur three or four months before. From this point of view, IMF assistance may have provided a critical window of opportunity for market participants to rebalance their portfolios and restore their liquidity. This is a plausible explanation for why, when it finally came, the devaluation's global fallout was surprisingly mild.

A Robust Trading System

The depression of the 'thirties was aggravated by the all-but-complete collapse of the world trading system. One country after another, starting with the U.S. in 1930, raised tariffs on imports from the rest of the world. The Smoot-Hawley Tariff, imposed in response to financial distress in the farm belt and lobbying by farmers, was particularly hard on agricultural imports. While the average tariffs of six European countries more than doubled between 1927 and 1931, the largest increase fell on imports of agricultural goods[16]. The quantitative restrictions imposed by exchange-control countries were more draconian still[17]. Developing countries dependent for foreign exchange earnings on exports of primary commodities were thus forced to default on their debts and turn inward, adopting import-substituting policies.

Today's international trading system has so far resisted this fate. Regional arrangements like NAFTA and Mercosur and the multilateral bindings and arbitration procedures of the WTO have worked to discourage countries in macroeconomic difficulty from turning their backs on international markets. The crisis countries of Asia and Latin America, far from turning away from international trade, have rededicated themselves to market opening. Until recently, exports were the only growing component of aggregate demand for the countries of Asia. Say what you will about the U.S.-EU Banana War, U.S. pressure for anti-dumping duties on steel, and Argentine calls for protection against the effects of a falling *real*, the world trading system has remained remarkably resilient in the face of protectionist pressures.

Continued Strong Policies in Emerging Markets

Latin America, which experienced its crisis in the 1980s, responded by upgrading its policies and institutions, better positioning it to cope with the crises of the 1990s. Argentina, Brazil and Chile strengthened supervision of their banking systems, imposed higher capital and liquidity requirements, and opened their banking systems to foreign participation. They streamlined their tax codes and improved tax administration while curtailing unproductive public spending in favor of health, education and infrastructure programs. Argentina strengthened corporate governance by adopting better disclosure systems and accounting standards. It and Mexico negotiated standby lines of credit with foreign commercial banks, and Argentina was able to secure further precautionary credits from the IMF. Chile moved further in the direction of exchange-rate flexibility, while Argentina adopted a currency board; both, in other words, evacuated the unstable middle ground of pegged-but-adjustable rates. Chile, and to an extent Brazil, discouraged short-term capital inflows using fee-based incentives.

For all these reasons, Latin America was less vulnerable when the Asian crisis hit. Ten years ago, it would have been hard to imagine the Argentine banking system successfully navigating the crisis and the peso's dollar link emerging un-

[16] *Liepmann* (1938) 413.

[17] Among the countries imposing exchange controls in the 1930s were Austria, Bulgaria, Czechoslovakia, Denmark, Estonia, Germany, Greece, Hungary, Italy, Latvia, Lithuania, Poland, Portugal, Romania, Turkey, and Yugoslavia.

scathed. There are few more dramatic illustrations of how dramatically the institutional framework has changed.

Thus, a global economic and financial crisis was averted by a combination of good policies, good institutions, and good luck. That's the good news. The bad news is that we cannot assert with confidence that the pieces will again fall into place in the event of another equally serious shock. This creates a critical need to further strengthen institutions and policies in the effort to make the world economy more robust.

4. Toward a More Robust World Economy

Reform begins at home. While some of the key steps needed to make the world a safer financial place require international initiatives under the umbrella of the IMF, the BIS and the G-7, emerging markets cannot wait for the development of the requisite consensus and will on the part of the advanced-industrial countries. I therefore focus in this section on what emerging markets themselves can do to create a more robust international system[18].

Strengthening Financial Institutions and Markets

A key problem in both the Great Depression and the financial difficulties of recent years was financial fragility[19]. The necessary response is to strengthen financial markets and regulatory structures at the national level. International initiatives can help (as I explain below), but this is first and foremost a task for national governments and independent regulatory agencies.

What is involved is no secret[20]. Supervisors should monitor the adequacy of banks' internal controls, external audits, loan and investment policies, and risk-management techniques to identify banks incapable of managing the risks to which they are exposed. They should verify that banks have management information systems in place which enable them to identify risky loan and investment concentrations. They should verify that banks are adequately managing liquidity and foreign exchange risks. Banks should lend on an arm's-length basis and attach realistic values to the assets on their balance sheets. They should be required to provide adequate and accurate information to their supervisors, who should be empowered to impose remedial and punitive measures, including revocation of the license to operate, in the event of noncompliance. Supervisory oversight should be strengthened by giving bank supervisors political independence,

[18] Here I summarize the conclusions and draw on *Eichengreen* (1999).
[19] As emphasized by *De Long* (1999).
[20] The particulars that follow are drawn from the Core Principles for Effective Banking Supervision (Basle Core Principles), which in turn build on *Goldstein* (1997). See also *Folkerts-Landau / Lindgren* (1998) and *Group of Twenty Two* (1998).

financial autonomy, legal immunity, and the power to conduct on-site inspections. Other desirable elements include limiting deposit insurance to small deposits, establishing a credible exit policy for unprofitable banks, and eliminating government guarantees where possible. They include the adoption of regulations requiring public disclosure of intermediaries' financial condition as a way of strengthening market discipline and helping depositors distinguish good and bad banks, thereby limiting the tendency for runs to spread contagiously throughout the system.

Achieving these objectives is no mean task, especially in emerging markets where regulatory policy is politicized and administrative capacity is underdeveloped. It took the better part of a decade for Chile and Argentina, two of the more successful cases, to make significant progress in the requisite direction. This is an argument for getting started[21].

Imposing Holding Period Taxes on Short-Term Capital Inflows

It is also an argument for levying holding-period taxes on short-term capital inflows where the prudential regulation of financial institutions has yet to rise to world-class standards. Recent experience has demonstrated too well that badly managed banks and open international capital markets are a combustible mix. Foreign funding gives banks gambling for redemption and otherwise seeking to take on excessive risk an additional way to lever up their bets. Government guarantees for banks regarded as too big to fail encourage foreign investors to provide those funds. But a disturbance to confidence may prompt these foreign investors to flee, and the short maturity of their loans provides ample opportunity for them to get out. Their rush for the exits can precipitate a crisis which brings down both the banking system and the currency.

This creates an argument for limiting or taxing bank borrowing abroad as a third line of defense against banking-system instability in countries where the first and second lines of defense – banks' own risk-management practices and regulatory supervision, respectively – do not suffice. And where banks can circumvent these measures by having the corporations do the borrowing and pass on the proceeds to them, broader measures may be required. Financial stability may have to be buttressed by a Chilean-style tax to limit short-term foreign borrowing by all domestic entities.

Viewing the issue this way makes clear why more and less developed countries should adopt different policies toward the capital account. To repeat an earlier point, the definition of a (financially) underdeveloped economy is one where the capacity to manage and regulate (financial) risk is underdeveloped. An emerging market is an economy where a substantial subset of the preceding conditions

[21] It is also an argument for vesting regulatory authority with independent agencies (possessing budgetary autonomy and staffed by experts appointed to long terms in office) as a way of reducing the degree of politicization.

apply. As economic and financial development proceeds, these conditions are removed, and the emerging market graduates to the club of countries with mature financial systems. At that point, the capital-inflow tax can be safely removed. Thus, the fact that none of today's advanced-industrial economies impose Chilean-style inflow taxes, preferring to partake of the advantages of an open capital account, hardly challenges the preceding argument. There is no double standard in arguing that emerging markets, where conditions are different, need to follow different policies.

Strengthening the Institutional Framework for Financial Markets

Better bank regulation and better policies toward capital flows will not be enough. To stabilize financial markets, it will also be necessary to strengthen the institutional framework within which they operate. This means upgrading auditing and accounting practices, corporate governance, and insolvency procedures. Inadequate auditing and accounting prevent investors from distinguishing good banks from bad and set the stage for economy-wide banking crises. Poorly designed or enforced insolvency procedures precipitate creditor grab races and cascading debt defaults. Inadequate corporate governance aggravates problems of principal-agent slack between shareholders and managers, allowing problems to develop and fester and sustaining suboptimal levels of investment. There is an urgent need to correct these conditions in order to restore the preconditions for growth and to insulate emerging markets from future crises.

Strengthening Monetary and Fiscal Institutions

Policy makers in emerging markets critically need to regain their freedom of action. Like Alan Greenspan, they need to be able to cut interest rates in order to liquify financial markets when they fear a credit crunch. Like central bankers who finally saw the light in the 1930s, they need to be able to boost money supplies when their economies descend into recession. And like Japanese policy makers today, they need to be able to make countercyclical use of fiscal instruments when monetary policy is not enough.

Unfortunately, policy makers in emerging markets have not been able to respond in this way. In one country after another, from Thailand to Indonesia, to Korea to Brazil, they have been forced to respond to the crisis in emerging markets and the resulting recessionary pressures by cutting budget deficits and raising interest rates, not by cutting rates and raising public spending as the Keynesian textbook would instruct. Were a country like Brazil to respond to slower economic growth by cutting taxes and increasing public spending, investors would flee, the currency would crash, and the resulting investment collapse and financial distress would only make the recession worse. Investors respond negatively because they perceive that governments lack fiscal and monetary discipline. Thus, governments with a history of fiscal laxity that respond by increasing their budget deficits similarly run the risk of being seen as having reverted to their bad old habits of running budget deficits and living beyond their means. And if investors rationally expect budget deficits to be monetized, then deficits today imply inflation tomorrow, encouraging the rational investor to take the first opportunity to get his money out of the country.

The solution in this case is to credibly signal that not just current policies but also future policies will be sound and stable by reforming the economic and political arrangements by which they are made. A large literature now establishes that better policy-making institutions produce better outcomes. For monetary policy the point is well known: more independent central banks are better able to resist political pressures to monetize budget deficits and generally run lower inflation rates. For fiscal policy, there are parallel arguments for creating an independent fiscal council empowered to set a ceiling for each year's budget deficit, along with automatic, legally-mandated procedures for what will be done if deficit spending threatens to broach that limit. Less ambitiously, fiscal reforms which vest more agenda-setting power in the hands of the prime minister or finance minister, thereby reining in the common-pool problem that arises in the presence of autonomous spending ministries and state governments (none of which has an incentive to fully take into account the impact of its additional spending on the deficit as a whole), have been shown to be associated with smaller deficits and debts. Similarly, measures that enhance the transparency of budgeting make it easier for voters to detect politicians who place self-serving goals above the national interest and hence produce better fiscal outcomes.

With these fundamental institutional reforms in place, markets will not conclude that deficits today mean deficits tomorrow, or that monetary expansion today means monetary expansion tomorrow. The freedom to use fiscal and monetary policies countercyclically will be regained.

Rationalizing Exchange Rate Policy

One lesson of the recent crisis applies to all emerging markets: crawling pegs, basket pegs, and adjustable pegs are recipes for disaster. Not only do governments have other priorities, as the markets are aware, but emerging markets are more volatile, their financial systems more fragile, their political systems weaker. These are all good reasons for investors to challenge emerging markets' currency pegs.

And if a government denies this reality and still attempts to peg its currency, it runs the risk of lulling banks and firms into the false belief that there is no need for them to hedge their exposures by purchasing contracts on the currency forward markets. Having accumulated unhedged foreign obligations, they will be thrust into bankruptcy when the peg collapses, as it ultimately will. For the vast majority of emerging markets, almost without exception, there is no prudent alternative from the point of view of crisis avoidance to greater exchange rate flexibility.

Someone in the audience will surely be quick to remind me of the Argentine alternative – a currency board or even dollarization – if I do not head him off. The single greatest advantage of a more flexible exchange rate, as I have argued, is that it encourages banks and firms to hedge their exposures. But if the exchange rate is not just pegged but locked in for the duration, it not longer matters whether banks and firms hedge against exchange rate fluctuations because there is a negligible probability that the exchange rate will change. But closing off all avenues for discretionary monetary policy and selling off the banking system to foreigners – the sine qua non of a currency board – is the sort of radical amputation of sovereignty that few societies are prepared to accept.

The vast majority of countries will consequently have to follow the other alternative of allowing their currencies to fluctuate more freely. If the exchange rate is allowed to move, banks and firms will learn to hedge their exposures. They will then have protection when it moves by an unexpectedly large amount.

Unfortunately, life with a fluctuating exchange rate is difficult for the typical emerging market, more so than for the U.S., Euroland or Japan. Because developing countries lack policy credibility, their exchange rates fluctuate wildly. And because the typical emerging market depends heavily on trade with the rest of the world, those fluctuations are highly disruptive.

Governments can address these problems by putting in place other measures to enhance their credibility. They can strengthen their fiscal institutions, giving the Finance Ministry the power to curb the fiscal excesses of the states and spending ministries. They can make their central banks truly independent. They can show the markets that they still have a coherent monetary policy strategy once the exchange-rate anchor is cut. The best way of doing this is for the central bank to adopt an inflation target for monetary policy, as Brazil has recently done. This is a significant breakthrough, being the first time the IMF urged a crisis country to adopt an inflation target rather than trying to defend an indefensible currency peg. Other emerging markets should follow suit and adopt inflation targets, the sooner the better.

Strengthening the International Financial Architecture

The agenda under this heading is limited but important. The first element is the need for international financial standards. High capital mobility makes it impossible to fix the international financial system without first fixing the domestic financial systems of countries active on international markets. But neither the IMF nor any other multilateral agency has the resources to micro-manage this process in 182 countries, or to design regulatory institutions that are sensitive to their different economic, cultural and legal traditions. The only practical approach is to develop and adopt international standards for acceptable practice, not just for bank regulation but also for auditing and accounting, corporate governance, and bankruptcy law as well. National practices can differ in their particulars, under this approach, but all must satisfy a common set of international standards.

Responsibility for designing standards cannot be delegated to the IMF, which lacks the resources and expertise. The lead must be taken by the private sector: by the International Accounting Standards Committee, the International Federation of Accountants, the International Organization of Supreme Audit Institutions, Committee J of the International Bar Association, and the International Corporate Governance Network. The multilaterals should of course participate in their deliberations. It is particularly important for the Fund to be involved to ensure that it assumes "ownership" of the standards it helps to set.

Promulgating standards is one thing, enforcing them another. Making the markets pay heed will require the IMF to issue blunt assessments of national practice. But lenders having a limited attention span, the IMF will have to reinforce market discipline by offering the carrot of concessionary interest rates on its loans to countries that comply, and by conditioning its programs on steps to bring national practice into conformance.

A second critical area concerns banks and capital flows. Everyone agrees on the need to strengthen banks' risk management and supervisors' oversight and regulation. But the sad truth in too many countries is that banks have a limited capacity to manage risk and that regulators have limited capacity to supervise their actions. This limited capacity is what defines a financially "less developed" or "developing" economy. Moreover, capital requirements in theory and capital requirements in practice can be two different things, given the inadequacy of auditing and accounting practices. And the political realities are such that bank capital is rarely written down. Consequently, revising the Basle Capital Standards to key capital requirements to the source of banks' funding as well as the riskiness of their investments is unlikely to prove effective.

There is also an argument, as noted above, for limiting short-term bank borrowing abroad where banks' risk-management practices and regulatory supervision do not suffice. The international policy community should become an unambiguous advocate of these measures.

A last area where there exists a reasonable degree of consensus is on changing the provisions of loan contracts. Avoiding both routine rescues and devastating defaults will require creating a more orderly way of restructuring problem debts. Majority voting and sharing clauses should therefore be added to loan contracts to prevent isolated creditors from resorting to lawsuits and other means of obstructing settlements, along with collective representation clauses specifying who will speak for the creditors in negotiations. This is the only practical way of creating an environment more conducive to restructuring negotiations.

Unfortunately, this is a process in which no borrower wants to be first, for fear of sending an adverse signal. The IMF will have to make clear that it will lend at more attractive rates to countries that issue debt securities with these provisions. U.S. and UK regulators should require the relevant provisions of international bonds admitted to trading on their markets.

5. Conclusion

While 1998 did not turn into 1931, the risk of a global financial crisis cannot be dismissed. A more serious crisis was averted last year by a combination of good policies and good luck. Quick cuts in U.S. interest rates taken against the backdrop of a strongly growing U.S. economy, a robust world trading system, and continued strong policies in many emerging markets helped the world economy to navigate these dangerous straits. But it is not certain that things will turn out so positively the next time. A Russian- or Brazilian-style crisis might occur against the backdrop of recession in the United States. There would then be less scope for cutting U.S. interest rates (which would already be low), and the U.S. would be less inclined to act as the world's consumer of last resort. The world trading system would be under greater stress. The leading central bankers might not respond so adroitly.

Emerging markets need to protect themselves from these risks by buttressing the stability of their financial systems. At the same time they achieve this, they can also contribute to the global public good of international financial stability. This means strengthening bank regulation, strengthening financial-market arrangements more generally, strengthening their monetary and fiscal policies, better regulating international capital flows, and rationalizing management of the exchange rate (except in a few exceptional cases, moving to greater exchange rate flexibility).

But better policies will lack credibility and durability if they are not embedded in better institutions. This means creating autonomous regulatory institutions insulated from political pressure, enhancing the independence of the central bank, centralizing fiscal policy making to attenuate free-rider and common-pool problems, and creating the forward and futures markets that will make it easier to live with floating exchange rates.

And emerging markets can continue to push for reform at the global level. The adoption of international standards not just for bank capital (the Basle Capital Standards) and financial supervision and regulation (the Basle Core Principles) but in addition for auditing and accounting, corporate governance and insolvency law will be critical for minimizing systemic risks. The incorporation of "collective representation" clauses in loan contracts to make it easier to restructure problem debts (as suggested by the Group of Ten in 1996) is necessary to create a viable alternative to ever bigger bailouts and devastating defaults. These should be the key components of the so-called "new international financial architecture".

But changes at the international level will take time to achieve. In the meantime, emerging markets have plenty to do.

References

Bordo, Michael / Edelstein, Michael / Rockoff, Hugh, Was Adherence to the Gold Standard a "Good Housekeeping Seal of Approval" During the Interwar Period?, unpublished manuscript Rutgers University and Queen's College, City University of New York (1998)

Caprio, Gerald Jr. / Klingebiel, Daniela, Bank Insolvencies: Cross-Country Experience (Policy Research Working Paper no. 1620) (Washington, D.C. 1996): The World Bank

De Long, J. Bradford, Why We Should Fear Deflation (Brookings Papers on Economic Activity, 1999), (forthcoming)

Dooley, Michael, A Model of Crises in Emerging Markets (NBER Working Paper no. 6300, December 1997)

Eichengreen, Barry, Golden Fetters: The Gold Standard and the Great Depression, 1919–1939 (New York 1992)

Eichengreen, Barry, Toward a New International Financial Architecture: A Practical Post-Asia Agenda (Washington, D.C. 1999)

Eichengreen, Barry / Fishlow, Albert, Contending with Capital Flows: What is Different About the 1990s?, in: *Miles Kahler* (ed.), Capital Flows and Crises (Ithaca 1998) 23–68

Epstein, Gerald / Ferguson, Thomas, Monetary Policy, Loan Liquidation, and Industrial Conflict: The Federal Reserve and the Open Market Operations of 1932, in: Journal of Economic History 44 (1984) 957–984

Fishlow, Albert, Lessons from the Past: International Capital Markets in the 19th Century and the Interwar Years, in: *Miles Kahler* (ed.), The Politics of International Debt (Ithaca 1985)

Folkerts-Landau, David / Lindgren, Carl-Johan, Toward a Framework for Financial Stability (Washington, D.C. 1998): International Monetary Fund

Frankel, Jeffrey A. / Rose, Andrew, The Endogeneity of the Optimum Currency Area Criteria, in: Economic Journal 108 (1998) 109–125

Friedman, Milton / Schwartz, Anna, A Monetary History of the United States, 1867–1960, (Princeton 1963)

Galbraith, John Kenneth, The Great Crash, 1929 (New York 1954)

Goldstein, Morris, The Case for an International Banking Standard, Policy Analyses in International Economics No. 47 (Institute for International Economics, Washington, D.C, April 1997)

Graduate, Charles J., Testimony Before the Committee on Banking and Financial Services (1 October 1998)

Group of Twenty Two, Report of the Working Group on Strengthening Financial Systems (Washington, D.C. 1998)

International Monetary Fund, Interim World Economic Outlook and International Capital Markets Report (Washington, D.C. December 1998)

Jayarante, Jith / Strahan, Philip, The Finance-Growth Nexus: Evidence from Bank Branch Deregulation, in: Quarterly Journal of Economics (August 1996)

Kaufman, George G., Bank Fragility: Perception and Historical Evidence, unpublished manuscript, Loyola University Chicago and Federal Reserve Bank of Chicago (1996)

King, Robert / Levine, Ross, Finance and Growth: Schumpeter Might Be Right, in: Quarterly Journal of Economics 108 (1993) 717–737.

Krugman, Paul, What Happened in Asia?, unpublished manuscript, MIT (1998)

Levine, Ross, Financial Development and Economic Growth: Views and Agenda, in: Journal of Economic Literature 35 (1997) 688–726

Liepmann, Harry, Tariff Levels and the Economic Unity of Europe (New York 1938)

Soros, George, The Crisis of Global Capitalism (New York 1998)

White, Eugene, When the Ticker Ran Late: The Stock Market Boom and Crash of 1929, in. *Eugene White* (ed.), Crashes and Panics: The Lessons from History (New York 1990) 143–187

Wicker, Elmus, Federal Reserve Monetary Policy 1917–1933 (New York 1966)

Schriften des Historischen Kollegs: Kolloquien

1 *Heinrich Lutz* (Hrsg.): Das römisch-deutsche Reich im politischen System Karls V., 1982, XII, 288 S. ISBN 3-486-51371-0

2 *Otto Pflanze* (Hrsg.): Innenpolitische Probleme des Bismarck-Reiches, 1983, XII, 304 S. ISBN 3-486-51481-4 *vergriffen*

3 *Hans Conrad Peyer* (Hrsg.): Gastfreundschaft, Taverne und Gasthaus im Mittelalter, 1983, XIV, 275 S. ISBN 3-486-51661-2 *vergriffen*

4 *Eberhard Weis* (Hrsg.): Reformen im rheinbündischen Deutschland, 1984, XVI, 310 S. ISBN 3-486-51671-X

5 *Heinz Angermeier* (Hrsg.): Säkulare Aspekte der Reformationszeit, 1983, XII, 278 S. ISBN 3-486-51841-0

6 *Gerald D. Feldman* (Hrsg.): Die Nachwirkungen der Inflation auf die deutsche Geschichte 1924–1933, 1985, XII, 407 S. ISBN 3-486-52221-3 *vergriffen*

7 *Jürgen Kocka* (Hrsg.): Arbeiter und Bürger im 19. Jahrhundert. Varianten ihres Verhältnisses im europäischen Vergleich, 1986, XVI, 342 S. ISBN 3-486-52871-8 *vergriffen*

8 *Konrad Repgen* (Hrsg.): Krieg und Politik 1618–1648. Europäische Probleme und Perspektiven, 1988, XII, 454 S. ISBN 3-486-53761-X *vergriffen*

9 *Antoni Mączak* (Hrsg.): Klientelsysteme im Europa der Frühen Neuzeit, 1988, X, 386 S. ISBN 3-486-54021-1

10 *Eberhard Kolb* (Hrsg.): Europa vor dem Krieg von 1870. Mächtekonstellation – Konfliktfelder – Kriegsausbruch, 1987, XII, 216 S. ISBN 3-486-54121-8

11 *Helmut Georg Koenigsberger* (Hrsg.): Republiken und Republikanismus im Europa der Frühen Neuzeit, 1988, XII, 323 S. ISBN 3-486-54341-5

12 *Winfried Schulze* (Hrsg.): Ständische Gesellschaft und soziale Mobilität, 1988, X, 416 S. ISBN 3-486-54351-2

13 *Johanne Autenrieth* (Hrsg.): Renaissance- und Humanistenhandschriften, 1988, XII, 214 S. mit Abbildungen ISBN 3-486-54511-6

14 *Ernst Schulin* (Hrsg.): Deutsche Geschichtswissenschaft nach dem Zweiten Weltkrieg (1945–1965), 1989, XI, 303 S. ISBN 3-486-54831-X

15 *Wilfried Barner* (Hrsg.): Tradition, Norm, Innovation. Soziales und literarisches Traditionsverhalten in der Frühzeit der deutschen Aufklärung, 1989, XXV, 370 S. ISBN 3-486-54771-2

16 *Hartmut Boockmann* (Hrsg.): Die Anfänge der ständischen Vertretungen in Preußen und seinen Nachbarländern, 1992, X, 264 S. ISBN 3-486-55840-4

17 *John C. G. Röhl* (Hrsg.): Der Ort Kaiser Wilhelms II. in der deutschen Geschichte, 1991, XIII, 366 S. ISBN 3-486-55841-2 *vergriffen*

Schriften des Historischen Kollegs: Kolloquien

18 *Gerhard A. Ritter* (Hrsg.): Der Aufstieg der deutschen Arbeiterbewegung. Sozialdemokratie und Freie Gewerkschaften im Parteiensystem und Sozialmilieu des Kaiserreichs, 1990, XXI, 461 S. ISBN 3-486-55641-X

19 *Roger Dufraisse* (Hrsg.): Revolution und Gegenrevolution 1789–1830. Zur geistigen Auseinandersetzung in Frankreich und Deutschland, 1991, XVIII, 274 S. ISBN 3-486-55844-7

20 *Klaus Schreiner* (Hrsg.): Laienfrömmigkeit im späten Mittelalter. Formen, Funktionen, politisch-soziale Zusammenhänge, 1992, XII, 411 S. ISBN 3-486-55902-8

21 *Jürgen Miethke* (Hrsg.): Das Publikum politischer Theorie im 14. Jahrhundert, 1992, IX, 301 S. ISBN 3-486-55898-6

22 *Dieter Simon* (Hrsg.): Eherecht und Familiengut in Antike und Mittelalter, 1992, IX, 168 S. ISBN 3-486-55885-4

23 *Volker Press* (Hrsg.): Alternativen zur Reichsverfassung in der Frühen Neuzeit? 1995, XII, 254 S. ISBN 3-486-56035-2

24 *Kurt Raaflaub* (Hrsg.): Anfänge politischen Denkens in der Antike. Griechenland und die nahöstlichen Kulturen, 1993, XXIV, 454 S. ISBN 3-486-55993-1

25 *Shulamit Volkov* (Hrsg.): Deutsche Juden und die Moderne, 1994, XXIV, 170 S. ISBN 3-486-56029-8

26 *Heinrich A. Winkler* (Hrsg.): Die deutsche Staatskrise 1930–1933. Handlungsspielräume und Alternativen, 1992, XIII, 296 S. ISBN 3-486-55943-5

27 *Johannes Fried* (Hrsg.): Dialektik und Rhetorik im früheren und hohen Mittelalter. Rezeption, Überlieferung und gesellschaftliche Wirkung antiker Gelehrsamkeit vornehmlich im 9. und 12. Jahrhundert, 1997, XXI, 304 S. ISBN 3-486-56028-X

28 *Paolo Prodi* (Hrsg.): Glaube und Eid. Treueformeln, Glaubensbekenntnisse und Sozialdisziplinierung zwischen Mittelalter und Neuzeit, 1993, XXX, 246 S. ISBN 3-486-55994-X

29 *Ludwig Schmugge* (Hrsg.): Illegitimität im Spätmittelalter, 1994, X, 314 S. ISBN 3-486-56069-7

30 *Bernhard Kölver* (Hrsg.): Recht, Staat und Verwaltung im klassischen Indien, 1997, XVIII, 257 S. ISBN 3-486-56193-6

31 *Elisabeth Fehrenbach* (Hrsg.): Adel und Bürgertum in Deutschland 1770–1848, 1994, XVI, 251 S. ISBN 3-486-56027-1

32 *Robert E. Lerner* (Hrsg.): Neue Richtungen in der hoch- und spätmittelalterlichen Bibelexegese, 1996, XI, 191 S. ISBN 3-486-56083-2

33 *Klaus Hildebrand* (Hrsg.): Das Deutsche Reich im Urteil der Großen Mächte und europäischen Nachbarn (1871–1945), 1995, X, 232 S. ISBN 3-486-56084-0

34 *Wolfgang J. Mommsen* (Hrsg.): Kultur und Krieg. Die Rolle der Intellektuellen, Künstler und Schriftsteller im Ersten Weltkrieg, 1995, X, 282 S. ISBN 3-486-56085-9

Schriften des Historischen Kollegs: Kolloquien

35 *Peter Krüger* (Hrsg.): Das europäische Staatensystem im Wandel. Strukturelle Bedingungen und bewegende Kräfte seit der Frühen Neuzeit, 1996, XVI, 272 S. ISBN 3-486-56171-5

36 *Peter Blickle* (Hrsg.): Theorien kommunaler Ordnung in Europa, 1996, IX, 268 S. ISBN 3-486-56192-8

37 *Hans Eberhard Mayer* (Hrsg.): Die Kreuzfahrerstaaten als multikulturelle Gesellschaft. Einwanderer und Minderheiten im 12. und 13. Jahrhundert, 1997, XI, 187 S. ISBN 3-486-56257-6

38 *Manlio Bellomo* (Hrsg.): Die Kunst der Disputation. Probleme der Rechtsauslegung und Rechtsanwendung im 13. und 14. Jahrhundert, 1997, 248 S. ISBN 3-486-56258-4

39 *František Šmahel* (Hrsg.): Häresie und vorzeitige Reformation im Spätmittelalter (mit Beiträgen von H. Boockmann, St. Bylina, W. Eberhard, K. Elm, V. Herold, I. Hlavácek, A. Hudson, H. Kaminsky, M. D. Lambert, J. Miethke, A. Patschovsky, F. Seibt, F. Šmahel, B. Töpfer, K. Walsh) 1998, XV, 304 S. ISBN 3-486-56259-2

40 *Alfred Haverkamp* (Hrsg.): Information, Kommunikation und Selbstdarstellung in mittelalterlichen Gemeinden (mit Beiträgen von G. Bönnen, R. Bordone, G. Fouquet, Chr. Hannick, A. Heinz, A. Linder, W. Meyer, M. Schwarz, R. van Uytven, J. Weitzel) 1998, XXII, 288 S. ISBN 3-486-56260-6

41 *Knut Schulz* (Hrsg.): Handwerk in Europa. Vom Spätmittelalter bis zur Frühen Neuzeit (mit Beiträgen von W. Blockmans, H. Braun, R. S. Elkar, A. Esch, S. Faroqhi, R. Holbach, F. Irsigler, M. Kintzinger, D. Kurze, P. Lourens, J. Lucassen, W. Reininghaus, J. Röhrkasten, L. Schmugge, Chr. Schuchard, K. Schulz, K. Wesoly) 1999, XIX, 313 S. ISBN 3-486-56395-5

42 *Werner Eck* (Hrsg.): Lokale Autonomie und römische Ordnungsmacht in den kaiserzeitlichen Provinzen vom 1. bis 3. Jahrhundert (mit Beiträgen von H. M. Cotton, W. Eck, H. Galsterer, J. Gascou, R. Haensch, H. Horstkotte, A. Jördens, E. Lo Cascio, S. Mitchell, D. Nörr, J. Nollé, M. Sharp, D. Thomas, H. Wolff) 1999, X, 327 S. ISBN 3-486-56385-8

43 *Manfred Hildermeier* (Hrsg.): Stalinismus vor dem Zweiten Weltkrieg. Neue Wege der Forschung / Stalinism before the Second World War. New Avenues of Research (mit Beiträgen von J. Baberowski, D. Beyrau, S. Fitzpatrick, G. L. Freeze, J. A. Getty, J. Hellbeck, M. Hildermeier, H. Kuromiya, S. Merl, D. Neutatz, S. Plaggenborg, G. T. Rittersporn, J. Šapoval, K. Schlögel, M. V. Škarovskij, R. C. Tucker) 1998, XVI, 345 S. ISBN 3-486-56350-5

44 *Aharon Oppenheimer* (Hrsg.): Jüdische Geschichte in hellenistisch-römischer Zeit. Wege der Forschung: Vom alten zum neuen Schürer (mit Beiträgen von H. M. Cotton, W. Eck, I. M. Gafni, D. M. Goodblatt, M. Goodman, M. Hengel, B. H. Isaac, H. Lichtenberger, M. Niehoff, A. Oppenheimer, P. Schäfer, L. H. Schiffman, M. Schlüter, D. R. Schwartz, G. Stemberger, G. Vermes) 1999, XI, 275 S. ISBN 3-486-56414-5

Schriften des Historischen Kollegs: Kolloquien

45 *Dietmar Willoweit* (Hrsg.): Die Begründung des Rechts als historisches Problem (mit Beiträgen von O. Behrends, S. Breuer, G. Dilcher, H. Hofmann, W. Kersting, P. Landau, J. Miethke, K. Seelmann, J. Weitzel, D. Willoweit) 2000, 345 S., ISBN 3-486-56482-X

46 *Stephen A. Schuker* (Hrsg.): Deutschland und Frankreich. Vom Konflikt zur Aussöhnung. Die Gestaltung der westeuropäischen Sicherheit, 1914–1963 (mit Beiträgen von M. Alexander, J. Bariéty, C. Buffet, G. D. Feldman, J. Gillingham, E. Glaser, D. Hüser, L. Kettenacker, M. Kipping, F. Knipping, P. Krüger, H.-J. Rupieper, G. Schmidt, St. A. Schuker, K. Schwabe, A. Sharp, D. Stevenson, M. Trachtenberg, C. Wurm) 2000, XX, 280 S., ISBN 3-486-56496-X

47 *Wolfgang Reinhard* (Hrsg.): Verstaatlichung der Welt? Europäische Staatsmodelle und außereuropäische Machtprozesse (mit Beiträgen von J. M. Abun-Nasr, G. Dharampal-Frick, X. Gu, M. F. Hamzeh'ee, H. Haury, J. Heideking, G. Krämer, Chr. Marx, J. Osterhammel, W. Reinhard, M. Riekenberg, R. Rothermund, W. Schwentker, Chr.Tapscott, H. W. Tobler, T. v. Trotha, P. Waldmann, A. Wirz) 1999, XVI, 375 S. ISBN 3-486-56416-1

48 *Gerhard Besier* (Hrsg.): Zwischen „nationaler Revolution" und militärischer Aggression. Transformationen in Kirche und Gesellschaft unter der konsolidierten NS-Gewaltherrschft (Herbst 1934 bis Herbst 1935) (mit Beiträgen von D. L. Bergen, G. Besier, A. Chandler, J. S. Conway, T. Fandel, F. Hartweg, H. Kiesel, H.-M. Lauterer, K.-M. Mallmann, H. Mommsen, I. Montgomery, G. Ringshausen, J. Schoeps, K. Schwarz, J. Smolik, M. Wolffsohn) 2001, XXVIII, 276 S. ISBN 3-486-56543-5

49 *David Cohen* (Hrsg.): Demokratie, Recht und soziale Kontrolle im klassischen Athen (mit Beiträgen von D. Cohen, J. Comaroff, J. Elster, C. A. Faraone, L. Foxhall, K.-J. Hölkeskamp, A. Maffi, J. Martin, W. I. Miller, C. Pattersen, G. Thür, H. Versnel) 2002, ca. 208 S. ISBN 3-486-56662-8

50 *Thomas A. Brady* (Hrsg.): Die deutsche Reformation zwischen Spätmittelalter und Früher Neuzeit (mit Beiträgen von Th. A. Brady, C. Fasolt, B. Hamm, S. C. Karant-Nunn, H. A. Oberman, H. R. Schmidt, E. Schubert, M. Schulze, T. Scott, H. Wenzel) 2001, XXII, 258 S., ISBN 3-486-56565-6

51 *Harold James* (Hrsg.): The Interwar Depression in an International Context (mit Beiträgen von Ch. Buchheim, F. Capie, P. Clavin, B. Eichengreen, G. D. Feldman, C.-L. Holtfrerich, H. James, A. Ritschl, M. Rosengarten, D. Rothermund, R. Skidelsky, S. Solomou) 2002, XVIII, 192 S., ISBN 3-486-56610-5

52 *Christof Dipper* (Hrsg.): Deutschland und Italien, 1860–1960 (in Vorbereitung)

53 *Frank-Rutger Hausmann* (Hrsg.): Die Rolle der Geisteswissenschaften im Dritten Reich 1933–1945. 2002, ca. XXX, 370 S. ISBN 3-486-56639-3

Schriften des Historischen Kollegs: Kolloquien

54 *Frank Kolb* (Hrsg.): Chora und Polis (in Vorbereitung)

55 *Hans Günter Hockerts* (Hrsg.): Koordinaten deutscher Geschichte in der Epoche des Ost-West-Konflikts (in Vorbereitung)

Sonderveröffentlichung

Horst Fuhrmann (Hrsg.): Die Kaulbach-Villa als Haus des Historischen Kollegs. Reden und wissenschaftliche Beiträge zur Eröffnung, 1989, XII, 232 S. ISBN 3-486-55611-8

Oldenbourg

Schriften des Historischen Kollegs: Vorträge

1 *Heinrich Lutz:* Die deutsche Nation zu Beginn der Neuzeit. Fragen nach dem Gelingen und Scheitern deutscher Einheit im 16. Jahrhundert, 1982, IV, 31 S. *vergriffen*

2 *Otto Pflanze:* Bismarcks Herrschaftstechnik als Problem der gegenwärtigen Historiographie, 1982, IV, 39 S. *vergriffen*

3 *Hans Conrad Peyer:* Gastfreundschaft und kommerzielle Gastlichkeit im Mittelalter, 1983, IV, 24 S. *vergriffen*

4 *Eberhard Weis:* Bayern und Frankreich in der Zeit des Konsulats und des ersten Empire (1799–1815), 1984, 41 S. *vergriffen*

5 *Heinz Angermeier:* Reichsreform und Reformation, 1983, IV, 76 S. *vergriffen*

6 *Gerald D. Feldman:* Bayern und Sachsen in der Hyperinflation 1922/23, 1984, IV, 41 S. *vergriffen*

7 *Erich Angermann:* Abraham Lincoln und die Erneuerung der nationalen Identität der Vereinigten Staaten von Amerika, 1984, IV, 33 S. *vergriffen*

8 *Jürgen Kocka:* Traditionsbindung und Klassenbildung. Zum sozialhistorischen Ort der frühen deutschen Arbeiterbewegung, 1987, 48 S.

9 *Konrad Repgen:* Kriegslegitimationen in Alteuropa. Entwurf einer historischen Typologie, 1985, 27 S. *vergriffen*

10 *Antoni Mączak:* Der Staat als Unternehmen. Adel und Amtsträger in Polen und Europa in der Frühen Neuzeit, 1989, 32 S.

11 *Eberhard Kolb:* Der schwierige Weg zum Frieden. Das Problem der Kriegsbeendigung 1870/71, 1985, 33 S. *vergriffen*

12 *Helmut Georg Koenigsberger:* Fürst und Generalstände. Maximilian I. in den Niederlanden (1477–1493), 1987, 27 S. *vergriffen*

13 *Winfried Schulze:* Vom Gemeinnutz zum Eigennutz. Über den Normenwandel in der ständischen Gesellschaft der Frühen Neuzeit, 1987, 40 S. *vergriffen*

14 *Johanne Autenrieth:* „Litterae Virgilianae“. Vom Fortleben einer römischen Schrift, 1988, 51 S.

15 *Tilemann Grimm:* Blickpunkte auf Südostasien. Historische und kulturanthropologische Fragen zur Politik, 1988, 37 S.

16 *Ernst Schulin:* Geschichtswissenschaft in unserem Jahrhundert. Probleme und Umrisse einer Geschichte der Historie, 1988, 34 S.

17 *Hartmut Boockmann:* Geschäfte und Geschäftigkeit auf dem Reichstag im späten Mittelalter, 1988, 33 S. *vergriffen*

18 *Wilfried Barner:* Literaturwissenschaft – eine Geschichtswissenschaft? 1990, 42 S.

Schriften des Historischen Kollegs: Vorträge

19 *John C. G. Röhl:* Kaiser Wilhelm II. Eine Studie über Cäsarenwahnsinn, 1989, 36 S. *vergriffen*

20 *Klaus Schreiner:* Mönchsein in der Adelsgesellschaft des hohen und späten Mittelalters. Klösterliche Gemeinschaftsbildung zwischen spiritueller Selbstbehauptung und sozialer Anpassung, 1989, 68 S. *vergriffen*

21 *Roger Dufraisse:* Die Deutschen und Napoleon im 20. Jahrhundert, 1991, 43 S.

22 *Gerhard A. Ritter:* Die Sozialdemokratie im Deutschen Kaiserreich in sozialgeschichtlicher Perspektive, 1989, 72 S.

23 *Jürgen Miethke:* Die mittelalterlichen Universitäten und das gesprochene Wort, 1990, 48 S.

24 *Dieter Simon:* Lob des Eunuchen, 1994, 27 S.

25 *Thomas Vogtherr:* Der König und der Heilige. Heinrich IV., der heilige Remaklus und die Mönche des Doppelklosters Stablo-Malmedy, 1990, 29 S.

26 *Johannes Schilling:* Gewesene Mönche. Lebensgeschichten in der Reformation, 1990, 36 S. *vergriffen*

27 *Kurt Raaflaub:* Politisches Denken und Krise der Polis. Athen im Verfassungskonflikt des späten 5. Jahrhunderts v. Chr., 1992, 63 S.

28 *Volker Press:* Altes Reich und Deutscher Bund. Kontinuität in der Diskontinuität, 1995, 31 S.

29 *Shulamit Volkov:* Die Erfindung einer Tradition. Zur Entstehung des modernen Judentums in Deutschland, 1992, 30 S.

30 *Franz Bauer:* Gehalt und Gestalt in der Monumentalsymbolik. Zur Ikonologie des Nationalstaats in Deutschland und Italien 1860–1914, 1992, 39 S.

31 *Heinrich A. Winkler:* Mußte Weimar scheitern? Das Ende der ersten Republik und die Kontinuität der deutschen Geschichte, 1991, 32 S.

32 *Johannes Fried:* Kunst und Kommerz. Über das Zusammenwirken von Wissenschaft und Wirtschaft im Mittelalter vornehmlich am Beispiel der Kaufleute und Handelsmessen, 1992, 40 S.

33 *Paolo Prodi:* Der Eid in der europäischen Verfassungsgeschichte, 1992, 35 S.

34 *Jean-Marie Moeglin:* Dynastisches Bewußtsein und Geschichtsschreibung. Zum Selbstverständnis der Wittelsbacher, Habsburger und Hohenzollern im Spätmittelalter, 1993, 47 S.

35 *Bernhard Kölver:* Ritual und historischer Raum. Zum indischen Geschichtsverständnis, 1993, 65 S.

36 *Elisabeth Fehrenbach:* Adel und Bürgertum im deutschen Vormärz, 1994, 31 S.

Schriften des Historischen Kollegs: Vorträge

37 *Ludwig Schmugge:* Schleichwege zu Pfründe und Altar. Päpstliche Dispense vom Geburtsmakel 1449–1533, 1994, 35 S.

38 *Hans-Werner Hahn:* Zwischen Fortschritt und Krisen. Die vierziger Jahre des 19. Jahrhunderts als Durchbruchsphase der deutschen Industrialisierung, 1995, 47 S.

39 *Robert E. Lerner:* Himmelsvision oder Sinnendelirium? Franziskaner und Professoren als Traumdeuter im Paris des 13. Jahrhunderts, 1995, 35 S.

40 *Andreas Schulz:* Weltbürger und Geldaristokraten. Hanseatisches Bürgertum im 19. Jahrhundert, 1995, 38 S.

41 *Wolfgang J. Mommsen:* Die Herausforderung der bürgerlichen Kultur durch die künstlerische Avantgarde. Zum Verhältnis von Kultur und Politik im Wilhelminischen Deutschland, 1994, 30 S.

42 *Klaus Hildebrand:* Reich – Großmacht – Nation. Betrachtungen zur Geschichte der deutschen Außenpolitik 1871–1945, 1995, 25 S.

43 *Hans Eberhard Mayer:* Herrschaft und Verwaltung im Kreuzfahrerkönigreich Jerusalem, 1996, 38 S.

44 *Peter Blickle:* Reformation und kommunaler Geist. Die Antwort der Theologen auf den Wandel der Verfassung im Spätmittelalter, 1996, 42 S.

45 *Peter Krüger:* Wege und Widersprüche der europäischen Integration im 20. Jahrhundert, 1995, 39 S.

46 *Werner Greiling:* „Intelligenzblätter“ und gesellschaftlicher Wandel in Thüringen. Anzeigenwesen, Nachrichtenvermittlung, Räsonnement und Sozialdisziplinierung, 1995, 38 S.

Schriften des Historischen Kollegs: Dokumentationen

1 Stiftung Historisches Kolleg im Stifterverband für die Deutsche Wissenschaft: Erste Verleihung des Preises des Historischen Kollegs. Aufgaben, Stipendiaten, Schriften des Historischen Kollegs, 1984, VI, 70 S., mit Abbildungen *vergriffen*

2 Theodor-Schieder-Gedächtnisvorlesung: Horst Fuhrmann, Das Interesse am Mittelalter in heutiger Zeit. Beobachtungen und Vermutungen – Lothar Gall, Theodor Schieder 1908 bis 1984, 1987, 65 S. *vergriffen*

3 Leopold von Ranke: Vorträge anläßlich seines 100. Todestages. Gedenkfeier der Historischen Kommission bei der Bayerischen Akademie der Wissenschaften und der Stiftung Historisches Kolleg im Stifterverband für die Deutsche Wissenschaft am 12. Mai 1986, 1987, 44 S. *vergriffen*

4 Stiftung Historisches Kolleg im Stifterverband für die Deutsche Wissenschaft: Zweite Verleihung des Preises des Historischen Kollegs. Aufgaben, Stipendiaten, Schriften des Historischen Kollegs, 1987, 98 S., mit Abbildungen

5 Theodor-Schieder-Gedächtnisvorlesung: Thomas Nipperdey, Religion und Gesellschaft: Deutschland um 1900, 1988, 29 S. *vergriffen*

6 Theodor-Schieder-Gedächtnisvorlesung: Christian Meier, Die Rolle des Krieges im klassischen Athen, 1991, 55 S.

7 Stiftung Historisches Kolleg im Stifterverband für die Deutsche Wissenschaft: Dritte Verleihung des Preises des Historischen Kollegs. Aufgaben, Stipendiaten, Schriften des Historischen Kollegs, 1991, 122 S., mit Abbildungen *vergriffen*

8 Stiftung Historisches Kolleg im Stifterverband für die Deutsche Wissenschaft: Historisches Kolleg 1980–1990. Vorträge anläßlich des zehnjährigen Bestehens und zum Gedenken an Alfred Herrhausen, 1991, 63 S.

9 Theodor-Schieder-Gedächtnisvorlesung: Karl Leyser, Am Vorabend der ersten europäischen Revolution. Das 11. Jahrhundert als Umbruchszeit, 1994, 32 S.

10 Stiftung Historisches Kolleg im Stifterverband für die Deutsche Wissenschaft: Vierte Verleihung des Preises des Historischen Kollegs. Aufgaben, Stipendiaten, Schriften des Historischen Kollegs, 1993, 98 S., mit Abbildungen

11 Theodor-Schieder-Gedächtnisvorlesung: Rudolf Smend, Mose als geschichtliche Gestalt, 1995, 23 S.

12 Stiftung Historisches Kolleg im Stifterverband für die Deutsche Wissenschaft: Über die Offenheit der Geschichte. Kolloquium der Mitglieder des Historischen Kollegs, 20. und 21. November 1992, 1996, 84 S.

Vorträge und Dokumentationen ohne ISBN erscheinen nicht im Buchhandel; sie können über die Geschäftsstelle des Historischen Kollegs (Kaulbachstraße 15, 80539 München) bezogen werden.

Schriften des Historischen Kollegs: Jahrbuch

Jahrbuch des Historischen Kollegs 1995:

Arnold Esch
Rom in der Renaissance. Seine Quellenlage als methodisches Problem

Manlio Bellomo
Geschichte eines Mannes: Bartolus von Sassoferrato und die moderne europäische Jurisprudenz

František Šmahel
Das verlorene Ideal der Stadt in der böhmischen Reformation

Alfred Haverkamp
„... an die große Glocke hängen". Über Öffentlichkeit im Mittelalter

Hans-Christof Kraus
Montesquieu, Blackstone, De Lolme und die englische Verfassung des 18. Jahrhunderts

1996, VIII, 180 S. ISBN 3-486-56176-6

Jahrbuch des Historischen Kollegs 1996:

Johannes Fried
Wissenschaft und Phantasie. Das Beispiel der Geschichte

Manfred Hildermeier
Revolution und Kultur: Der „Neue Mensch" in der frühen Sowjetunion

Knut Schulz
Handwerk im spätmittelalterlichen Europa. Zur Wanderung und Ausbildung von Lehrlingen in der Fremde

Werner Eck
Mord im Kaiserhaus? Ein politischer Prozeß im Rom des Jahres 20 n. Chr.

Wolfram Pyta
Konzert der Mächte und kollektives Sicherheitssystem: Neue Wege zwischenstaatlicher Friedenswahrung in Europa nach dem Wiener Kongreß 1815

1997, VIII, 202 S. ISBN 3-486-56300-9

Schriften des Historischen Kollegs: Jahrbuch

Jahrbuch des Historischen Kollegs 1997:

Eberhard Weis
Hardenberg und Montgelas. Versuch eines Vergleichs ihrer Persönlichkeiten und ihrer Politik

Dietmar Willoweit
Vom alten guten Recht. Normensuche zwischen Erfahrungswissen und Ursprungslegenden

Aharon Oppenheimer
Messianismus in römischer Zeit. Zur Pluralität eines Begriffes bei Juden und Christen

Stephen A. Schuker
Bayern und der rheinische Separatismus 1923–1924

Gerhard Schuck
Zwischen Ständeordnung und Arbeitsgesellschaft. Der Arbeitsbegriff in der frühneuzeitlichen Policey am Beispiel Bayerns

1998, VIII, 167 S. ISBN 3-486-56375-0

Jahrbuch des Historischen Kollegs 1998:

Peter Pulzer
Der deutsche Michel in John Bulls Spiegel: Das britische Deutschlandbild im 19. Jahrhundert

Gerhard Besier
„The friends ... in America need to know the truth ..."
Die deutschen Kirchen im Urteil der Vereinigten Staaten (1933–1941)

David Cohen
Die Schwestern der Medea. Frauen, Öffentlichkeit und soziale Kontrolle im klassischen Athen

Wolfgang Reinhard
Staat machen: Verfassungsgeschichte als Kulturgeschichte

Lutz Klinkhammer
Die Zivilisierung der Affekte. Kriminalitätsbekämpfung im Rheinland und in Piemont unter französischer Herrschaft 1798–1814

1999, 193 S., ISBN 3-486-56420-X

Schriften des Historischen Kollegs: Jahrbuch

Jahrbuch des Historischen Kollegs 1999:

Jan Assmann
Ägypten in der Gedächtnisgeschichte des Abendlandes

Thomas A. Brady
Ranke, Rom und die Reformation: Leopold von Rankes Entdeckung des Katholizismus

Harold James
Das Ende der Globalisierung: Lehren aus der Weltwirtschaftskrise

Christof Dipper
Helden überkreuz oder das Kreuz mit den Helden. Wie Deutsche und Italiener die Heroen der nationalen Einigung (der anderen) wahrnahmen.

Felicitas Schmieder
„... von etlichen geistlichen leyen“. Definitionen der Bürgerschaft im spätmittelalterlichen Frankfurt

2000, VI, 199 S., 7 Abb., ISBN 3-486-56492-7

Jahrbuch des Historischen Kollegs 2000:

Winfried Schulze
Die Wahrnehmung von Zeit und Jahrhundertwenden

Frank Kolb
Von der Burg zur Polis
Akkulturation in einer kleinasiatischen „Provinz“

Hans Günter Hockerts
Nach der Verfolgung
Wiedergutmachung in Deutschland: Eine historische Bilanz 1945–2000

Frank-Rutger Hausmann
„Auch im Krieg schweigen die Musen nicht“
Die ‚Deutschen Wissenschaftlichen Institute‘ (DWI) im Zweiten Weltkrieg (1940–1945)

Ulrike Freitag
Scheich oder Sultan – Stamm oder Staat?
Staatsbildung im Hadramaut (Jemen) im 19. und 20. Jahrhundert

2001, 250 S., 16 Abb., ISBN 3-486-56557-5

Schriften des Historischen Kollegs: Jahrbuch

Jahrbuch des Historischen Kollegs 2001:

Michael Stolleis
Das Auge des Gesetzes. Materialien zu einer neuzeitlichen Metapher

Wolfgang Hardtwig
Die Krise des Geschichtsbewußtseins und der Aufstieg des Nationalsozialismus

Diethelm Klippel
Kant im Kontext. Der naturrechtliche Diskurs um 1800

Jürgen Reulecke
Neuer Mensch und neue Männlichkeit. Die „junge Generation" im ersten Drittel des 20. Jahrhunderts

Peter Burschel
Paradiese der Gewalt. Martyrium, Imagination und die Metamorphosen des nachtridentinischen Heiligenhimmels

2002, ca. 200 S. ISBN 3-486-56641-5

www.ingramcontent.com/pod-product-compliance
Lightning Source LLC
LaVergne TN
LVHW010548300926
849162LV00002B/271